THE BOY
ON THE
SHED

THE BOY ON THE SHED

A Memoir

PAUL FERRIS

HODDER &
STOUGHTON

First published in Great Britain in 2018 by Hodder & Stoughton
An Hachette UK company

2

Copyright © Paul Ferris 2018

A CIP catalogue record for this title is available from the British Library

ISBN 9781473666702
eBook ISBN 9781473666726
Tradeback ISBN 9781473666719

Typeset in Plantin by Hewer Text UK Ltd, Edinburgh
Printed and bound by Clays Ltd, St Ives plc

Hodder & Stoughton policy is to use papers that are natural, renewable and recyclable products and made from wood grown in sustainable forests. The logging and manufacturing processes are expected to conform to the environmental regulations of the country of origin.

Hodder & Stoughton Ltd
Carmelite House
50 Victoria Embankment
London EC4Y 0DZ

www.hodder.co.uk

For Conor, Owen and Ciaran; the shining stars of my life.
And for Isla, the sunshine, who came along at the perfect
time and is blissfully unaware of just what she means to me.

ACKNOWLEDGEMENTS

WRITING A memoir should be a solitary and perhaps a lonely pastime. In my case it has been anything but that. I would like to thank my wife Geraldine for sharing every step of the journey with me. For reading and re- reading the early drafts. For believing in me, encouraging me, and supporting me.

Thank you to Guy Rose for his enthusiastic and wholehearted belief in the manuscript I sent to him. He made me a promise and he kept it.

Roddy Bloomfield, my editor at Hodder and Stoughton, and his colleague Fiona Rose deserve special mention. Roddy has been a warm, generous and inspirational presence since he first introduced himself to me. I have drawn great strength from his belief in my story, and his suggestions and guidance have only served to enhance it. Fiona has worked diligently and professionally to ensure my story has been presented in the best possible way. A special thank you to publicist Karen Geary for all her hard work and commitment to ensuring my story is read.

I must thank Newcastle United and the Evening Chronicle for their permission to use their photographs.

A sincere thank you to Alan Shearer for the kind foreword and much valued friendship.

To my brothers and sisters: We've lived a lifetime apart but you are always in my heart. Finally, I want to thank my parents Bernadette and Patrick. Their story ended far too soon. I hope by telling mine that I gave life to theirs once more.

PHOTO ACKNOWLEDGEMENTS

THE AUTHOR and publisher would like to thank the following for permission to reproduce photographs.

Newcastle United FC, Newcastle Evening Chronicle, Owen Humphreys/PA Archive/PA Images, PA/PA Archive/PA Images, Clive Brunskill/Allsport/Getty Images Sport, Allsport UK /Getty Images Sport, Clive Brunskill/Getty Images, Harry Goodwin/Paul Popper/Popperfoto/Getty Images, Colorsport/REX/Shutterstock, Dan Sheridan/INPHO/REX/Shutterstock, Matthew Ashton/REX/Shutterstock, Trinity Mirror / Mirrorpix / Alamy Stock Photo, Allstar Picture Library / Alamy Stock Photo, Mirrorpix

All other images are from private collections.

FOREWORD

I FIRST MET Paul in a hospital in Manchester more than twenty years ago. I had just been transferred from Blackburn Rovers to Newcastle United for a world record fee of £15m. Every transfer in football entails a medical examination but the scale of the fee ensured this was one big medical.

There were various representatives of Newcastle United present and Paul was there as the physio. He did not push himself to the front, he was a little bit shy, but when he spoke he was warm and engaging. He was very professional.

We struck up a relationship immediately, not least because I had to fly off on Newcastle's pre-season tour directly from the hospital. That meant Paul was given the task of driving my car to Newcastle. It was a Jaguar and Paul was laughing, bemused: 'What are all these buttons?'

Looking back, Paul was obviously a seriously talented footballer when he was a boy. He came over from Lisburn when he was sixteen, and physically and emotionally you could almost say he was a child. I know from my own experience there is a massive difference between being sixteen and seventeen in professional football.

Yet just look at the company he kept: in that Newcastle United squad of 1982–83 there were four forwards – Kevin Keegan, Chris Waddle, Peter Beardsley and Paul Ferris. No wonder Paul found it hard to get into the team, and in an era when there was only one substitute. In the *Rothman's Football Yearbook* for that season, there is also a Newcastle apprentice called Paul Gascoigne.

Paul Ferris was part of the excitement of all this, but by the time I met him that career opportunity had been cruelly ended by injury. I was not meeting Paul Ferris: footballer, I was meeting Paul Ferris: physiotherapist. I soon discovered I was meeting Paul Ferris: good man.

I always feel the need to know if I can trust someone when I meet them. I quickly found I could with Paul. He is honest, reliable, intelligent, likes to laugh, likes to be serious and is incredibly hardworking. He's all that.

When I sustained a bad ankle injury a year after joining Newcastle, it meant I had six or seven months' recuperation. Every day of those months I spent with Paul, so our bond, our friendship, deepened.

In terms of my playing career, I felt robbed of those months, so I can begin to understand how Paul must feel about his lost playing career.

We remained great friends after I stopped playing. It was no surprise to me that he left medicine for the law and immediately immersed himself in it and made a success of it. It was also no surprise to me that he wrote a book and started talking about writing a second one while doing the first.

Then, I interrupted his legal progress when I was offered the job of managing Newcastle United towards the end of the 2008–09 season.

Paul came with me, back to St. James' Park. Officially his role was as Head of Medical Department but he was much more than that. He is a person I trust, whose judgement I trust.

It has not been good to see his health suffer, but I know he will come through because he is a fighter. A fighter and – as you will see – a writer.

Alan Shearer
Newcastle upon Tyne
November 2017

CHAPTER 1

THE DAY I nearly died started like every other day. That's the thing about dying. It comes along right in the middle of living and ruins everything. The other thing about dying is that sometimes even when you are in the middle of doing it you don't truly believe you are. It's not like I thought: *This is it. I'm dying here.*

But I was. And I nearly did. I was forty-eight.

It's not as if I didn't have warning signs. I did. I had plenty. I didn't ignore them either. I'd been getting severe chest pains for two weeks. I'd been to the doctor and even the cardiology clinic at my local hospital. I wasn't a smoker or particularly overweight and I was a regular exerciser. What I did have was a very bleak family history of heart disease. But in spite of my history, the cardiologist had assured me that all was well. He had checked my eyes, taken my blood pressure and I had had an ECG. He was pretty unequivocal:

'You seem a bit anxious Mr Ferris, but I can assure you there's only a one in a hundred chance these pains are caused by your heart. We will book you in for further tests to put your mind at ease. Please don't worry, though. We're only doing them to put your mind completely at rest. Get on with your life as normal.'

So I did; as much as the chest pains would permit. I basically carried on with my life as if I'd be here forever. I worked as hard as I could, drove the length of the country for a family wedding – I even travelled to Dubai and back in one day for business. On the morning I nearly died, I did what I always do. I had breakfast in a rush, told my kids off for squabbling, kissed my wife and raced off to work. I sat in traffic like everybody else that day. Flicked between the channels to try and find a song I recognised, which is considerably less often the older I get – *thank God for Spotify*. Van Morrison eased my journey. I got to work with minutes to spare and prepared for another day in the office.

I was, and still am, the MD of a new health and fitness company. It has been a long and very winding road to get here. My friend and colleague, Rob Lee, formerly of Newcastle United and England, was in the office that day. He was a manager of one of our new centres and was in Newcastle ahead of playing in a testimonial game that evening. I offered him a lift to a local golf club to meet the others so they could have a catch-up on old times ahead of the game. We turned into the tree-lined drive of the club and were discussing a work-related issue that was causing me some stress at the time. I'd previously been Rob's physiotherapist for many years at Newcastle United, which had also led to us becoming good friends. But on this occasion I was talking to him as his boss. We were both struggling with the new arrangement. We were speaking calmly enough on the surface, but on the inside I was definitely feeling irritated. My chest began to let me know just how agitated. As we parked outside the golf club he looked at me.

'You all right?'

My chest was getting tighter by the second. 'Yeah, I'm all right. My chest's a bit sore. Why don't you go and have a cup of coffee and I'll follow you in a minute when it settles down?'

He moved to get out of the car. 'You sure you're all right?'

By now the pain was getting severe. Maybe that was the point when I should've realised something was seriously wrong? But I had had the cardiologist's reassurance. I also had an image of heart attacks that involved left arm pain, sweating, breathlessness. None of these symptoms were mine.

'Yeah. I'm fine.'

So I sent him away.

I tried to relax my breathing as I'd done the previous times the pain had come. I got out of the car and leant on it for a little while to see if the change in position would miraculously ease the vice-like grip in the centre of my chest. I got back in the car and the vice became a burning spear that was pushing right though my chest and pinning me to the chair. My eyes welled with tears without my permission. I picked up the phone and found Rob's number. It didn't ring. I tried again. Nothing. I didn't think I'd get from the car to the club. I sat. I wiped the uninvited tear from my cheek and tried again.

'Hello I thought you'd . . .'

'Rob, you'd better come. I think I'm having a heart attack.'

I crawled over the gear stick. My chest was on fire.

Rob jumped into the car.

'Jesus, you look awful. What d'you want me to do?'

I stared straight ahead. 'Take me to the nearest hospital please.'

I wasn't thinking straight. The nearest hospital was 10 miles away. A clear head would have asked him to call an ambulance. A clear head would have asked him if he knew CPR just in case. But I wasn't a clear head. I was a frightened child. In a situation that was beyond my comprehension. The sun flashed on and off in my eyes as we sped through the trees. We turned out of the club towards the village of Heddon. Something about the pain changed. It didn't necessarily get more severe but something about it changed. I felt fearful and tearful at the same time. I wanted to throw up. I knew 10 miles was too far.

'Please pull over and call an ambulance, Rob, and call Geraldine. I don't think I'm going to make it.'

I heard him speaking on the phone. He was asking me questions and answering the operator's questions. I could hear panic in his voice. I was annoyed with myself that I'd put him in this position.

'*How old are you?*'

'He's forty-eight.'

'*How would you describe the pain?*'

'He says his chest is burning. He feels like he's being pinned to the chair.'

'*On a scale of one to ten, how severe is the pain?*'

When I told him he panicked. 'It's nine and a half. It's nine and a half!'

Rob was grey at the best of times but when we pulled the car over he looked white from his head to his boots. The paramedics arrived. An ECG, four aspirin and some morphine later, I was signing a form to undergo an emergency angioplasty. I signed under the line that read: *This procedure can lead to dizziness, headache, stroke and death.*

I tried to lighten the mood. A bad habit of mine.

'Have you got one that stops at dizziness and headaches?'

The pointy registrar looked unimpressed . . .

'You really have little choice but to sign this one.'

I took the pen. Stopped with the wisecracks and signed the form. I kissed Geraldine. I told her I'd see her shortly and was wheeled to theatre to have a stent inserted into my main coronary artery and stop my heart attack from killing me. It wasn't until everyone had gone home, and I was left in a ward with three men all over seventy, that the gravity of the day's events fell heavy on my aching chest. As I lay in the half-light, listening to my neighbours having a world-class farting competition, uncomfortable questions began fighting their way through the fog of my medication. *Why me? Will my life be shorter now? Old before my time?*

It felt as if life as I'd known it had changed and I could never go back to how it was. The illusion of certainty that convinced me I'd live forever was obliterated on one cloudy September morning. I'd been introduced to my own mortality. I fumbled for my phone on the cabinet and nearly knocked over the jug of water balancing on the edge of it. I sent Geraldine a message.

I loved her, really loved her, and was grateful for the life we'd shared till now. I was proud of the three boys we'd created and nurtured.

I pulled the curtains around my bed. I lay there in the darkness – wired up, tearful, and inhaling seventy-year-old shit. I tried to sleep but the pain in my chest and the restlessness in my head wouldn't let me settle. My mind was in overdrive. It was determined to take me on a journey. It darted here, there and everywhere, but then settled on a destination. It wanted to take me home. Not to Geraldine and my boys. Not to our home in the Northumberland countryside. But home to Ireland. To the place of my birth. To where I came from.

I could see a boy. He was six years old. He wore a red shirt and black shorts. His face was covered in mud and freckles and his knock-knees rubbed together with every step he took. He slipped unnoticed out of the back door. He looked at the big wall of the shed, tall in front of him. He wanted to climb it but he was scared he wasn't big enough yet. He was frightened he might fall. But he needed to climb it. He had no choice. He put his foot on the first step. His fingers found a gap and he slipped them in. He pulled himself up. His foot found its hold. He was on his way now. Halfway there his foot slipped. His knee collided with the concrete and it tore his skin from his kneecap. His blood trickled down his shin and into his sock. He thought of going back but was scared to look down. His knee was throbbing now. But he couldn't go back.

He had to keep climbing. It was the only way. He wanted to cry but big boys didn't do that. On he moved. One step at a time. He felt for the lip at the top. To get both hands on it he had to let go of the wall. He took a deep breath and jumped. He caught the ledge with both hands. His other knee made contact with the wall and he had a matching pair. He pulled himself to the safety of the roof and lay back to stop his heart from leaping out of his throat. He sat up and tucked his muddy bloody knees under his chin. He was where he needed to be now. He looked down through the kitchen window and breathed a sigh. He could see her.

She was smiling and singing to herself. He was happy now. He knew that if he could see her then she couldn't leave him. God wouldn't take her from him if he was watching over her. God had already tried. Tried to take her while he was sleeping right next to her. God gave her a heart attack when he wasn't watching. He'd tried to steal her away from him before he was ready. He wouldn't let God do that again. And God wouldn't be so cruel as to take her when he was watching. He needed her to stay. It was his duty to keep her safe. To make sure she lived. Today was his first climb to the top. He knew if he was there, watching, then she would never leave him. Her name was Bernadette and he climbed the shed every day.

CHAPTER 2

I WAS BORN in the summer of 1965 in Lisburn, Northern Ireland. Just before the onset of the Troubles in 1969. I was the youngest child of Patrick and Bernadette Ferris. We lived in a 1960s council house on the edge of the town. We were one of the few Catholic families who lived on the Protestant Manor Park estate. Lisburn was, and still is, overwhelmingly Loyalist and staunchly Protestant. Like everywhere else in this tiny remnant of the British Empire, the town and its people were tossed in the wind of political turmoil during that dark period in Ireland's recent past. My childhood was framed by it.

We were a happy family. My father worked as a labourer for Ford Motor Company in Belfast and my mother, like most of the town, worked in Hilden Mill, until her first heart attack, aged forty-one, meant she could no longer walk any distance without severe pain in her chest. I wanted for nothing. Love and affection were available in abundance. While money clearly wasn't, it never felt that way. Four themes ran through my childhood. Dominated it, shaped it, and sculpted the person I would become. They've at times cast a murky shadow or shone a bright light that has determined the paths I've chosen. I've battled against their influence on many occasions but I know that more often than not I've failed to overcome their grip on me. I've made life-altering decisions based on these four constants of my childhood. I've fought against them, but have never been able to outpunch them. They're unconnected in many ways and intertwined in others. Some have had more influence than others but each is indelibly woven into my life's journey. So what were these four cornerstones that have dominated my outlook and framed my world view?

The first was my mother's ill health, which I became aware of as soon as my consciousness was developed enough to appreciate how fragile life can be. I lived my entire childhood in fear that my most precious gift – her love – could be gone at any moment.

The second was the Troubles, which scarred my childhood and adolescence and helped shape my political beliefs to this day.

The third was the Catholic Church into which I was indoctrinated at an early age and I've been fighting against its dogma ever since.

Finally, there was football. It seems so trivial when I write it here next to the other three. But football has dominated my life since I first played for my school team, aged eight, because I was the only 'left-footed' boy available that day, until I left Newcastle United for the third and final time in the summer of 2009 having spent a total of eighteen years of my working life there over a twenty-eight-year period. I played for the club between 1981 and 1985. I was a physiotherapist there between 1993 and 2006. I went back as part of the management team in 2009, even though I'd left in 2006 vowing never to return. Football has been far from trivial in my life. Despite crying myself to sleep every night as a lonely sixteen-year-old boy all those years ago aching for nothing more than to go home to the love of my family, I still live in Newcastle upon Tyne because of football. My children were born and live in the city because of football. I've lived for thirty-one years in exile from the country of my birth because of football.

I sometimes wish it were more trivial but football and Newcastle United have had an enormous influence on my life. I was the youngest player ever to play for the team when I made my debut as a terrified sixteen-year-old boy. I was an integral part of the medical staff under Kevin Keegan, Kenny Dalglish, Ruud Gullit, Bobby Robson and Graeme Souness. I was the invisible man in Alan Shearer's management team and stood beside him as he took what I hoped would be his first steps into a long and successful managerial career. When he accepted the challenge of trying to keep Newcastle in the Premier League during the disastrous season of 2008–2009, I was proud to be there with him. I have some unforgettable memories of my time at Newcastle United. I've met some remarkably talented people. Great people. Decent people. There have also been many dark periods – unsavoury characters, unchecked egos. I'm grateful that my livelihood no longer depends on the whim of a failing manager or the prevailing mood of the moment at the club. Football was a big part of my life but I'm glad the page has turned.

I was three years old when the Troubles began. They were so much a part of my life that it's been all too easy to look back on them and think I wasn't really affected by them. But undoubtedly I was. My whole family was. My brothers, Joseph and Eamon, left Ireland in the early 1970s – not to find work, but because they'd been left with no other choice. When walking through the town one evening they were stopped by a group of men wearing balaclavas. They had hoods placed over their heads. Guns pointed at them. They thought they'd be shot there and then. They were forced to do 'press-ups' to exhaustion and were told if they stopped then the trigger would be pulled. Their crime? They were Catholics in the early 1970s, and had fallen in love with Protestant girls in Lisburn. They were ordered to end their relationships, or they'd be murdered. Rather than do so, they fled Ireland with their girlfriends. One minute they were in my life and the next they were gone. Lisburn wasn't a big town in those days. It was one of those places where everybody knew everybody. My brothers recognised the voice behind the balaclava. It was some-one they'd known all of their lives. It was also someone they knew to be a member of the newly formed UDA (Ulster Defence Association) – an organisation originally created to defend Protestant Ulster from the threat of the IRA. They knew the threat was serious and they knew they had to go. Whispered conversations and my mother sobbing at the kitchen table after they left for the airport were my only indications that anything was wrong in my world.

I remained largely protected from the polarisation of the two communities and the unspeakable atrocities that were a part of daily life in Northern Ireland in the 1970s. Lisburn was eight miles from Belfast, where most of the trouble was occurring. It was a pleasant market town that had grown around a once thriving linen industry. The large Protestant community lived in harmony with the very small Catholic minority. But in spite of this relative peace, it still had its share of bombings, sectarian violence and brutal kill-ings. We were in the unfortunate position of being part of the small but very visible Catholic minority. We occupied a larger four-bedroomed end-link property on our street of eight houses. Almost all of the end-links on our estate housed large Catholic families. We mixed freely with our Protestant neighbours most of the time. But then there was the 'Marching Season,' the time of year leading up to the celebrations of the Protestant King William of Orange's victory over the forces of the Catholic King James in 1690. Everything was different then.

'What's a Fenian bastard?'

I would have been around seven years old when standing at the sink peeling potatoes next to my mother on a sunny day in early July.

'You're wasting half the potato cutting it like that.'

At 4 feet 11 inches tall, she was small in stature, but big in heart and personality. Kind and loving in one sense, but fierce, protective, and argumentative in another. I never once remember getting the better of her in any discussion or argument. I don't recollect anybody doing so. If she was frightened of anyone or anything she did a remarkable job of hiding the fact. She would allow you to have your point, she'd listen, and then let you know why she was correct in the first place. She had a strong sense of right and wrong and was a shrewd judge of character. Because of her ill health, I felt an urgency to be near her and I could sense she felt that way about me. Her biggest fear was that she'd not live to see me grown up and independent.

'What's a Fenian bastard?'

She took the knife with half a potato on it from my hand.

'Where have you heard that nonsense?'

I started to cry. 'The older boys at the bonfire told me I wasn't allowed to collect wood 'cos I was a Fenian bastard.'

She sat me down and provided me with my first understanding that I was born on a troubled island and that we lived in a world that was dominated by religious and sectarian bigotry. I was called a 'Fenian bastard' on many occasions after that. Sometimes I'd be chased home from the Catholic school by gangs of kids shouting the limited number of obscenities they knew. They never caught me, but I can still feel the fear when outrunning them all the way to my back gate. Leaping over it to the sanctuary of our patch of back garden. (Some of them would be playing football with me in the park an hour or two later as if the 'chase' had never happened.) My mother sitting at night in the tiny kitchen listening to the 'police messages' on the transistor radio, and the snippets of news reports on the latest bombings or shootings were my main inklings to the desperate times we were living in. That all changed on a warm August night in 1976.

It was one of those brilliant summer days that seemed to last forever. I'd played football for hours with my friends in the park next to our home. I got to stay up late to watch *Guns for San Sebastian*, where fugitive Anthony Quinn disguises himself as a priest and helps villagers fight against a group of violent Indian intruders. I'd witnessed my first on-screen hero. My mother made 'potato-apple bread' – my favourite – apples, wrapped in flour and potatoes, baked, then smothered in butter and sugar. I shared a bed with my brother Tony in those days, much to his distress – he was four years older than me and spent his night's drawing imaginary lines down the middle of the bed. My straying limbs could never cross the line on pain of a swift knee to the thigh that would render my leg well and truly dead. We'd only just settled down, after our regular telling-off from my father, who had his own nightly ritual of threatening us with his belt if we didn't go straight to sleep. The threat never actually worked as he didn't once ever go through with his promise. As I was drifting off, the bed, the walls, and the entire house shook like we'd been hit by an earthquake. We jumped out of bed and raced downstairs. There was no one in the house. The front door was wide open and we could see the street was full of people. I could see my mother talking to Annie, our next-door neighbour.

'Get back inside you two.'

'What was the bang?'

She moved towards us and pushed us back though the front door.

'Get off the street. Standing there in your underpants.'

'Mammy, I'm scared.'

To my surprise the words came from Tony. I looked at him. He was shivering. She put her arms around him as she ushered us off the street.

'Was it a bomb, Mammy?'

'I don't know. Annie says she thinks it happened somewhere in Lambeg.'

She walked into the kitchen and put on the police messages. Through the crackling reception we could hear the panicked emergency services mustering and heading for the site of the enormous explosion. It had occurred 5 miles from our home but was big enough to make my bed shake. My mother peeped around the kitchen door to where we were seated side by side on the bottom stair.

'Go to bed and I'll be up in a minute. There's nothing to be scared of. It happened in Lambeg. Say a prayer that no one is hurt.'

I don't know how long we lay awake in bed after that. It felt like minutes, but it must have been longer before I finally drifted off. I awoke to the sound of glass breaking and a loud explosion. I could hear footsteps on the stairs and my father appeared at the bedroom door. He was waving his hands.

'Get up, get up, and get downstairs now!'

His fear became my fear. I jumped out of bed and followed him the few steps to the half landing of the stairs. He stopped before we turned the corner to make the rest of our way.

'Go straight out the back door and run to Agnes's house.'

Agnes and Felix O'Neill, and their eight children, occupied the four-bedroomed-link directly behind our house. The houses consisted of four small bedrooms upstairs. A staircase that turned on a half landing. A back kitchen that couldn't accommodate the smallest of tables without blocking both the doorway in and the doorway out. A thin hallway with a bathroom next to the front door. Off the hallway were two rooms. One was our living room and the other our sitting room. The sitting room was at the front of the house and was used only for special occasions. When we turned to head the rest of the way downstairs I could clearly see that this was a very special occasion. The sitting room was on fire. Flames and thick black smoke were billowing into the hall where my heavily pregnant sister Denise and brother-in-law Kieran were throwing buckets of water into the blaze. I stood for a moment and watched transfixed by the dancing flames engulfing our 'good room'. I watched the futility of their efforts as the heat from the inferno forced them back towards me in the hall.

'Get them out of here!'

My father was shouting. I don't know if he was worried for our safety or if he just didn't want us to witness their hopeless efforts to prevent our home from burning to the ground. He pushed us out of the back door and for the second time that night I stood in my underpants in the street. This time there were no neighbours milling around. No one at all. I ran to Agnes's house and banged on the door. I saw a light inside. She gave us tea and bread and put us to bed. There were six of us sleeping head to toe – me, Tony and four of her own. When I woke up I was soaking wet. I thought it was sweat at first but when I touched my underpants I realised I'd wet the bed. I felt the bed. There was a puddle all around me. I moved my body to lie on top of it in the hope that no one would know. I lay on that spot till all the others got up, then I slipped downstairs and I, my shame and my wet underpants sneaked past the three important-looking council officials standing in our kitchen. They were offering my parents a home in the Twinbrook estate on the edge of Republican West Belfast. It was a Catholic ghetto that had rapidly become a breeding ground for the IRA. It didn't take long for the council men to realise that Bernadette wasn't in the mood to be burnt out of her home. She had no desire to raise her two young-est children somewhere guaranteed to radicalise them. She'd rather stay in the town she was born in and bring her children up the way she wanted.

After changing my underpants and hiding the evidence. I walked fully clothed into what used to be our sitting room. The 'good settee' was now a hollow shell. The rest of the furniture was gone. Just black lumps of charcoal on the floor. The ceiling was black, the walls were black. The air was a mixture of smoke and chemicals.

'Don't just stand there with your arms the one length. Help me move this.'

My mother brushed past me, all aprons and rubber gloves. She picked up the edge of what used to be our good settee. A piece of charred wood broke off in her hand. She started to laugh but forgot to tell her tears.

'What happened, Mammy?'

I already knew most of the answer. The older O'Neill kids had told me last night before I wet their bed. There were well-worn charcoal tracks running from her eyes to her neck.

'We were petrol-bombed, son.'

'Why?'

'Why? Because we're Catholics.'

'Why us, though? The O'Neill's are Catholics too. They weren't petrol-bombed. Did we do something wrong?'

She looked at me with a mixture of helplessness and anger. 'No. They burnt eleven other houses last night too. We did nothing wrong. We're decent people. We're innocent people. We didn't deserve this. You don't deserve this. Never forget who you are. Never let things like this change who you are. The people who did this are scum. If they knew us they'd never do this to us. But they don't know us. Don't want to know us. But they can never beat us. Never frighten us. Never make us like them.'

She was holding me too tightly. I could feel her heart beating fast against me. I always felt safe when I could feel her heart beating against me. I could trust her with anything. So I told her my secret.

'Mammy, I wet the bed.'

It was the first of many wet beds I slept in. In the weeks and months that passed, I would regularly wake in the night soaking wet. When I wasn't being wakened in a puddle of my own making, I would be stirred in the night by the red glow of my mother's cigarette as she peered out of my window. She could barely see through it past the giant wardrobe that my father had positioned in front of it the morning after the attack. It stayed there for two years. She spent the hours of darkness standing there helping the wardrobe protect her child. It wasn't the only window that was blocked off. My father spent every night putting boards up on all of the windows he felt were vulnerable to any attack. Every morning they would come back down and we would carry on with life as if everything was normal. But it wasn't. The country was in the grip of violent paramilitarism on both sides and our daily life was dictated by the ebbs and flows of the conflict. If there was an IRA attack then there would be a UDA/UVF attack. In Lisburn, the Catholic community was an easy target. Several innocents lost their lives in appalling circumstances. Beatings, petrol bombings and vigilantism were part of the fabric of growing up there in the 1970s. Hooded men wearing facemasks regularly marched in drill outside our home. They were the local UDA. Often including off-duty members of the Ulster Defence Regiment, they effectively controlled the town. My father would regularly nod and say hello as we walked past the commander of the organisation. My mother would berate him for doing so.

'How can you speak to him? You know what he is. He probably knows who petrol-bombed our house. He probably ordered it.'

He would get annoyed at her. 'I speak to him because it's the polite thing to do. There's no point in going out of our way to antagonise him or anybody else. We've got to live here.'

My father was a well-known and very popular member of the Catholic community in Lisburn. Indeed, of the entire community. The pub and the church competed for his affection and the church often lost. I would often find him on his knees with his head buried into a cushion where he'd fallen asleep saying his prayers after drinking a few bottles of Guinness throughout the evening. He was a quiet, intelligent man when sober, and the life and soul of the party when drunk. He loved my mother with a passion and took pride in the achievements of his children. He worked all of his life and never once laid a finger in anger on me or any of his children. He left the disciplining to my mother and she was an expert at it. He was popular and friendly with our Protestant neighbours. It caused him great angst that no one came to help us on the night we were petrol-bombed. It hurt him even more that no one even mentioned it afterwards. It was as if it had never happened. My parents loved each other dearly. Despite many years of marriage they would often cuddle up on the chair and were always openly affectionate with each other and us. They would go out once a week on a Saturday night when my sister Denise would babysit me and Tony. One night there was a knock on the door. Denise opened it tentatively. It was a girl who lived at the top of the estate.

'Come quickly, your mammy and daddy are fighting.'

Denise started to run and paid no attention to my following her the short distance to the top of the estate. I expected to see my mother and father engaged in some sort of drunken fisticuffs. At eleven years old I was aware enough to be very embarrassed even at the thought of it. We approached a crowd of maybe fifteen or twenty people forming a circle. As we got there it parted to let us through. I could see two figures lying on the ground. I recognised my mother, bloodied and bruised, and trying to get up onto her feet. My father was flat on his back behind her. Denise moved towards them.

'Could somebody help me, please?'

She was pleading with the spectators.

'And call an ambulance.'

My mother and father hadn't been fighting after all. They'd been attacked and beaten up by eight men who had been drinking all day at a Loyalist marching event. They'd had the misfortune of walking out of the only Catholic club in the town just as the men were passing by. Words were exchanged and that was enough for them to break my father's ribs, my mother's arm, and leave them both in a bloody tangled mess on the ground for their children to scoop up.

The sitting room was crowded with people when the local commander of the UDA made his way into our home. Three of his colleagues followed. He spoke to my father first. 'I'm so sorry this has happened to you, Paddy. Rest assured this was nobody local. I'll do my best to find out who did this. I'll make sure they know this is unacceptable.'

My father shook his hand and was about to answer.

'Get out! Get out of my house! You're not welcome here! Get out!'

My mother was on her feet in an instant. She was pushing him with her unbroken arm; all 6 feet 2 inches of him. He tried to reason with her. 'Bernadette, I know . . .'

She just kept pushing him – screaming at him. 'Don't Bernadette me! Get out of my house and take your cronies with you! You've no place here and we don't need you here!'

He looked at my father as she bundled him out of the door.

'I'm really sorry, Paddy. I'll get to the bottom of this.'

With that she pushed him out the front door with her good and bad arm. He never did get to the bottom of it. We never did find out who was responsible.

CHAPTER 3

THESE EVENTS weren't the narrative of my childhood. Rather they were punctuations to it. Ours was a happy home and, my visits to the top of the shed apart, I was a contented child. My sisters Elizabeth and Denise helped my mother raise me. They took me everywhere with them when she was too ill to do so. We holidayed in Donegal every year. I'd look forward to these trips for months. When the day came, we'd pile into whatever wreck my father had recently bought. When he'd finished tinkering with every part of it, we'd set off three hours late on what seemed like the longest journey ever attempted. My father would sit on newspapers to help him peer over the dashboard. He'd get himself into a comfortable viewing position. This was usually hunched forward and squinting through his thick glasses and the top half of the steering wheel. My mother would spend the whole trip in a blind panic, popping angina tablets under her tongue, muttering something about Jesus, Mary and Joseph, and begging him to slow down. He loved his driving. He just wasn't very good at it. Every car he ever drove he claimed was 'pulling to the left'. Usually after we'd ended in a ditch or a hedgerow.

There could be four or five of us in the back seats depending on which friends we were allowed to bring. We were all elbows and corned-beef sandwiches. Whenever I dared to look out of the front window it would be just as my father was attempting to overtake another old banger on the road. I don't think he ever fully grasped the concept of overtaking. He'd wait for the gap in the traffic on the other side of the road. When it came, he'd let the opportunity pass and only then would he commence his manoeuvre. Right at the moment the ongoing traffic approached us. We usually completed an overtaking manoeuvre to the sounds of three car horns blaring.

We'd drive through border checkpoints, take in the wild beauty of Barnesmore's Gap, and head through Donegal town to our regular destination. Mrs Malarkey's guesthouse was perched on top of a mountainous forest, 2 miles out of town. We could see the rooftop in the distance as we turned up the steep tree-lined drive to get to it. It would have made the perfect setting for a Hammer House of Horror movie. When we reached the gate, the great white structure that was her luxury guesthouse sat imposingly at the end of a half-mile gravel drive. We had a ritual. I'd get out, open the gate excitedly, and jump back in the car. I'd then get back out again, close the gate, and get back in. With the beautiful old property standing proudly in the distance straight ahead of us, my father would turn the car sharp right and park it under a hayloft next to the gate. Under the same hayloft stood what must have been the oldest caravan in current usage in all of Ireland. It lived there because the roof leaked in so many places that it needed the protection of the extra roof. My father would bring me up to the house, where the old lady would smile at me and give me biscuits. He'd pay her; she'd pass him the key and we were on our holidays. I loved everything about those days.

My mother and father were always content to be 'down south' – their term for across the border. Tony and I were free to roam the forest and fields. We'd play Dead Man's Fall by throwing ourselves off the hay bales onto the other bales below. The imaginary weapon of choice would determine the theatrics of the fall. My favourite was the dagger. It allowed me to hold it in my stomach, stagger right and left and then perform a full somersault to my untimely death below. We made rope swings, carved our names in trees and used cowpats as targets to score points by dropping stones into them from all angles – we earned better scores for direct hits from further distances. I was blissfully happy. When we were in Donegal, I never wanted to go home. I would have stopped the clocks if I could. Even the chores didn't feel like chores. I can still feel the gravel crunching under my feet as I skipped along, two steps one way, two steps the other, from the caravan all along the drive and around the back of the house. All the while, happily swinging the 'shit bucket' I'd just collected from the outhouse next to the caravan. I'd skip the empty bucket all the way back, just in time for my father, newspaper in hand, to rush past me to get rid of last night's Guinness.

If the days were good then the nights were better. Every night we'd go to the Talk of the Town bar. We'd get sweets on the way in. The entrance to the bar was a shop. Not just any sweets but 'down south' sweets. They were different. Even Cadbury's chocolate was a different shape and seemed to taste better. We'd find a table and I'd drink Cavan Cola and eat Tayto Cheese & Onion crisps until my stomach hurt and my mouth burned. But the best bit was the music. I got to know and love the old Irish ballads and traditional music and the stories that accompanied them. I'd still be singing 'Whiskey on a Sunday', 'Carrickfergus', or 'Finnegan's Wake' weeks after we returned home. That love of Irish music – all music – seeped into my bones on those holidays and has been my trusted companion ever since. We arrived at the pub early and stayed late. The 2-mile journey home in the blackness of the unlit road was a nightly adventure, as Arthur Guinness was a big presence in the car with us – menthol sweets were never far from my father's lips when driving us home. We only once encountered a Garda officer. When I say encountered, I mean we saw the light on the back of his bicycle out of the front window. Then we saw the light on the front of his bicycle out of the back window as we watched him pulling it out of the hedge accompanied by the familiar soundtrack of my father muttering about the car *pulling to the left* and my mother *Jesus, Mary and Josephing*. When we got back we'd light the oil wicks in the caravan. We always got supper and would always play cards. It'd be daylight when we were bedding down for the night.

The mornings would be spent preparing to visit one of the many beautiful beaches in Donegal. Leckie and Rossnowlagh were my favourites. Often we'd only just be on our way when the first drops of rain would hit the windshield. In an instant we'd change direction and head for my father's favourite pub, O'Gorman Arms in Bundoran. There we'd spend the afternoon playing pool and, in my case, feeding the jukebox with my father's change until he'd had enough of me asking. I heard my first Bob Dylan and Van Morrison on that jukebox. Even today when I hear songs that I first heard in that smoke-filled bar room, it transports me to the innocence of those days. Harry Nilsson's 'Without You' and the Drifters' 'Save the Last Dance for Me' were my mother's regular requests. I'm with her every time I hear them.

There was a freedom and joy in those holidays that I wished would last forever. The songs and stories, the places and people – all of it – intoxicated me. The tensions of the Troubles in the north disappeared as soon as we crossed the border. They were completely erased by the long days and longer nights. I was cocooned and safe. My parents seemed younger, happier, and healthier. Nothing could spoil my bliss. Nothing. Well, when I say nothing . . . there was one thing. One thing always spoilt it for me. It was unavoidable. I couldn't escape it. Even daydreaming my way through it didn't help me avoid the tedium of it. Yes, the one thing absolutely guaranteed to burst my bliss bubble was Mass.

Bloody Mass. Bloody boring Mass. Bloody boring bloody Mass. Even on holiday we never missed Mass. Mass and prayers were as much a part of my existence as eating and breathing. I spent half of the 1970s kneeling in the living room mumbling 'Holy Mary Mother of God the Lord is with thee,' as we recited the Rosary after dinner. The rest of the time was split between my nightly prayers, my morning prayers, and going to Mass. Every Sunday we shuffled into the same pew on the back right of the giant Catholic Church on Chapel Hill. The same families sat all around us. I hated going. It was an hour of pure torture. Ritual chanting, sore knees, and an occasional elbow in the ribs just as my eyes betrayed me. The elbow from the left was my mother and the one from the right was my father. I'm sure they spent their whole time just waiting for my lids to droop and then *whack*. Some masses were worse than others. It all depended on the priest. If you got the parish priest, *Oh Jesus!* His sermons could last for an eternity. He was small, rotund, red-faced and possessed a monotone drone guaranteed to get me a smack in the ribs as soon as he *staaarrted speeeeaaaking reeeaaally sloooowlly*. He had an unfortunate habit of dipping his head to everyone he met. That earned him the nickname Noddy. If his sermons were boring, he was worse on his regular visits to school. I attended the local St Patrick's secondary school – a result of failing my 11-plus exams during the height of the petrol bomb, bed-wetting, and wardrobe over the window period. We'd stand in the assembly hall, the whole school, while he addressed us for an hour every Friday morning – usually informing us of the many ways we could get ourselves into Hell. Every monologue was accompanied by the sound of bodies hitting the floor as the combination of an inadequate breakfast and no air-conditioning took its toll on the regular fainters. It was an education listening to him, albeit a rather warped one at times.

'I'd like to talk to you all today about why many of you may be breaking the sixth commandment.'

Low murmuring in the room as 600 children worked their way through the first five to get to . . . *Thou shalt not commit adultery?*

More murmuring as confusion took hold.

'You don't need to be married to commit adultery.'

He was really getting into it, in full drawl now – every single word, every last syllable being stretched to breaking point for added effect. 'You can break the sixth commandment when you're on your own. In your bedroom or your bathroom. Touching your private parts is breaking the sixth commandment. Breaking the sixth commandment is a mortal sin. Mortal sin is punishable by damnation to Hell.'

That was the bad news. The good news?

'If you have broken the sixth commandment then you can still be saved from Hell's fire. Confess your sin and genuinely repent and Our Lord will forgive your evil.'

So there it was. My first realisation that masturbation existed . . . and was an evil just below murder on the scale of dastardly deeds guaranteeing a one-way ticket to Satan's bosom. He didn't just leave it there though. At the end of every confession over the next four years he'd always finish with a question:

'Have you broken the sixth commandment?' *He was asking me to add sins to my confession? I mean, Jesus Christ Almighty!*

The trouble was it seemed to me that everything was a bloody sin. Every action or natural instinct was a sin to some degree. Even being born and dying before you got baptised was a sin. My whole childhood was an invitation to feel guilty. I was encouraged to feel guilty about the greatest gifts of life – falling in love, feeling passion and desire for another human being; loving and wanting to be loved in return. God forbid you had an immoral thought before marriage.

When married, you were to make love only to procreate. Don't even think about doing it for pleasure. Definition of Irish Catholic foreplay? *Brace yourself, Bridget!*

Priests were the rock stars of our community. They had a direct line to God Almighty. Whatever they said or did was followed to the letter not just by my parents but by everyone. The church would organise youth discos every Sunday night in a little club behind the priests' house. I loved those nights. I would listen to the chart countdown on the radio in excited anticipation for the new Number One to be announced. Then an hour later I'd be at the disco wearing too much of my father's best aftershave and patches of my mother's foundation. A vain attempt to hide my ever-growing post-pubescent whiteheads from spoiling my chances of anybody even talking to me, never mind breaking the sixth commandment with me. Halfway through the night, Noddy or one of his brothers would stroll around the hall separating those of the opposite sex who were lucky enough to meet a girl and be holding hands or, better still, kissing. The end of the night was usually accompanied by an announcement that the local Protestant gang was waiting outside. We'd exit the building en masse, running frantically in all directions in the hope that the one or two thugs outside would catch somebody else and beat them up instead. Why we didn't just walk out together, all one hundred of us, and chase them off, I'll never fathom. The Catholic Church was all-pervasive in my childhood and adolescence. Mass – *mortal sin if you miss it*; confession – *only chance of repenting your evil ways until the next time*; sex education – *don't do it, don't think about it, and don't touch yourself while thinking about it*; Youth Club disco – *don't stand too close, hold hands, or kiss.* It was unbelievably easy to get into Hell when I was younger. I was so frightened by the prospect that I even started attending some non-compulsory masses. I think I was storing up anti-Hell points. At one of those masses my life changed forever.

The church had organised a service for all the young boys and girls from the parish. I'd gone with my friend – I think as much to see the girls as to listen to the priest mumbling. We were sitting at the end of the pew when the congregation made its way to the altar in an obedient procession to receive Communion. I recognised them all. Boys I played football with. Girls from my class. I looked to my right, just as an unfamiliar figure walked slowly past my seat. I turned away as quickly as I'd looked, but not before I'd made eye contact with the prettiest smile I'd ever seen. She had black hair, big brown eyes and a shy demeanour. When she caught my eye, I felt my chest tighten, my stomach turning, and my face flushing. She was the most beautiful girl I'd ever seen. I was sure she'd smiled right at me. I turned to my friend.

'That's my girlfriend.'

He swivelled his head. 'Who?'

'The girl with the dark hair there.'

He wasn't convinced.

'What's her name?'

Shit. He had me.

'We've only started going out together.'

He whispered in my ear.

'Not only is she not your girlfriend but she never will be.'

'Why not?'

'Cos she heard you saying that and is now thinking you're some sort of creep.'

I didn't look up.

'Please tell me she didn't hear me?'

'Afraid she did and she and her friend were laughing as they walked past.'

I'd blown it before even finding out her name.

In the days and weeks that followed she dominated my thoughts and my conversations. I'd get butterflies in my stomach just at the thought of her smiling at me. I found out her name and that she attended the local grammar school. I saw her once or twice in town. I thought she'd smiled at me once from a distance but couldn't be sure. My weary friend finally snapped.

'Just get on with it and ask her out, will you?'

I was sitting with him in my formerly petrol-bombed sitting room. The charts were on the radio and we were getting ready to go to the disco.

'I can't.'

'What do you mean you can't?'

'I've never spoken to her. She probably doesn't even know I exist.'

He was getting annoyed now. 'You've been boring me for weeks with stories about her smiling at you more than once. Did she smile at you or not?'

I was getting annoyed now.

'Of course she did. Well . . . I'm sure she did. She didn't just have wind, you know?'

He was heading out to the hallway. 'Where's your phone book?' He already had it in his hand as he came back in.

'You know her name. You know her Da's. This shouldn't be difficult.'

Before I could speak he was walking towards the phone. I chased after him and pulled his arm.

'What are you doing?'

He showed me the page. 'Three numbers match that name in the entire phonebook. Hers must be one of them.'

I could feel a mixture of fear and excitement building in my chest. He was on a roll.

'She's never heard you speak?'

'Correct.'

'You don't know if she knows your name?'

'Correct.'

He started dialling the first number. 'The way I see it is this. If she answers and I say "Hello, it's Paul here," she's either going to say "Paul who?" Or "Hello, Paul." If it's the first answer I'll hang up. If it's the second answer then you've got yourself a girlfriend. She'll think I'm you and I'll arrange the date for you. It's ringing!'

I was pacing up the narrow hall in one direction and my stomach was moving in the other. I can't remember much else after he asked to speak to her.

'It's Paul here.'

He turned towards me as he said it. I could see he was raising his hand. He flicked his thumb out and gave me a huge grin. *She knew my name. She was saying yes to a date. She could meet me tomorrow at seven.* It was 12 October 1980. She was thirteen and I was fifteen.

Geraldine McCaugherty became my childhood sweetheart and my first love that day.

CHAPTER 4

S HE LOOKED so peaceful, sleeping on the little sofa in our tiny box of a front room. She was curled up, lying on her right side, with her left hand under her chin. A photograph taken many years ago hung behind her head. It was of a smiling beautiful teenager with the entire world in front of her. It was *her*. Before marriage, the passing of time, and seven children had distorted the image. I was five years old and hungry. I tried to waken her. Usually she'd make me toast and jam or a sandwich when I got dropped off from school. But today was different. When I balanced my way along the garden fence *like the expert tightrope walker I'd become*, I could usually see her shaking her head in mock disgust. I leapt off the gate *like the world-class long jumper I was*. I landed softly and stood to attention just as any self-respecting Olympic gymnast should. She wasn't at the kitchen window to witness my awe-inspiring athleticism as usual. But she was always there. In the whole two years I'd been going to school she was always there. I opened the back door and called her.

'Mammy, I'm back.'

There were no sandwiches on the messy table, no toast browning under the grill. I pushed the living room door open and saw her sleeping. *Sleeping when I was starving?*

'Mammy, I'm back.'

I found her on the settee. I shook her arm but she didn't stir. I was so hungry I left her there and went back to the kitchen. Two slices of burnt toast later I was sat on the floor in front of her watching *Scooby Doo* in black and white. I fell asleep with my head under her chin.

'How long's she been sleeping for?' There was urgency in my father's voice.

'I don't know, I . . .'

He was lifting me off the floor.

'It doesn't matter, son. Get Agnes or Annie and get them to phone the doctor.'

That was my mother's first heart attack. She was forty-one and I was five. I didn't know it was a heart attack. No one ever told me. I just knew something was very wrong in our house. Something was wrong with my mammy. Her movements were slower after that. She couldn't walk too far. She loved to dance but from that point she had to sit down after one quick waltz round the floor with my father. She never said anything to me, but she held me tighter than before and for longer than before. For my part it was like a magnetic force pulled me to her. I wanted to be beside her all of the time. She'd get annoyed with me sometimes.

'Get down off that shed and stop staring though the bloody window. Go and play with your friends.'

But I'd just get back up again and sit there for hours. Watching her through the kitchen window. I was frightened that if I let her out of my sight God would take her. So I implored him not to. I'd take the crucifix from the upstairs landing. Place it on a chair outside my bedroom and pray. And pray. And pray. At night, sometimes I'd wake in a panic and imagine she was dead. I'd creep out of bed, creak open my door, tiptoe to my parents' bedroom and watch through the darkness to see the bedclothes rising up and down. One night I awoke to a commotion. I could hear her struggling for breath. She was in pain. I froze with terror. My heart was pounding out of my chest.

All my praying in vain? This was it. She was dying.

I could hear my father. He was panicking. I regained my courage and jumped out of bed. I burst through their bedroom door, distraught by now.

'Mammy, are you all right?'

There was silence. Then they both sat up. My father shouted first. 'Jesus Christ, son. She's all right. Get back to bed. Now will you get out and shut the door.'

I had a mother with angina and a father with asthma. I never did venture into their bedroom again.

They were a loving couple. They'd hold hands; she'd sit on his knee. They'd kiss on the lips. *My friends' parents didn't do that.* After dinner and the Rosary, they'd curl up on the sofa together. My father never tired of telling me how beautiful Bernadette Corrigan was when she was younger. She never disagreed. She still had a beautiful face, even then, after the first heart attack. Wide eyes, high cheekbones and a warm smile. She carried a little weight, they both did. Their small frames couldn't disguise it and a diet of potatoes and fried meat ensured it stayed that way. I never had any doubt they loved each other. Especially my father. He loved her. He idolised her. He wasn't one for grand gestures. He was a loyal husband and father, who believed it was his job to provide for her and for us. He believed in hard work, modesty and decency. His formal education ended aged fourteen when he was forced to get a job to help support his family. His formal education might have ended prematurely but he was full of knowledge. He could recite rhymes – naming every country in Europe. He was an avid watcher of any political debate; especially those involving the Troubles. He would perform complex mental arithmetic and come up with the exact pay-outs for his multiple bets on a Saturday morning. After her heart attack I found myself with him more often. A lot of my time was spent kicking my feet at the betting shop, kicking a football in a pub car park, or drinking a coke in Mooney's pub while he gulped his Guinness when we should have been in the butcher's or baker's.

'Do you know Guinness is the only drink mentioned in the Bible, son? Jesus said those who are not for us are *a Guinness*.'

It was his favourite line and I had no reason to doubt him. I never doubted him. Until the day he was supposed to take me to Mass and he didn't. Instead we drove to the other side of town – paying no attention to oncoming traffic as usual. Once through town we turned left, then right, then left again and stopped outside an unfamiliar house in an unfamiliar street.

'Where are we, Daddy?'

He swivelled on his newspapers and looked at me earnestly over his thick glasses.

'Can you keep a secret, son?'

I was uncomfortable now. I didn't know how to answer. I was ten and old enough to know this was wrong. He dipped his hand inside his jacket and leaned towards me in the back seat. He was brandishing a key.

'This is the key to my other house.'

I felt sick.

'Promise you won't tell your mammy about this?' I thought I was going to throw up. He got out of the car. I didn't follow him. I wanted my mammy.

'For Jesus sake, Paul. Get out of the bloody car and come on.'

I followed him through a small rusting gate, up two broken steps and through an overgrown garden. He raised the key to the lock that was sitting loosely in the ageing door. The rain started to fall heavily outside as we entered the dark hallway, and I could feel my stomach begin to betray me as we walked up the stairs. I could hear laughter as we reached a closed door at the top. Adult laughter and excited children screeching. My mind was in a fog. *How could this be happening? How could my daddy do this? Was this my other family behind that door? How quickly could I get home and tell my mammy?*

He pushed the door open and I followed him in. *We were in the same room as my other family.* I held on to his arm. My eyes fixed firmly on the knotted and dirty wooden floor. A strange voice was speaking to me now. I raised my head.

'What can I get you to drink, son?'

I looked around the room. There were two children playing with some cards at a table by the window. They were a little younger than me. The only other thing in the room was a long wooden bar with two men sitting on one side and the man on the other side who offered me the drink.

'You must be the wee footballer your da' is always bragging about?'

The man closest to me was smiling at me. He was skinny with thick dark hair.

'I'm Raymond and this is John.'

The other man got off his stool. He was tanned and handsome. He brought me across to the other kids. We stayed for the exact length of time of the Mass we'd missed. My daddy laughed, drank, and talked animatedly with his friends. I played cards with their children. We were driving home now.

'Where was that, Daddy?'

He was leaning forward, eating menthol sweets, and peering through the steering wheel. 'That's the Hibs Club.'

'Is it a pub?'

He smiled at me.

'As far as your mammy's concerned, it's Mass, son.'

I kept his secret. *Even if it did cost me a mortal sin for missing Mass.*

The following week I was playing football when a large explosion scared the interest in the game out of me. I ran home to find my mother in the kitchen listening to the police messages. I went to my room to get changed but fell asleep on my bed instead. I walked downstairs two hours later and found them in the living room. My mother was sitting on his knee. His head was buried in her chest. His shoulders were heaving. A UDA bomb had destroyed the Hibs Club and two men had been killed. They were Raymond Maze (aged thirty-three) and John Tennyson (aged twenty-seven).

I saw my father crying for the first time.

CHAPTER 5

I DON'T REMEMBER a time before football. Every day I played with a ball. When there wasn't a ball, then a crunched-up tin can, a bag of my mother's washing or a balloon were always in danger of a good kicking. I'd spend hours roaming the house, juggling a balloon with any body part, to keep it from hitting the floor. I'd play every day after school in the recreation centre next to our house. My brother and his mates would be there. They were four years older than me but made no exceptions for that. It could be fifteen-a-side on a tiny patch of grass. To get a touch of the ball at all was a rarity. To get it and not be cut in half by some clumsy big lump was a miracle. I became a master at skipping lunging feet, at stopping, changing direction rapidly, and back again just as quickly. The playground at school during lunchtime was a free for all with fifty screaming boys chasing one tennis ball. I'd watch the stampede, marauding one way then another and bide my time. Then I'd find my way through the uncoordinated throng, get the tiny ball and try to keep it for as long as I could. I seemed to be able to move faster than my friends, to anticipate their movements and react to them.

'Could I speak with Paul Ferris please?'

I looked up from my books to see Mr Murray, the P7 teacher, standing at the front of my P5 classroom. I was a good student, never one to misbehave; even the thought of it churned my stomach. My mind was racing. *Am I in trouble?* I followed him outside the classroom into the cloakroom crammed with winter coats. He had a round face; a kind face in corduroy trousers.

'Don't look so worried, Paul.'

I did '*worried*' very well. It was a *Hell* thing.

'I've been watching you playing football in the yard. You're very good. The school team has a game today against Forthill. I'd like you to play. You're left-footed, aren't you?'

My heart was pounding. *The school team?* The school team was for eleven-year-olds. The big boys. I was eight.

'I can't, sir, my sister's picking me up after school and I will . . .'

'Don't worry about all that. I'll sort things out with your sister. Now do you want to play or not?'

It was the most exciting question I'd ever heard in my short life. Did I want to play for the school team? With the big boys? The heroes of the entire school? Of course I did. But . . .

'What's the matter, son?' He leaned towards me. He had a kind face and bad breath.

'I don't have any boots, sir.'

He laughed. 'You worry too much. I'll drive you home when your sister gets here and we can get your boots.'

He had misunderstood.

'No, sir. I mean I don't have any boots.'

Two minutes later we were outside his office and my head was buried in the stagnant Lost and Found box. Two hours later I was standing on the left wing, in a shirt that was meant for an eleven-year-old, holding my shorts up with my right hand, staring at my lost and found boots which must have been discarded by Bigfoot himself, when the hailstorm started. Freezing, lashing rain and howling wind combined to spray hailstone bullets against my defenceless thighs. I barely touched the ball, didn't know where to run, or what to do. I spent most of my time worrying as usual that I'd never be picked again. Never be picked to stand in a giant's boots, getting pelted by hail bullets and playing for my school team.

Then it happened.

The invisible ball somehow found itself in unknown territory, 10 yards in front of me. I started to chase after it. It was rolling towards the left side of the 18-yard box. If I could get there before the lanky full back running alongside me I knew exactly what I would do. My heart was pounding out of my chest and my shorts were slipping down my thighs. My hail-battered legs reached it just before him. I pulled my left foot back to shoot and was glad Sasquatch's boot stayed on my foot. I threw my leg forward with all my might to strike the ball just as the full back slid to block the shot. Then I stopped and placed my foot right on top of the ball. He skidded past. His friend rushed to his rescue but before he could settle himself I flicked the ball over his right foot and ran around his left side. The goalkeeper was rushing at me. Without moving the ball I exaggerated a full movement to my left, and he dived in the direction of my body. I stood still. Looked up at the empty goal in front of me. And one touch later I was in love.

If I was in love with football as a boy I had a brief fling with boxing. My brothers all played football and they all boxed. So I was sent off, reluctantly at first, to the ABC Boxing Club, which sat perched on the River Lagan at the bottom of our town. For a small club it had produced some very significant fighters from its tired little gym. It was all very strange to me at first. But once I got used to the smell of stale sweat and the weight of the enormous gloves I really got into the swing of it. I loved the training – hitting the heavy bags, dancing around the ring, sparring with my friends. My first fight came along very quickly. It was a Friday night and the tiny gym was packed with parents, and thick smoke. (Not my parents – they had a prior arrangement at Mooney's pub. *They had lots of prior engagements there.*) My knees were knocking as I climbed through the ropes. My gloves felt like they were made of concrete. My opponent was a skinhead from Belfast who didn't smile much, I tried to give him my best 'I'm nice don't hit me too hard' look but he was all grimaces and punching himself in the face. The bell rang and he ran towards me. He threw a punch, I swerved – he missed. For three rounds he threw a punch, I swerved – he missed. The ref raised my hand, which was more than I'd done the whole fight, and I was on my way home with a shiny medal and a dilemma. Was I going to be Kevin Keegan or Muhammad Ali? I knew I could play football but now I was a boxer too!

'I'm not going to bloody boxing to sit and watch someone punching the shite out of my child,' she said.

My father was annoyed with her.

'Come and support your son, Bernadette.'

I butted in.

'Please, Mammy. Everybody else's mammy and daddy will be there.' That always worked. 'Anyway, I'm so fast nobody can hit me. The wee skinhead I fought last week hit himself more than me.'

When the day came I was so proud stepping through the ropes with her in the front row. *One fight, one win.* No knocking knees and the concrete removed from my gloves. My opponent was a big skinny thing with a mop of curly hair and a buck-toothed grin that he shared shyly with me as we touched gloves. The bell rang and he loped towards me. He threw a punch, I swerved – he missed. Then he hit me with his other hammer right on the nose.

Wow.

It stung a little and made my eyes smart. He threw another. I swerved straight into the same hammer.

WOW.

I felt my nose squash against my face. It made my eyes water. I'd only just recovered and worked out not to swerve into the big hammer when he threw the jab again and hit my non-swerving nose again.

Jesus Christ, WOW.

My watering eyes sent an instant signal to my brain. My shoulders starting heaving. The next thing I remember the ref had his arm around me and was taking me out of the ring. I didn't look up. 'The winner is . . .'

Big tall gangly thing with buck teeth. Fight stopped due to the next Muhammad Ali crying like a baby.

I did that all the way downstairs to the changing room – until my mother came in. 'Stop your crying and let's get out of here. I've never been so bloody embarrassed in all my life. It's safe to say you're not a boxer, son.'

I stood up, wiped my eyes and took the loser's medal she'd collected for me. It looked just like the winners' one from the week before, only there was no star surrounding the image of the two boxers in the middle.

'Boxing's all right until the other person hits you. Then it's shit.'

She moved towards me. A middle-weight with angina. 'Stop your bloody swearing.' She raised her hand to clip me round the head. I swerved – she missed. It was my last act as a boxer.

CHAPTER 6

I F MY boxing career was halted in its tracks, *due to too much crying*, then my football one was rapidly developing. A losing argument with my sister that Adidas had three stripes, and not four, ensured I was the not-so-proud owner of my first pair of boots – Woolworth's Winfield's. Santa could also get confused in our house sometimes. I once bounced out of my front door on my new Space Hopper only to be confronted by three of my laughing friends on theirs.

'Why's yours blue?' I didn't have a chance to answer.

'And why has it got glasses?'

Jesus, the shame! Santa had brought me the only blue, glasses-wearing Space Hopper and he got all my friends the orange one. The Pogo Stick the following year was a problem, too. My friends would be pogo-ing happily to their hearts' content on theirs while I would be trying to do the same on mine. Theirs had a nice soft spring that allowed them to spring up and down all the way along our back alley. My spring was so firm that I think my Pogo Stick was basically just a stick. One bounce, maybe two, and I was off it and on the ground. My bleeding knees ensured my love of pogo-ing waned by Christmas night.

As my footballing prowess became more apparent I moved on from Woolworth's Winfield's, mainly because one of the soles fell off in one game and flapped about like a dislocated jaw and couldn't be repaired. I passed through a Gola phase and onto *Patrick Keegan's*. I loved them, not because they were great boots but because I idolised *him*. Kevin Keegan was my hero and Liverpool was my team. Everybody in my family and in my town supported Man United but Liverpool was my team. If I was playing with my friends in the park I was always Kevin Keegan. If I was practising on my own in the garden, I would run like him and provide a full commentary as I weaved my way through imaginary defenders before reeling off in triumph after dispatching the ball past the despairing dive of the invisible keeper. I did dump him briefly during two World Cup tournaments in favour of Gerd Müller – *twisting and turning, and always scoring* – and Mario Kempes – *all long legs, flowing locks, and ticker tape* – but in the main I was a loyal disciple. I'd watch him in games for Liverpool and England then go straight outside the following day, and copy the darting runs off Toshack's flicks, the one-twos with Trevor Brooking, or impossible twisting headers against Italy. He broke my heart when he left for Hamburg. Kenny Dalglish eased the pain but there was something about Keegan. He was the first superstar to enter my consciousness and make me want to be a footballer. And believe that I could be.

When I wasn't watching football, or trying to be Kevin Keegan in the park, I was scoring goals. Firstly for my school team, St Aloysius, and then soon after for Lisburn Youth. Lisburn Youth changed the course of my life. In the early 1970s Northern Ireland was in the brutal grip of tit-for-tat sectarian violence. Every IRA atrocity was followed by a UDA/UVF one. Lisburn was an ugly town to live in. Against this backdrop a group of enlightened friends in Alexander's pub at the edge of town, decided to create a cross-community football team to bring children together in the hope that football would play a small part in educating tolerance and understanding between both sections of the divide.

Eddie Coulter, a Protestant labourer, Jim Kerr, and Sean Ricard, a Catholic factory worker and teacher, were later joined by Les King and Robbie Walker. Together they changed the lives and attitudes of the many children that joined their little club. I don't think even they knew what a profound and positive impact they had on the lives of so many, me included. I joined Lisburn Youth when I was nine years old and was very quickly nurtured to play with the older boys. I played for the Under-11s in my first year. Football felt easy to me. I was lightning fast, was small, and could change direction and stop and start sometimes before my opponent had started to follow my initial movement. If we won 3–0, I would score two. If 6-0, I would score five. I knew before every game that we would win and I would score. I'd go home after games and get the familiar question from my father: 'How many today?'

Bursting with pride, I'd reel off the number for him. I lived for Saturday mornings. *Zorro* and *Champion the Wonder Horse*, on TV, followed by the long walk to the Barbour playing fields to play for my team in the morning, and the older team in the afternoon. I loved the noise of the boots on the wooden floor in the changing room, the smell of wintergreen, and even pouring hot orange over my boots to stop my toes from falling off in the icy winter mornings. I lived and breathed it all. When the early game was over, me and Marty Crossey would share fish and chips and ice cream from the Royale. We'd eat them sitting on the swings, in the derelict old park opposite the chippy. I met Marty on the first day I turned up for training and instantly knew we'd be friends. He was a year older than me – tall and gangly and too sensible by far for a ten-year-old. I looked up to him all through my time at Lisburn Youth. The days in the park eating fish and chips cemented our friendship through the years. The team quickly built a reputation for winning. Every league, every cup, every tournament, we would be there at the end, in the final, winning the cup. I'd be there, man of the match, top goal scorer, winning goal in the cup final. I was lost in a world of football. When we weren't playing, we were training. We had no facilities and used to train on a Tuesday night in the old markets area of the town. We'd enter the old sheds where the market had been that morning. We'd clear the debris and rotten fruit and veg out of the way, turn two stalls on their sides and train on the solid concrete floor. I loved the training but lived for the games. I'd hover on the wing waiting for Marty or one of the others to feed the ball to me and then I'd be off, all instinct, speed, and twisting and turning, the coaches on the side roaring their encouragement.

'Take him on, wee man.'

'He can't live with you.'

'Cross it. Shoot. Pass it. Brilliant, wee man. Can you? Can you?'

And then cheers when the inevitable goal went in.

'So you did, wee man.'

'So you did.'

So you did. Those three little words were my favourites in the whole world. They meant success, approval, reassurance, belief, confidence. When I heard them my chest swelled, my head buzzed, and I felt like I could do anything. I'd take the slaps on the back from my team-mates, race back to the halfway line and get ready to do it again. I did it so often before the age of eleven that I woke up one morning with my mother screaming at the top of her voice from the bottom of the stairs.

'Paul, get down here now. Get up. Get up.'

I slipped out of bed and into the freezing dark bedroom. My bedroom was always freezing. The whole house was – except for the living room, where the coal fire was. When the fire was lit the living room was warm but then my bedroom above it would fill with thick smoke that poured out of the unused fireplace next to my bed. The room was always dark on account of the giant wardrobe covering its only window.

'Paul, where the bloody hell are you? Get down here now.' She was scaring me now. I was racking my brains to work out what I'd done to get myself into trouble. I pulled on my Manchester United shirt – the result of another lost argument with my sister who insisted it was the same as a Liverpool shirt because they were both red.

My parents were sitting on the sofa when I peered around the door. My mother looked like she'd been crying. *I was definitely in trouble.* Maybe they'd found the packet of Rich Tea biscuits I'd stolen from the VG store on Longstone Street? I'd hidden them in the hedge at the end of our front path. Every night, for two weeks, I'd sneaked out and brought one in to dip in my tea. I'd dipped for too long a couple of times lately, and the remnants were mulch at the bottom of my cup. *Had I incriminated myself for failure to dispose of the evidence?* I sat on the chair opposite. She had a letter in her hand. She'd definitely been crying. I got ready to confess. *Always better to confess. Show remorse.* My hands were wet and my stomach heaving. *Just say it. Tell them you're a thief. Get it out.* My mouth was dry.

'Mammy, I sto . . .' She didn't let me finish. Instead she stood up and handed me the letter. I looked for signs that it was from the police. I recognised the crest and read:

Dear Mr Ferris,

I am writing on behalf of Manchester United Football Club. I have watched your son Paul play for Lisburn Youth on several occasions and have been very impressed with his performances. I'd like to offer him a one-week trial at the club's Cliff Training facility during the next school holidays. If this is an opportunity that you would like him to take, could you please let me know at your earliest convenience?

Yours sincerely,

Bob Bishop

Manchester United Football Club

I looked up and she was definitely crying. *Good crying. Not, my youngest son's a thief and going straight to jail (and Hell) crying.*

My father spoke for them both. 'Do you know what this means? Bob Bishop wants you to go to United. Bob Bishop discovered George Best, son, and he wants you to go to United. I've always said footballers are born not made and you're a natural, son. We're so proud of you. Our Paul going to Manchester United.'

I'd never felt so happy. Sitting there in my Manchester United shirt, with my Manchester United letter in my hand. The joy of making my parents proud made me feel 10 feet tall. In my head I was already playing at Old Trafford, getting slaps on my back from Sammy McIlroy and Gordon Hill, with the manager shouting in my ear.

'So you did, wee man.'

'So you did.'

'What did you steal?' The lights of Old Trafford faded and my thoughts turned to my mouldy stash in the hedge. *Always better to tell the truth. Confess. Show remorse.* My tongue didn't agree.

'I . . . I stood on something sharp in my bedroom. I . . . I . . . I don't think I cut my foot but it was really sore. I'll go and see if I can find it.' I bounded up the stairs, taking them three at a time. I front-flipped onto my bed and lay there with the letter in my hand. The thought of my mother's temper had scared the truth clean out of me. I squinted at the crest in the darkness. I was going to Manchester United.

I thought about my biscuits in the hedge and my lie to my mother. *I was going to Manchester United . . . and heading straight to Hell.*

CHAPTER 7

THE WEEKS leading up to the next school holidays passed in a blur. New boots, new clothes, new pyjamas, new suitcase, and new popularity at school. When the day finally arrived my father drove me in his latest death-trap. We headed out of Lisburn and up the mountain towards Aldergrove airport. The snow was falling lightly across the headlights as we started ascending the winding 14-mile drive. By the time we got to Dundrod, my father's car was really pulling to the left. Every corner he turned to the right, the car paid no attention, and continued in a straight line, or veered off to the left. We got stuck. The snow was blanketing down by now. I placed my freezing hands on the front bonnet while he reversed with one leg on the road and one on the accelerator. I could hear him cursing the snow under his breath. He'd later find out it wasn't the snow's fault after all. He drove me the whole way there, and himself the whole way back, in a car without a working steering column. For the first time in his life his car really was pulling to the left and my mother wasn't there to curse her way through it.

As we approached the airport terminal, I could see an old man with three boys huddled against the wall just outside the entrance. We hurried towards them. After my father's tenth apology for being late the old man shook my hand. 'You must be my flying winger?'

He wore a tatty old trench coat, his thinning white hair was blowing in the wind, and most of his teeth were a distant memory. He looked just like Clarence Odbody- the guardian angel from It's A Wonderful Life.

'I'm Bob. Let me introduce you to my boys.'

He motioned towards the three boys eyeing me suspiciously from behind his back. I nodded and they all nodded back. Two were definitely my age, eleven at most. Both slightly taller than me. *Everybody was.* The other must have been fifteen at least. He was a giant compared to the rest of us. 6 feet maybe? He looked a bit like my friend Marty. He looked like Marty would have looked if he'd been brought up on the Shankill Road, had a skinhead, and was four years older. I felt a pang of something I'd not felt before as I watched my father walk off into the distance and on his way to completing his miracle of driving a car down a mountain with no steering column. My legs felt a little weak as I stood at the check-in with my new acquaintances. I'd never been away from my parents before, never been on an aeroplane before, and never been anywhere with people I didn't know before. I was excited to be going but anxious to be leaving my father. As we walked towards Departures the older boy spoke to me.

'You play for Lisburn Youth?'

He sounded younger than fifteen. When I looked at him his face was younger than his size. He had kind eyes and smiled at me. 'We play you next week.'

I was glad of the conversation.

'Who do you play for?' I asked.

He laughed.

'Well, it's a bit of a mouthful. I play for East Belfast Liverpool Supporters Club.'

I was more confident now. 'Jesus. How d'you fit that on the shirts?'

'We don't. It's EBLSC for short.'

I realised then who he was. Sean and Les had been talking about us playing them soon. We were top of the league by a long way but they were second. We were a team but they had one player. One player that everyone was talking about. I didn't tell him I knew who he was.

'I'm Norman. Norman Whiteside. My friends call me "Smiley".'

He was two months older than me. An eleven-year-old man.

We stayed in Salford Polytechnic's halls of residence, where I had my first (and last) meat and potato pie. I closed the door to my room at the end of the long hallway, staring too long at some gruesomely ghoulish artwork on the wall. I switched the light off. Then quickly back on. I lay in the dim light fretting about my mother and her health. When morning came I felt like I hadn't slept. My drenched pyjama bottoms told a different story. I peeled them off and hid them in my case. I washed myself and pinned the St Christopher medal my mother gave me, inside my fresh underpants. I picked up my boots and headed to training with the thirty other trialists – wondering if anyone else had scared themselves shitless, hardly slept, pissed the bed, and had a safety pin down their underpants?

After getting over the shock of seeing and speaking to actual footballers, living breathing footballers I'd only ever seen lose to Liverpool, I was now in the changing room with the other boys. It was noisy with excited chatter. It was like they'd known each other all of their lives and not merely just shared one rancid meat and potato pie supper. There were boys from Ireland, Scotland, Wales, and accents from all over England. Some were more confident than others. Some more excited than others. One boy from Nottingham walked around with his willy standing to attention the whole morning and every morning after that. *Noddy would have had a field day with him*. I think it was at that moment when I realised I was different from the other boys. Not obviously so. Not walking around with my willy pointing to the sky. Just different. Quieter. Gentler. Timid maybe?

Shy definitely. Stiflingly. Gut-wrenchingly, shy.

I wanted to be in the room with them there at Manchester United. But I wanted to be anywhere else but there too. I wanted to talk to the other boys, *apart from Stiff Willy*, but the words just wouldn't come. So I sat in crushing silence while they all made friends until it was time to train. When we trained it wasn't like Lisburn Youth. There was no Marty Crossey. No knowing looks from my coaches. This was every man for himself. I was unable to get the ball for the first two days. No one passed to me and I stood on the wing, help-less and hopeless, my hands down my shorts twiddling my St Christopher. I'm sure the coaches must have thought Bob Bishop had lost his mind. As the week progressed, I spoke with more of the boys and got to know the coaches; I eventually found my voice and got better and better. I played so well on the last day that the coach called me over after training and asked if I'd like to come back in the next school holidays. *Not bad for a non-sleeping, bed-wetting mute.*

If I got better as the week progressed, Norman was head and shoulders above everyone from day one. Not just in stature but in ability too. I'd never played with or against anyone like him before. I was proud of how well he did against the English, Scottish and Welsh boys. Being Catholic or Protestant didn't matter outside of Ireland. We were the same – we were Irish. They would have signed him there and then if they could. Two weeks later I met him again at the Barbour playing fields in Lisburn. We were playing EBLSC. I was walking to the pitch with Les King, my manager. I was trying to explain what I'd witnessed in Manchester.

'Nobody's that good, wee man. He looks like a big lump.'

Les was listening but he wasn't hearing me.

The game finished Lisburn Youth 6 – EBLSC 4. I scored my customary hat-trick. Norman scored all four of their goals, including a volley from the halfway line, and nearly beat us by himself.

CHAPTER 8

'For Jesus' sake, will you leave Kieran alone?'

It became one of my mother's most used lines. Kieran was Kieran Moran, who came into my life when I was seven years old and has been a constant presence ever since. A denim-clad, long-haired music fan, who started going out with Denise when he was sixteen and would later become my brother-in-law. But he was much more than that to me. He never once said no when I pestered him to play football with me in our little patch of side garden. He would be at one end of the narrow strip and me at the other. We would play Long Booting. I'd hit the ball as hard as I could to try and score past him and he would do the same with me. In the early days he would trundle his shot towards me and I would smack mine with all my might but barely reach him. Every day we'd play. As I got older and stronger the games became more competitive. When I started to win regularly he moved the goalposts literally. He took me over to the recreation centre and increased the distance so I could hardly reach again. His desire to beat me really helped my ability to strike the ball accurately.

Joseph and Eamon were living in England when Kieran and Denise started dating. My brother Tony was four years older than me and regarded me as a bit of a nuisance. He was always being forced to bring me with him when he was going out to play football with his mates and would sometimes take his frustrations out on my shins. Patsy, my eldest brother, was into drinking heavily and

squeezing my knee viciously when drunk. I tended to avoid him
when he was drinking, unless I was passing him in the street on a
Saturday afternoon, when he was guaranteed to be really pissed.
Then I'd go out of my way to cross the road to meet him. He'd be
bouncing off the walls.

'Hiya, Patsy.'

He'd stare at me through the fog. Recognise we were related. Do
his best impression of a weeble and fill my two hands with all the
change from his pockets. I'd be straight to the shop and fifteen
minutes later my jaw would hurt from stuffing myself with toffee
dainties and penny chews. It was very different if he was at home
after a night out. He would grind his teeth and pit his wits against
me. And take pleasure from breaking my spirit. He was seventeen
years older than me. One night, when there was just me and him in
the living room, he sat down beside me, gripped my skinny leg just
above my knee and squeezed it so hard and for so long that tears
welled in my eyes.

'Let go, Patsy. You're hurting me. Let go, please.'

He squeezed harder.

'Please, Patsy.'

Nothing.

He just sat, staring at the TV, grinding his teeth, and squeezing
my eight-year-old leg as hard as he could. I tried to wriggle away.
Tried to prize his clamp off me. I couldn't move him. Until I gritted
my teeth and nipped him as hard as I could. I felt his grip slacken a
little. Got my fingers under his thumb and yanked it with all my
might. He yelled and let go. I jumped from the chair, was on the
move, and screamed at him through my tears. 'Fuck off, you vicious
bastard and leave me alone.'

I was barely at the living-room door and he was staggering to his
feet after me. I ran along the narrow hallway into the bathroom and

bolted the door. He banged it and banged it. I sat on the floor with the toilet at my back and wedged my feet against the door. I could see the bolt rattle and move every time he slammed his fist against it. 'I'll fucking kill you, you wee bastard. If I get my hands on you I'll fucking kill you.'

He stopped banging but I didn't move. I sat there with my back hurting from the toilet seat, my bum numbed from the hard floor and my legs burning from the pressure of the door. I woke up with my father screaming at me for spending too much time in the toilet when he was busting for a *merry and bright*.

I had good reason to be frightened of Patsy. He had a reputation as a hard man. His wife's bruises also indicated he didn't care who he hit. I once watched him break my father's ankle by repeatedly slamming a car door on it while me and Tony sat terrified in the back seat. When I was a little older, I witnessed him in action again. I was babysitting for my brother Eamon, who had come home from England, and lived on Longstone Street. It was getting late and I was desperate for him to come home so I could get some sleep before football in the morning. I heard a commotion outside and peeped through the blinds. I could see four figures arguing loudly straight across the street. One man was leaning against the window of a little terraced house. There was a woman standing next to him. The other two men had their backs to me. The woman's arms were wind-milling everywhere and she was spewing swear words like a demented banshee. The man leaning on the window was pushing at the man in front of him. In the half-light I recognised that the man being pushed was Patsy. I'd only just established that when he lunged forward and head-butted the big man through the living-room window of the house. The lights were on and there were people in the room. He climbed through the window and was on top of the other man using his fists as pistons on his face. He was still throwing punches when he was being pulled out of the window. He was like a wild animal. I felt like I was going to throw up. My legs started trembling and didn't stop until Eamon came through the door.

There were many other incidents. He once got high on Poteen and pills and was causing mayhem at the top of our street. My only knowledge that something was wrong was walking into the living room the following morning. My mother was lying on the sofa. He was kneeling in front of her pleading, praying, apologising – and saying that it would never happen again.

What was never going to happen again was that he was never going to punch her again, never going to pull her hair out in clumps; never going to not recognise her in a drug induced state and never again going to tear her dress off her body. He'd never again beat up his angina-riddled mother when she intervened to try and stop him fighting anybody and everybody in front of him.

It wasn't just physical violence with him. I shared a bed with Tony, and one night Patsy came in and told us to be quiet. We watched him walk out the door and close it behind him. We lay talking, and giggling, for another hour afterwards. But when I turned around to go to sleep he was there, kneeling by my bed with his eyelids turned inside out, just staring wildly at me. I screamed so loudly that my father raced up the stairs. *I almost shit myself. Physically shit myself.* He'd opened the door to leave but hadn't. Instead he'd ducked down, crawled back in, and shut the door from inside the room. He'd never left the room. Then he'd crept along to my bed and stayed there silently waiting for his moment the whole time. He was married with a child of his own at the time. I've been scared of the dark ever since – I slept with the light on after that and still do sometimes when I'm alone in the house or a hotel room.

Kieran filled the role of big brother. He played football with me when I'm sure he would rather have been doing anything but. He came to my games and watched me play. He encouraged me and was proud of my performances. He took me to Northern Ireland games. It was a big adventure, the train journey from Lisburn to Windsor Park, buying souvenirs and hot dogs before kick-off. We'd stand in the Kop listening to the Loyalist sectarian chanting and I would get to catch glimpses of my heroes between the moving heads in front of me. I saw Kevin Keegan in the flesh for the first time and half the Liverpool team who played for England at that time. It was exhilarating. Kieran was a big influence on me in many ways and I loved being around him. He loved his music and shared that with me. Our house was full of music before Kieran ever stepped into it. There was a big radiogram that ran along the entire length of the living room. It was filled with The Rolling Stones, The Beatles, The Who, Bob Dylan (Joseph and Eamon); The Kinks (Patsy); Motown, Amen Corner and the Monkees (Elizabeth); T Rex, (Denise); Patsy Cline and Country Albums (Mammy); The Dubliners and Irish Albums (Joseph). I loved them all. I woke up one night in the living room and to my embarrassment my mother and father were playing the cassette recorder I'd spent the night performing into. Andy Kim's 'Rock Me Gently' and Glen Campbell's 'Honey Come Back' (complete with the talking bit) didn't sound nearly as good coming out of the recorder as they did going in.

Kieran introduced me to other music, including Simon and Garfunkel, Gallagher and Lyle, Lynyrd Skynyrd, James Taylor and Clifford T Ward. Along with his brother Paul, he seemed to hear of all the new bands before anybody else and he was always introducing me to stuff I'd never heard before. With Kieran around, my football going well, and my newly discovered love of music, I was content. I never did go back to United. Several stubborn conversations with my parents and they eventually gave in. The halls of residence, my painful shyness, and the boy with his willy in the air, all dampened my desire to ever return. It was 1978, Christmas was coming and all was well in my world. Then my mother had her second heart attack, *and third, fourth, fifth and sixth.*

CHAPTER 9

BY THE time she'd finished having heart attacks, including one cardiac arrest, and after three weeks in hospital being brought in and out of sedation, she was functioning on less than half of her heart's capacity. She also developed unstable angina. I developed sores on my knees from praying to the crucifix on the upstairs landing, my eyes hurt from crying myself to sleep and my spirit was shattered at the thought that I'd lose the most precious thing in my entire universe. I visited her in the hospital. Seeing her lying helpless, unconscious, with tubes and wires everywhere increased my fear and anxiety so much that I couldn't go back. Even when my father told me she was OK I still couldn't go back. I just wanted her home. When she came home she was different. Smaller. Slower. Less than before. If she couldn't walk far before, now she could barely walk any distance at all without stopping to wait for her chest pains to subside, or to pop a pill under her tongue to ease the suffocating tightening in her throat. I never left her side. My friends would call for me to go out and play and she'd tell me to go, but I always found homework, or chores to do. The fear of her not being there meant I couldn't let her out of my sight. I felt that if I was with her then she wouldn't be able to leave me. I lived in constant fear that she would die. If she did I wanted to be with her. *To go with her.*

She still did all the things she had done before, but she rested more, slept more, and stayed in the house more. When she did go out, it would take an age to get there. We would stop every five minutes so she could catch her breath. On a windy day I would sometimes hold an umbrella in front of her and she would hold on to my arm as we crawled along to the shops. I'd have to stop myself from walking too fast or she would let me know by pulling on my arm. She was forty-nine, but she was an old woman. The picture on the wall in our living room was the only glimpse of what she had been. In it, she was smiling shyly, head tilted, curls around her cheekbones, and wearing make-up for the first time in her life. She was fifteen in the photo and looked like a Hollywood movie star. My father would tell me stories of how they first met – of her beauty, her smile, and her dancing. On the few occasions I was at a social event with them he'd take her hand and walk to the dance floor. They'd get into position and then, just for a fleeting moment, they'd glide as one, gracefully around the room. Their eyes fixed on each other, their hands locked, their bodies as one. I'd see the people they once were right there in front of my eyes and then all too quickly they were gone again. It was always over as soon as it had begun. She'd have to stop. Her angina was strangling the life from her. I wished I had known her when she was younger. I wished I had known her when she was healthy, invincible and ready to take on the world.

My father would tell me stories about her father. He was a violent alcoholic who had suffered a head injury during his service in the First World War. He returned home with some souvenir shrapnel embedded in his skull. He would regularly beat her mother. He once sat her on the hot stove in the kitchen and held her there. He'd sometimes throw the whole family out and my grandmother would walk her four children around the streets until he fell asleep in his drunken stupor and they could creep back in and sleep till he was sober. At fourteen my mother fought her father; she fought him to stop him beating her mother, her brothers Patsy and Josie, and her sister Alice. She stood up to him and let him beat her instead. I knew my father's stories were true because that spirit was still there, despite her fragile heart. She wasn't afraid of anyone or anything. She was gentle but could be fierce – especially if anyone threatened her family. My father would say he didn't know what she saw in him and she would smile and agree. But it was clear she loved him as much as he did her. He was five years older than her and already had a job when they met. She lived in Hilden and he was from the Low Road. In those days there was nothing but a long dark track separating the two areas. He was 5 feet tall and so scared walking the lane that he used to light his cigarette, and hold it above his head to convince any would-be attackers he was 6 feet 2 inches instead. They courted for five years but fell in love at the dances. Every weekend they'd be at one dance or another and every weekend they'd glide their way to a prize. You could still see their grace in their fleeting moments before she'd pull his arm and he'd walk her slowly back to her seat.

My father worked night shifts for Fords Motor Company. I'd wake every morning to the smell of him cooking scallops in the pan downstairs (thin slices of potato fried in lard and smothered in salt and vinegar). At nights after my homework I'd sit with her, curled up beside her, listening to her heart beating. We'd talk about anything. I'd tell her I didn't want her to die. She'd promise she'd asked God to spare her until I was old enough to look after myself, until I was reared. She made me feel I was capable of anything. She taught me the importance of decency – to be kind to myself and others – to stand up to those who behaved badly. Sometimes at night when I'd wake shivering with fear from my latest nightmare she'd let me climb into her bed. She'd snuggle up behind me and she'd take my hand and I'd be asleep before my head touched the pillow. On nights when my father was home she'd tell me to curl up behind his back and then she'd do the same to me. I'd wake up soaked with sweat, and gasping for air. I'd gently pull the blankets down and suck for air. I never complained, in case they wouldn't let me back in again.

She started smoking the day my father stopped. He was twenty-three and she was eighteen. It was the sophisticated and grown-up thing do. Thirty years later my daily – sometimes twice daily – routine after school was to run to McFarlane's shop to buy 20 No. 6. Or 20 Embassy Pure Virginia. Or 20 Embassy Regal King Size. Or 20 Benson and Hedges. Or 20 Silk Cut. Or 20 Park Drive. They had to be filter-tipped 'cos she said that protected her. After the latest heart attacks, I'd buy her Solent menthol cigarettes because she said they were better for her. I loved going because most times she'd let me have a penny or two from her change which I'd spend on toffee logs, toffee dainties, or candy longs. One day while in the shop I got her cigarettes as usual and two toffee logs for myself. As I was leaving I spied Mrs McFarlane coming around the counter carrying a big cardboard sign. She stood it up. It was taller than her and me. It read:

Cadbury's Curly Wurly
A chewy caramel ladder draped in delicious milk chocolate.

'Would you like one? Mrs McFarlane snapped me from my chocolate-induced trance.

I looked at my toffee logs, which had suddenly lost their lustre. They looked tiny compared to this new chocolate ladder to heaven in front of me. I looked at the 12p change in my right hand and my toffee logs in the other.

'How much are they?'

She was opening a box full of long thin strips.

'3p.'

I looked again at my toffee logs. I was tired of toffee logs. All thoughts of my mother's anger and the deceit I was about to commit which would nudge me further down the road to Hell were replaced by my overwhelming desire to taste this new exciting bar of choc-olaty toffee goodness.

'If I give you back my toffee logs and 2p will that be OK?'

She handed me the bar and took my logs and my mother's 2p. I was outside the shop in an instant. I sat on the little wall between two spikes that were designed to maim anybody who was careless enough not to look before putting their bum down. I peeled the wrapper off and sniffed the chocolate into my lungs. I stared at the zig-zag pattern of the toffee ladder. *Compared to my toffee logs this was huge.* As I bit into it the chocolate fell off and I caught most of it and stuffed it into my mouth. The toffee stretched into long gooey caramel strands that melted slowly in my mouth then combined with the chocolate and stayed there for ages. And that was only the first bite. I ate the rest of it with my head pointing to the sky for fear of spilling any of the chocolate to the pavement. As I started walk-ing home the first pangs of guilt pricked my bliss. By the time I'd reached my front door I was firmly in Hell and going to cause my mother another heart attack. I fully intended to confess until she was standing right in front of me. I gave her the cigarettes and short-changed her. I was halfway down the path, relieved that I had got away with it but still a bit distressed that I was going to Hell.

'Paul.'

'Yes?'

'Come here a second.'

I was back in front of her now.

'Where's the rest of my change?'

I didn't look up as I started to explain. 'There's this new choco-late bar called a Curly . . .'

The stinging in my ear told me I should have looked up.

'What have I told you about stealing?' She slammed the door. I walked down the garden path past my hedge that had previously held my stolen Rich Tea. The pain in my ear was already easing. I thought of the ten minutes I'd spent eating my Curly Wurly. It wasn't worth an eternity in Hell. But a slap around the ear?

It was definitely worth that.

CHAPTER 10

'WHAT'S USLTER?'

My mother was standing at the sink washing breakfast dishes when I pushed through the back door.

'You're late for school. What are you on about?'

'Come outside and I'll show you.'

She followed me out in her dressing gown, tea towel in hand. I took her around to the side of the house and pointed to the gable wall. There in red paint in giant dripping letters was scrawled:

FOR GOD AND USLTER

We stood staring at it for a little while. She started to head back to her dishes.

'That's the work of an illiterate bigot. And that's why you should stick in at school.'

It was such an unusual event. It was 1980. I was fifteen and my mother's heart condition had become part of normality for me. The Troubles never really troubled me much anymore. The wardrobe was back against the wall. The petrol-bombing was a distant memory. My brothers were home from England and married to the girls they had done their press-ups for. My football was getting better the older I got. I was quick and strong and had grown, or 'filled out' as my mother would put it. I'd discovered new interests to distract me from football and the fear of my mother dying – music and girls. I loved music. Every night I'd listen to Radio Luxemburg into the early hours, frantically taping songs as soon as I recognised the first few bars. I had cassettes full of songs with either no intro or with some late-night DJ babbling all over them. Girls had stopped being irritants to be avoided at all costs, though my shyness ensured I still never got too close to them. And I loved school.

After the disappointment of failing my 11-plus during the petrol-bombing, parents getting beaten up and mother having a heart attack period, I quickly settled into a routine at my new school, St Patrick's. I was placed in the top class at eleven, and was top of that class every year after that. I loved school because I was good at school. In tests it didn't matter if you were quiet or shy. If you knew the answer, you got top marks. My secondary school leaving age was sixteen. No A level option. I'd decided I would pass my nine O levels with A grades, and then go to Rathmore Grammar School to complete my A levels. It was a well-worn path for the brightest kids from St Patrick's. I was very fortunate at school – Sean Rickard, my Lisburn Youth manager, was also one of my teachers. He must have spoken well of me in the staff room, as I felt the teachers were really on my side and willing me to do well. Sean encouraged me at every opportunity. He believed in me and made me believe in myself. I felt anything was possible with my football and my school. I'd signed schoolboy forms with Bolton Wanderers and spent every school holiday training next to Burnden Park. I'd watch Peter Reid, Sam Allardyce, Willie Morgan, Alan Gowling and the others training for their next match and I'd eat pie and chips and Supermousse in the main stand every day after training. I was always glad to get home after my trips away. I was guaranteed an apprenticeship at sixteen – which meant I'd leave home and live in Bolton. It was there on the horizon but I never really paid too much attention to it. I never really thought it would happen because I really believed I was on my way to Rathmore and then Queen's University. Nobody in my family had ever been to university and I was sure I was going to change all of that.

One day, as I entered my fifth and final year, I was called into the headmaster's office. When I left I was wearing a shiny new badge – I was the head boy of the school. I raced home to tell my mother, but when I got there, she told me she had some terrible news. Bolton had sacked their manager and all of his staff. I'd received a letter. *I was no longer guaranteed my apprenticeship at the end of the year. I wasn't going to be a footballer after all.* I feigned enough upset to convince her I was devastated, then skipped upstairs and front-flipped onto my bed. I studied my shiny badge and felt pretty content. I was relieved I wouldn't be leaving home after all. I smiled at the thought of Queen's. I'd be the first person in my family to go to university – now that would be really something. I'd never wanted to leave home in the first place. But this desire not to go had taken on an urgency lately. *I couldn't go.* Not now. Not ever. The thought of moving to England, away from my home, my family, my mother, had always been a troubling one for me. But now there was a bigger reason. Something had happened to me in the last year that had changed everything. Changed who I was. How I felt. What I wanted. Geraldine McCaugherty had said yes to my friend's offer of a date. Since that day we'd walked and talked, held hands and kissed, promised and planned our way to this point. I couldn't even imagine moving to England for one day without her, never mind going there forever.

I didn't get off to a good start on our first date. My choice of Hawaiian shirt, white pleated trousers, and black and white winkle picker shoes, caught her off guard, I think. Or it might have been my mother's necklace that I decided to top it off with. If that wasn't bad enough, my multi-coloured underpants, which were completely invisible when I put them on, were suddenly lit up in all their technicoloured glory by the fluorescent lights of the disco. As ABBA were belting out 'Super Trouper,' the lights were illuminating my pants so much I had to spend the whole night pinned against the wall just to stop people pointing. I was so nervous that when I first looked at her I had to quickly look away. My face was burning and my hands were shaking. I was sure she'd made some terrible mistake and checked with her that it was me she was expecting. When she smiled at me she was even prettier than I had imagined in my head. She had big dark brown eyes, and a beautiful wide smile. She was younger than me and maybe just as shy as me. Not too shy that we didn't speak, but shy enough that we didn't say much. We were two children playing at being adults. My heart thumped when I saw her and didn't slow down the whole night. *I think the light shining on my underpants contributed to that.* When I walked her home and we'd reached her house, I asked if she'd like to see me again. The four sticks of Wrigley's Doublemint I'd been chewing all night – *just in case I got to kiss her* – obstructed my tongue a little, caused me to salivate too much, and made me sound like I had a speech impediment. But in spite of that, she said yes – and then kissed me and my Doublemint.

We saw each other at every opportunity after that. This usually meant me walking from my school through the town to the bus stop in Market Square, where she would get off with all the other kids from Rathmore. I'd then walk her back through the town to her house opposite the chapel on Brookvale Rise. Her parents owned their own home and she was at the grammar school. That was enough to make me worry that maybe I wasn't good enough for her. At weekends we'd walk. We'd walk for miles and end up in Hillsborough Park. There we'd sit, hold hands, tease and laugh with each other and then all too soon we'd have to start the long journey home. Occasionally we'd steal an evening together, when she skipped her piano lesson, or Girl Guides. We'd sit in the freezing darkness of the recreation centre next to my house and hold on to each other to keep the chill from our bones. She was easy to talk to. I could tell her anything; my hopes and dreams, my fears about my mother. I could tell she had a good heart. She was kind, understanding, clever, and really really pretty. When I wasn't with her I would close my eyes and conjure up an image of her in my head. When I'd see her next she'd be more beautiful than any image I'd managed to create. I would daydream about her when I should have been studying and think about her when I should have been concentrating on the match I was playing in. At night my recordings from Radio Luxembourg became songs for us. Dire Straits' 'Romeo and Juliet' became our song. Then I heard 'Brown Eyed Girl' one night and thought Van must have written it for her. When I was training or playing for Lisburn Youth I'd get reports from Marty of how he'd met her in the canteen or corridor at school.

'Did you tell her how many goals I scored?'

He'd just stare at me, shake his head and smile. 'No. We were too busy talking about where we were going on our first date.'

'Really?'

'Of course I bloody told her. She's as bad as you. All she wants to talk about is you. I don't see what all the fuss is about myself. But each to their own, I suppose.'

I really wanted her to know about my football. I was a bit embarrassed about being Head Boy, in case it made me seem a bit uncool. The football thing would hopefully tip the scales the other way. On a bitterly cold and rainy day in January I got the opportunity to show her for myself. Rathmore were drawn to play St Patrick's in a schools cup competition. It's all we talked about at Lisburn Youth in the weeks leading up to the game. Marty and a few of the others would be on one team and me on the other. Geraldine said she'd come and watch. The game was at the recreation centre. I could see the bench where we regularly sat just behind one of the goals. In the distance I could make out the rooftop of my house. As kick-off approached I could see her and a friend sheltering under an umbrella and walking towards the pitch. I felt more nervous than I had ever felt on a football pitch. But if the thought of Geraldine watching me potentially lose to her school team made me nervous, it was the person I noticed standing half-hidden under the tree in front of her that set my knees trembling.

In all my time playing and scoring goals for Lisburn Youth, my post-match ritual was the same. I would go home or to Mooney's pub and find my father. He'd then ask the simple question and I'd proudly tell him how many. In all that time, that was my ritual because he never once came to watch me play. I used to ask him to come but he'd say something about not being one of these 'pushy parents' shouting on the touchline. He seemed convinced by his own reasoning. I had strong suspicions that the kick-off time far too often clashed with opening time at Mooney's. On a dark and rainy afternoon in January the two people I wanted to watch me play most in the entire world were standing yards apart as the referee blew his whistle. We were 1–0 down in two minutes, courtesy of a Marty Crossey goal before I'd even touched the ball – but I needn't have worried too much. When I did get the ball I set off on one mazy dribbling run after another and didn't stop until I'd rounded the hapless goalkeeper and scored. I just repeated again and again and again. When the final whistle blew. I shook hands with Marty.

'You bastard.'

I shrugged my shoulders. 'My girlfriend and my da' were watching. Sorry, Marty.'

He laughed. 'I'll let you off as long as this is never mentioned again?'

I agreed and looked under the tree for my father. He wasn't there. Had he missed it? Gone home early? Or was the call of Mooney's too enticing? I felt a rush of disappointment. All that effort. Lung-busting runs. All those goals. And he'd missed it?

'You were fantastic.'

I took my gaze from the empty space under the tree. Geraldine's friend's eyes were bulging with excitement as she spoke to me. 'Really frigging fantastic.'

I looked at Geraldine's face and could tell I never had to worry about being Head Boy again. Her boyfriend's team had obliterated her school team. All of the cool footballers in her school had just lost 15–1 to her boyfriend's school. Marty, who was my biggest champion and best friend, had just watched me score nine times against him and his mates. Her friend was looking at me like I was Kevin Keegan ... *I felt like Kevin Keegan.* But my father had gone ... he'd missed my greatest moment. Nine goals in one game was a big event for me. I'd scored three, four and five before, but *nine*?

I walked the short distance to my house still in my soaking school kit and my bootlaces thick with clagging mud. I slipped my boots off at the back door and pushed it open into the kitchen. It got half-way before hitting a familiar block. My father was in his chair at the small kitchen table. The table and chairs only fitted in the room when no one actually sat in them. When they were occupied they made getting in and out a challenge even for my wiry frame. I squeezed past him and into the room, which smelled of home baking. My mother loved to bake – she was very good at it. She lifted a giant mince pie out of the oven just as I managed to wriggle past his chair. She surveyed my muddied kit.

'Jesus, would you look at the state of you? Go and get yourself washed. Your dinner's nearly on the table.'

My eyes weren't on her. My father was sitting behind the *Belfast Telegraph* he was reading. I could just see the top of his Brylcreemed head. I waited for him to speak. Where was the familiar question? If he hadn't bothered to stay, he could at least ask me the question? I couldn't bear the suspense any longer.

'Did you not stay and watch the game, Daddy?'

He folded his paper. I could see that his hair was wet with rain and not Brylcreem. He took his thick glasses off and sat them on his newspaper.

'I did, son. I watched the whole thing. Left just as the final whistle blew.'

I felt a flutter of excitement in my chest. *He'd watched the whole thing? All the mazy runs, all the goals, my best ever performance and he'd witnessed the whole thing?* I'd put on a show and it was a monumental triumph. I looked into his eyes. He was staring intently at me now. He had a quizzical, pained expression like he was trying to break wind but his bum wouldn't let him.

'Can I ask you something, son?'

I got it now. I knew what was bothering him. It was the third goal. When I'd picked the ball up on the halfway line and slalomed my way past the entire opposition before knocking it to one side of the advancing goalkeeper and running around the other side. Then I'd stopped abruptly as I was about to shoot, ensuring the clumsy centre-half slid right past me and the post as well, allowing me to tap into the empty net. No wonder he was confused; even I didn't know how I'd managed that! I think it was because I was showing off for him and for Geraldine. Showing them what I could do on a football pitch. That's definitely what it was. I waited for him to either break wind or ask me how I'd scored that goal, or nine goals in one game. He didn't break wind, kept the same pained expression and asked me a different question. 'Son . . . do you never bloody pass the ball?'

His paper rose to his face. He was oblivious as my heart travelled in the opposite direction. My mother's mince pie lacked its usual flavour that day.

CHAPTER 11

THE SUMMER of 1981 was a turbulent one in Northern Ireland. The hunger strikes in the Maze Prison 3 miles from my home were dominating the news and political agenda. There was a standoff between the British government and IRA inmates, over the latter's right to be regarded as political prisoners. Bobby Sands had been elected to parliament in April while on hunger strike, and then died in May. 100,000 people attended his funeral in West Belfast. Margaret Thatcher showed little sympathy for the manner of his death:

'Mr Sands was a convicted criminal. He chose to take his own life. It was a choice that his organisation did not allow to many of his victims.'

Riots erupted across Belfast and Derry. More hunger strikers died. More riots ensued. Still Margaret Thatcher steadfastly refused to negotiate a settlement with 'criminals'. In spite of international condemnations and pleas to do so, she stood firm while ten hunger strikers starved to death for the right to be regarded as political prisoners and not 'criminals'. I hated her for it. I hated her for her arrogance and unwillingness to talk to men who were starving themselves to make their point. The very act of starving themselves to death to highlight the strength of their convictions was a political statement in itself. I didn't for one second believe that Northern Irish prisons were filled with burglars, muggers, and bank robbers. They were bursting with prisoners on both sides who had committed acts of political violence. To label it as anything else was a complete absurdity. A deliberate distortion of the reality I was living in. I'd been brought up to abhor violence from wherever it came. There was no sympathy in my house for anyone who committed acts of violence as a political weapon – I lost count of the number of times my mother or father would condemn the IRA as murdering terrorists. The hunger strikes changed the conversation in school and at home. How could the prime minister just let people starve to death, no matter who they were or what they'd done, and not even speak with them? How could she let a sitting member of parliament die and not attempt to negotiate? After Sands's death, the other hunger strikers contested and won various elections north and south of the border. I followed the progress of the hunger strikes on the nightly news. I talked with friends at school. I questioned my father on the legitimacy of both sides of the argument. I felt strongly that I knew where the blame lay for the deaths of the hunger strikers. It lay with Margaret Thatcher and the British government. I was becoming politically aware.

My mother sat me down on more than one occasion to ascertain how far my sympathy with the plight of the hunger strikers extended. She was reassured that my interest was not in running off to join the IRA, but that I felt there was an injustice happening on our doorstep and the prime minister was displaying a cruel and uncaring attitude to the plight and suffering of fellow human beings. I didn't care whether they were terrorists or not. I didn't understand how our government would let anyone die in our prisons without at least trying to find a resolution. I think my views worried my mother and she was concerned that I was becoming radicalised by the unfolding events. She was desperate for my football to be a pathway to a better life. Away from the daily murder, bombings and bigotry she had grown so tired of. She saw no future for me – for any of us. She wanted a better life for me and was pinning her hopes on me moving to Bolton when I was old enough to take up my apprenticeship as a footballer. She felt I had a better chance at life outside Ireland; especially if she wasn't going to be around to look after me. She had been devastated when the Bolton offer didn't materialise. More so now that the province had erupted again in the wake of the hunger strikes. She needn't have worried. A future with Geraldine and getting into Queen's University were very much at the top of my agenda.

I told Geraldine about the Bolton thing while we sitting on the floor in her living room making tapes of our favourite songs.

'That means you're not going?'

I was twirling a pencil through the middle of the cassette, trying to rescue our days' work after her father's hi-fi had chewed Cliff Richard up right in the middle of 'Miss You Nights'.

'That means I'm not going.'

She threw her arms around my shoulders and knocked me to the ground. We lay there holding each other in the silence with the unravelled cassette trapped between our bodies. My moving to England had been a cloud over us ever since the day I had mustered all the courage I had and whispered 'I think I love you' in her ear three months after we met. She made me remove the 'think' and told me she loved me back. We were so young that I don't think anybody took us seriously. Even when we'd spend every bit of spare time we had together. My parents had taken her to Donegal with us that summer. We'd upgraded from the caravan to a small two-bedroomed chalet opposite my father's favourite pub. My mother, who could be a tough judge, liked her right away. They struck up a relationship instantly and developed a bond of their own. I shared a bedroom with my parents and she slept in a tiny room wedged between the kitchen and the bathroom. I awoke one night to see my Guinness-filled father disappear into the bathroom next to her room in the silence of the night and lay there squirming with embarrassment while he produced a bowel movement that sounded like ten machine guns being fired simultaneously.

He commentated on every bullet. I thought it was never going to end. The smell of it reached my nose before he staggered back into bed and was snoring before he was lying down again. I lay there soaked in sweat with the hot smell enveloping the room . . . and thought about her in the tiny room right next door to the war zone. I prayed that she was asleep and had missed his Guinness torpedoes. I mentioned it to her at breakfast and she said she didn't know what I was talking about. But the crimson flush in her cheeks when my father walked out of the bedroom and sat beside her at breakfast told me she'd heard every last bomb. If she still loved me after that then I knew we had a chance.

As I lay on the hard floor of her living room and the spectre of my moving to England had vanished, I didn't want to be anywhere else in the world but right where I was, feeling her breathing softly against me. The sound of her mother's key in the front door ruined the moment and any chance of redeeming the unravelled cassette. We were sitting upright on chairs opposite each other before she'd finished turning the key. I was too shy to stay long and talk to her mother, so I took my damaged cassette and headed the 1 mile walk to my home. Leaving Geraldine's house and walking past the other houses on her small private estate was an entirely different experience to entering the Manor Park council estate where I lived. It was even more evident in the summer months. As soon as I'd turn into the estate, I'd be met with a sea of red, white and blue. Every house, apart from the very few Catholic ones, would be teeming with flags – Union Jacks, Ulster flags or Vanguard flags. Some had one or the other, many had them all hanging from special attachments that enabled them to fly five or six flags at once to really demonstrate their patriotism to Queen and Country. It didn't stop at the flags either. The pavements were also coloured red, white and blue. There were grammatically incorrect slogans on the sides of the houses courtesy of our resident illiterate bigot. It all combined to ensure that I never felt much love for the place I was born or brought up in. I loved my family home but I felt unwelcome in our council estate. Most days I'd run the gauntlet of abuse from a small group of men who always congregated at the back of an alley I had to walk past to get home. *Fuck off, you wee Fenian cunt. Taig bastard. IRA scum.* The more drunk they were, and the more of them there were, the louder and longer the abuse would last. I never made eye contact and always kept my head down. I only exhaled after I was sure they'd let me past again. They'd let me pass every day for five years but I still had the memory of the day I smiled nervously at one of them when I was eleven.

'You laughing at me?'

He didn't break his stride as he walked towards me. He pushed me against the fence. He was three or four years older than me. He hadn't brushed his teeth, his face was dirty and he had an orange rim around his lips.

I tried in vain to save myself. 'I wasn't laughing, I was just . . .'

His friends egged him on. They were all crowding around me now. 'Fuckin' smack the Fenian bastard. Go on . . . knock him out.'

I could feel my legs turning to jelly and my stomach sinking. I wasn't getting away this time.

So without further encouragement he punched me hard in the mouth. It was much worse than any boxing punches I'd experienced – even the ones that made me cry and ended my fledgling career. I felt my lip press against my front teeth and then spring back. As I was tumbling over the fence, I could taste the saltiness of my blood combined with the dirt from his fist. I started to get up with blood pouring on to my Man United shirt that should have been a Liverpool shirt. They were walking up the alley, arms around each other. As I climbed to my feet, my tears completing the cocktail in my mouth, I smelt something foul. I looked around to see if I could identify the source. The back of my shorts was wet. I felt the damp patch and brought my fingers to my nostrils.

The smell! It was like nothing I'd ever smelled before. I started retching immediately and threw up right next to the decomposing and rancid dead bird I had just been punched on to. None of them ever hit me again but the memory of the punch and the dead bird was enough to fill me with dread every time I scurried past them.

There had been no sign of my tormentors as I made my way from Geraldine's house with my damaged cassette. I'd only just got through the back door when I could hear voices in the front room. By the time I got to the hall I recognised Robbie Walker's voice. I knew they were talking about me and I knew what they'd be talking about. I shook his hand and sat on the sofa next to my mother. He continued talking to my parents. *The scout from Linfield wanted me to sign. Because I was from Lisburn he'd assumed I was a Protestant. Because I was a Catholic I couldn't sign for Linfield. They didn't sign Catholics. The scout had a friend who was a coach at Newcastle United. He had arranged for me to have a trial there at the end of the month. My mother was talking about the hunger strikes and the lack of a decent future for any kids growing up in Northern Ireland in these times.*

There were lots of nods, smiles and handshakes. My mother and father were very excited – their hopes and dreams for me were alive again. There was a still a chance for me to 'get across the water' after all. They called Kieran in from the living room. He was the only Newcastle United fan I'd ever met. He was still talking to me about Malcolm Macdonald, Jackie Milburn and Hughie Gallacher as I was dialling Geraldine's number to tell her the news. The Troubles, religion and football had all combined in one conversation to potentially alter the course of my life. It made our plans from that afternoon seem like nothing but childish fantasy.

My leaving home and leaving home soon was looming larger than ever on my horizon.

CHAPTER 12

As I RAN at the last defender I could see my team-mate to my right screaming for the ball. I looked up and moved as if to pass it to him. The defender anticipated the pass and moved all his weight on to his left side so he could narrow the space. I sensed his movement and flicked the ball to my left and was past him with just the keeper to beat. I put my head down and drilled it into the far corner. The game was only five minutes old and I'd already scored a goal that was sure to impress anybody watching. I was on the ball again now, weaving my way towards goal again. The same team-mate was running alongside me.

'Pass it. Pass it. One-two. One-two?'

He was gesticulating widely. He was right. The same defender stood rooted in front of me. A quick one-two with my screaming arm waver and I'd be past him again and have my second goal of the game. I slipped the ball to the right of the statue and into the path of my team-mate and then quickly moved to the left. It was my turn to scream now. 'Yes. Yes. Give me it. Give me it!'

The pass didn't come. *No one-two?* I was clear through on goal. Instead my team-mate just stopped and put his foot on the ball. He then stared straight at me as he shouted, 'Fuck off. If you don't pass to me then I'm not passing to you.'

With that he turned his back on me and passed the ball in the opposite direction. I'd never experienced that before or since on a football pitch. We won the game and I knew I'd done enough to impress but I was still troubled by what had happened. We were in the old clubhouse now. I brought my Coke over to the table where he was sitting. He was younger than me – fourteen, maybe? He was sitting at the centre of the group – holding court and telling stories. He seemed very popular with the other boys. As I approached he looked up. I was ready for the fight. He stood up so that he was in my face now. He was a little smaller than me, had chubby cheeks that were still bright red from the exertions of the game. His teen-age spots were inflamed and looked like mini craters ready to erupt at any second. He had a crooked smile. *He was smiling at me?* He held out his hand. 'Sorry about before, mate. I was just a bit pissed off when you didn't pass to us the first time. No hard feelings, man. You played really well. Have me seat and I'll grab another one. What's your name again, mate?'

His apology was warm and sincere and his smile was infectious. I switched my Coke into my left hand and shook his firmly with my right. 'I'm Paul. Paul Ferris. What's your name?'

He let go of my hand and dragged a chair and placed it next to the one he'd vacated. We sat down. 'I'm Paul, too. Paul Gascoigne. Me friends call me Gazza.'

I sat listening in complete silence as they swapped stories. Not 'cos I was too shy – I just couldn't understand a word any of them were saying. I watched closely for the moments they laughed and then I laughed with them. Occasionally, one of the boys would ask me a question and, after repeating himself slowly three or four times, I'd eventually understand what he was trying to say. Their accents, especially when they were talking rapidly and all at the same time, were simply impossible for me to comprehend. I'd never heard anything like it in my life. It was *howay* this and *howay* that. *I'm fog and howay man I was fog. Pass the bullets and Who nicked me ket?* They sounded like they were singing the words to each other. Every sentence began with *Howay* and every sentence ended with *man. Howay* meant *come here* in one sense, and *fuck off* the next. Then it could mean *I don't believe you* in one instant, and *you're joking* in another. Everybody spoke in plurals – *us* replaced *me* in every utterance, and whole words were changed to something else entirely. The word *divvent* seemed to have replaced *don't* completely in their strange language. Some words were only used as part of a complete phrase. *Haddaway* was one such word. I worked out pretty quickly it was essential that it was always to be followed by *and shite*. Otherwise it made no sense at all.

The game took place at Whitley Bay FC and was the only match I played during my trial. I didn't even last the whole game, courtesy of a flying boot to my nose. I had an unfortunate habit of being a little too brave (or stupid) for my own good. I was a left-winger and wingers were supposed to be a bit 'soft'. I made sure no one could ever say that about me. If a full-back kicked me I would just get up and run at him again and try my best to kick him back. Usually that meant leaving my foot in the air just after he'd struck the ball – guaranteed every time to let him know I was there. On this occasion in my desire to impress on the trial I'd done that with my face instead. I played for forty minutes with a cotton plug up each nostril until my breathing got so bad I couldn't continue. I only had one training session the day before the game and flew home to Ireland the morning after. The trial was cut short because I'd been selected to play for the Northern Ireland Under-18s against Scotland. It meant I'd been selected just after my sixteenth birthday and before I'd joined a professional club, but also interfered with my attempts to impress Newcastle United. On the plane home when I replayed my performances in the training session and the game, I knew they had been good, but was convinced that I'd not been there long enough for anyone to make a decision about me. Two weeks passed after I got home and I had no contact. So I just settled into my familiar routine of school and finding ways to be with Geraldine as often as I could.

I was eating my dinner in the kitchen when my mother answered the phone in the hall. She shouted for me and asked me to join the call on the extension in her bedroom. I sat on the end of her bed, picked up the dusty green receiver, and recognised the voice of the person singing his words down the line. In a thick Geordie accent, not helped by an inability to pronounce his R's, Brian Watson, the scout who'd driven me to the airport a fortnight before, was delivering a monologue to my mother.

All the coaches had been very impressed with my ability and attitude in training and the game. I had natural talent, was quick and brave and had fitted in well with the other boys. They had watched me play for Northern Ireland and that had confirmed that they wanted me to sign as an apprentice footballer at Newcastle United. I would earn £20 a week and they would put me in 'digs' in a nice part of the city. It was a great opportunity for any lad and he had no doubt I would be a big success.

As I lay listening in the darkness of my parents' bedroom I was filled with a mixture of dread, fear and excitement. I was always excited when I realised I'd done enough to impress professional clubs with my ability. I would always try my best when I was on trial. I never really thought about the consequences of playing well. That it would result in me leaving home, my family, Geraldine. When that thought did arise, I would suppress it by reassuring myself that there was still a lot of time between now and my leaving school. I'd only just started the second year of my O levels – I would have months left to decide what I wanted; before I had to confirm that I would accept any offer. *Plenty of time*. Then right at the end of his monologue Brian snapped me into the present.

'We'd like him to start on the first of November.'

First of November? That was less than two weeks away.

I thought about leaving Geraldine, my mother, my family, my life. I could feel my chest tighten and my stomach go with it. All my fears exploded from my mouth. 'What about my school work? My O levels? I'm not due to leave school until next July. I've only just turned sixteen. Aren't all the other apprentices a year older than me? Haven't they already done their exams? The school won't let me leave!'

His answers came thick and fast. I could finish my O levels in Newcastle. Education was very important. I was entitled to leave school the day I turned sixteen. The other apprentices were a year older technically but some of the younger ones were only two or three months older. They'd done their exams but I could do mine too on a day release scheme. The school had no choice but to let me leave if I wanted to go.

By the time he'd finished dismissing my every objection all I could say was thank you. He hung up and I lay there in the familiarity of my parents' bedroom: the enormity of the call sinking in and my heart sinking with it.

I was leaving home. It was actually happening. I had no choice.

Was I really moving away from my family, leaving Geraldine and everything I'd ever known? And was I going in less than two weeks? Every part of me knew there, in that moment, that I didn't want to go; that I didn't want to be a footballer and didn't want to leave school. I wanted to stay at home. I wanted to be near my mother. I was frightened that if I wasn't there then she wouldn't fight to stay alive. I wanted to be with Geraldine. I knew there was no way she could still be my girlfriend if I lived in a different country from her.

I could feel my fear turn to despair. Then my despair moved on to anger.

I wasn't going. I wasn't leaving. I would decide my own fate.

I'd go downstairs and tell them all it was my life, my future, and I was staying where I was, and doing what I wanted. I was feeling better now. Back in control. I'd made my decision; there'd be no more trials. No more offers. I was going to Rathmore and Queen's and that was that. I bounced off the bed and headed downstairs to tell my mother my plans. When I got there she wasn't in the house. The back door opened. She came in with Agnes O' Neill.

'I was telling Agnes the good news and she wanted to come and congratulate you. I've spoken to your daddy and he's really proud of you. Denise and Kieran are coming round in a minute. Go and phone your Uncle Josie – he will be so excited for you.'

I hugged Agnes and walked along the hall to phone Josie.

CHAPTER 13

I WALKED ALONG the unfamiliar hall towards the red door that stood at the very end of the narrow passage. In all my five years at St Patrick's I'd never ventured here. The sign on the door said 'Mr Magee'. Mr Magee was the designated careers officer at the school. I didn't even know we had a careers officer until that morning when one of the other teachers recommended I go and see him. She'd congratulated me on my news and made her suggestion after ten minutes of listening to my confusion. I didn't really know Mr Magee, but I was surprised to find out he was the careers officer. He only ever taught the kids who weren't very bright, or those who had learning difficulties, or those who were just plain difficult; naughty boys who were deemed too disruptive for the normal school curriculum. I had a friend who was one of them. We used to joke that he would one day be a great bin man. He and his friends would walk past my window when I was in class and then walk back carrying bins. Then they'd be back again with empty bins. Every single day they just walked backwards and forwards with bins and Mr Magee.

'Come in.'

I'd barely brushed the door with my knuckles and he was calling me from behind it. I pushed it open and nearly hit him with it. What I thought was a room was little more than a store cupboard. The tight space was filled by Mr and Mrs Magee and two chairs. He beckoned me to sit. When I did, my knees were touching his until I moved them to my left and he moved his to his right. We

With Geraldine at Lisburn Youth's Awards Dinner. I was 15 and she was 14. I left for Newcastle four months later.

My mother as a young girl. Beautiful and full of life. It hung in our living room when I was a child and still hangs in mine today.

The only photo of Geraldine I had with me the day I left Ireland for Newcastle.

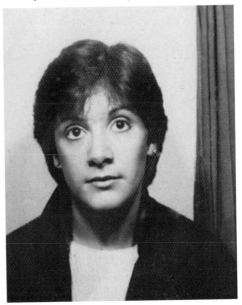

Lisburn Youth's all conquering under 13 team. My friend Marty Crossey is middle row back right. I am front left, aged 11.

Closing in on goal for Lisburn Youth under 13's. The best days of my childhood.

My Father Patrick and my mother Bernadette as I remember them from my childhood

Kieran Moran came into my life when I was 7 years old and has been an important presence ever since.

Norman Whiteside. The boy who was already a man when I travelled to Manchester United with him aged 11.

Above: Scoring at the Gallowgate end at St James Park. The fulfilment of a dream. I was sure it was going to be the first of many. It ended up being the only one. But what a feeling.

Left: Embracing the eighties. A world class mullet.

Right: With Geraldine at St James park on match day. She moved to Newcastle days after I injured my left knee. I would never fully recover from the injury.

Above: Third from left front row on the day I badly damaged my left knee. My crutches are to the left of the photo. My leg had to be bent into position. I was in plaster by the end of the evening.

Below: Chris Waddle beating his man which he did with ease time and time again. He grew from non-league footballer into one of the most gifted players of his generation in a few short years.

Above: My boyhood hero Kevin Keegan.

Left: Jack Charlton. The manager when I scored my only goal for the club.

Right: Paul Gascoigne whose star was on the rise just as my mine was falling away. A warm, kind, and generous soul who possessed a remarkable gift

Above: Peter Beardsley. The best player I ever played with. A footballing genius in my eyes.

Left: The day my hero became my teammate. Kevin Keegan pictured with Manager Arthur Cox. Two of the most genuine, honest, and talented individuals I met in all my time in football.

Above: Newcastle United boarding a plane bound for Bermuda in 1985. I'm in the centre of the photo. Paul Gascoigne (and his prize mullet) is on my right shoulder.

Left: Geraldine and my mother Bernadette pictured in my family home at Christmas 1986. My mother is 58 but looks twenty years older. I was shocked and distressed when I saw her. She died five weeks after this photo was taken.

Below: Paul Moran. Kieran's brother. A loving husband and father and a victim of a senseless murder. His death convinced me that I should never return to Ireland to raise my young family.

shuffled back and forth before finally settling for touching knees. He was a giant of a man and was made bigger still by the confines of the store cupboard. He had black curly hair and thick glasses, which made his eyes change size depending on whether he was looking through them or over them. He smiled warmly as I sat down.

'Young Ferris. I hear congratulations are in order? You're going to be a famous footballer, I gather? Mr Rickard tells me you're some player. We've never had a footballer from St Patrick's before. The school's very proud of you. I think Mr Kearns said he wants to hold a special Assembly for you before you go? Not too often our Head Boy leaves us to be the next George Best now, is it? Look forward to seeing you on *This is Your Life*. Say hello to Eamonn Andrews for me now, won't you?'

I thought he was never going to stop. I moved my knees again in one last push for freedom. My left leg settled uncomfortably jammed between his thighs. And I made my rehearsed pitch. I didn't deliver it nearly as well as I had when walking around the yard at lunch-time.

'I don't want to go. I want to stay here and finish my O levels and then go to Rathmore and do my A levels and then go . . .'

He looked at me like I'd just told him I'd murdered the head-master. 'What? Not going? Not going to be a footballer? Most kids would give their right arm for this, son. It's a once in a lifetime opportunity for you. For your family. Anybody can do O levels – very few can be footballers.'

I tried to move my left leg but it was stuck. 'I think I can get really good grades and then do the same at Rathmore. Then I want to be the first person in my family to go to Queen's. I can still play football in the Irish League. My brother plays for Distillery.'

'Distillery? Shower of shite, son! Sorry . . . I mean that's not the same standard or the same opportunity you have here. You can get your O levels any time. Go to university any time. You'll never get another chance like this if you live three lifetimes. My advice to you is to grab it, son. Grasp the nettle. Grab on with everything you have and take this golden opportunity to get out of this God-forsaken dump. What good is an education in this place? There are no jobs, no prospects, and gangs of murdering bastards roaming the place that would snuff your life out without a thought for you or your family. Son, you are young, you're probably a bit frightened, but please hear what I'm saying to you. Take this chance. Go and never look back and never regret your decision. There is nothing here for you and there never will be.'

With that my knee was released and I was being ushered back into the hallway even more confused than when I'd left it to sit in the cupboard. Mr Magee didn't know it but he was my last hope. I thought if I could get the careers teacher on my side then when I faced the awkward conversation with my parents that he would step in and tell them I was too good a student to throw away my education. That in his opinion it was vital that I get all the qualifications I could get. But his advice was the same advice I got from every adult I spoke to – my Lisburn Youth coaches, my teachers and my family. *Only a complete fool would turn down the opportunity to become a professional footballer.* I was taking up a two-year apprenticeship with a guarantee of nothing at the end of it, but everybody I spoke to treated it as if I'd been offered a one-way ticket to fame and fortune. It's not that I didn't want to be a footballer. I did. I'd wanted to be a footballer since I scored my first goal for St Aloysius. It's just that I didn't want to move to a different country to have to become one. I obviously knew that I had to move to England to achieve my dreams but I'd lived in a state of denial around the practicalities of that. But now it was real. I was leaving school in two days and leaving home soon after. I left Mr Magee's office and trudged the long walk home in the rain.

I wasn't alone. Since the call last week I had had a constant companion. It was with me in the morning when I awoke and still there when I put my head on the pillow at night. When I was with people it would settle into the background, but I could sense its presence. It was very noisy when I was on my own. Like today, walking home in the late October rain. It sat right in the middle of my chest. Under my ribcage. In my heart. I noticed it when I'd been lying on my parents' bed straight after the call and it had never left me since. It was like something had come into my parents' room, slipped inside my body while I was lying there and taken up residence under my ribs. It squeezed my heart and made my chest ache. Not ache like I'd just been kicked by a frustrated full back, but ache like my heart was being squeezed and held tight and my lungs were being prevented from filling with air. I'd spent the last week with this pain that wasn't a pain making me feel like throwing my guts up every time I thought about what was to come. It had an accomplice on the outside too. Right at the same time it slipped unnoticed inside me; its companion messed with the time. Made whole days seem like hours and hours like minutes. Everything was on fast forward and I couldn't get it to pause, not even for a second. It wouldn't slow down to let me breathe. My hours spent with Geraldine felt like minutes. I'd just arrive to meet her and spend my time worrying that this was the fourth last time or third last time or second last time we'd be together. Before I knew it, our time was up, and me and my strangled chest would be home and in bed with another day gone. I'd try to steal time with my mother too. Sit with her. Hold on to her for as long as I could, but time wouldn't let me. It hurtled me and my shallow breathing right past every moment I tried to snatch. And now my time was running out. My chest let me know it. Every racing minute of every day. Before I knew it I was meeting with Geraldine for the last time. The last time we'd be together before she and my parents would take me to the airport tomorrow and I'd be gone.

The thing about first loves or childhood sweethearts is this – everybody has one. We all remember our first kiss. The first rush of joy that another soul loves us for who we are. The thrill of realisation that the person you think is the most special thing on earth feels the same way about you. The intensity of it and the innocence and purity of it are feelings that never leave us. First love matters. It helps shape who we are, how we relate to others, what we are like as a partner. But first love ends. Everybody knows that. Yes, something remains, but it's not love. It's nostalgia at best. Something to look back on fondly or with embarrassment. A rite of passage and nothing more. We all have a childhood sweetheart. Even the name conjures up innocence long consigned to the past. As adults we are sometimes guilty of trivialising it. Of forgetting what it was like. All those feelings? We dismiss them as child's play. Not real. Just part of growing up. But when you are living them they are very real. They are the single most important thing in the world. In my case the thought of losing Geraldine was right up there with the fear of losing my mother to another heart attack. So when I sat holding her hand on her parents' sofa the day before I was due to leave I never wanted to let it go. I would have stopped the clocks and stayed there with her forever. She'd been my girlfriend for over a year. A year is a long time when you're fifteen. I couldn't remember what my life was like before. I loved being with her. Music sounded better when she was listening with me. I would have given up my life for her. I couldn't bear the thought of life without her. I didn't have the words to tell her how I felt. I was too limited in my vocabulary to articulate what she meant to me. She was a part of me. So instead I let the singers sing their songs to her. Tell her better than I ever could just what she meant to me in that moment. As our time was running out our conversations got more urgent, frantic:

This wasn't the end for us. If we loved each other then nothing could keep us apart. We'd see each other at Christmas and have the whole summer together. We'd talk on the phone every day and write letters once a week. When she was old enough and her parents would let her she'd come and visit at first and then come and live in Newcastle with me when she'd finished her A levels.

I meant every word with all of my heart, but deep inside me, under my rib-cage, my new companion was crushing my heart with all its might. Deep down inside me it was letting me know that this was the end of us.

I'd go to England. We'd ring each other a few times. Write once or twice. Her friends would get boyfriends they could actually go on dates with. Their boyfriends would have friends. She was beautiful. It was inevitable. I was losing her. I was leaving. And losing Geraldine's love was the price I would pay.

My heart was disintegrating from the loss of her. I was already missing her, while she was sitting right beside me. I listened to Roberta Flack telling her far better than I ever could what I felt the very first time I had laid eyes on her. What I would always feel.

CHAPTER 14

I TOSSED AND turned in the creaking old bed. I didn't know how long I'd been awake or what had awoken me. My brothers and sisters had all been at the house to say their goodbyes. I'd tried one last time to talk with my parents but to no avail. Now, as my eyes adjusted to the darkness, I could make out the familiar features of the room I'd be sleeping in for the last time. To my left was the old fireplace, which had never been lit, but still belched out thick, choking smoke at random forcing me out of my bed and into another room for the night on many occasions. The big wardrobe, which had been my protector in the years after the petrol bomb had destroyed our front room, filled the entire length of the wall to the right of my bed. The curtains, where my mother would stand in the dead of night with an ever-present red glow arcing from her side to her mouth, were right in front of me. I swept my legs around the bed in search of my regular tormentor.

I found it all too easily. The sharp spring that had burst its cover nearly two years before was sticking into my right leg as it had done at least once a night since it had introduced itself to me. This sparse room had been my nightly home for all of my life. I'd shared it with Tony at times but mostly it was all mine. I'd known nothing else. I was safe here; in this ancient bed that I'd converted into a swimming pool on many occasions. *I think the spring was its attempt at a rebellion against its nightly soaking.* Behind my head was the thin wall that separated me from my parents' room. The comfort of that had rocked me off to sleep on many a troublesome night over the years.

Particularly in times when I knew my mother wasn't very well. Hearing them talking and laughing made me feel that everything would be OK. The thought was just beginning to work its magic again, on this most difficult of nights, my last at home, when I was disturbed by an unfamiliar sound. I could hear furniture moving and rustling. It was emanating from our living room downstairs.

I crept out of bed and walked quietly down the stairs as far as the landing. The living-room door was open. The light was on. I could see the suitcase I'd packed earlier still sitting on the sofa where I'd left it. Only it wasn't how I'd left it. The lid that I'd sat on, and struggled to zip shut, was wide open again. Had I forced too much into it and had it burst open again? I walked the rest of the way down the stairs and stepped around the half-open door. The case was completely empty. All the clothes I'd crammed into it earlier were now spread out across the cramped living-room floor. The only thing not on the floor was my favourite shirt. It was being held to my mother's face instead. She was kneeling in the middle of everything I possessed. She didn't hear me enter the room. I watched her for a moment in silence. She was rocking gently backwards and forwards and was making a low murmuring sound. I thought she was praying into my shirt. I wasn't sure what to do and started to back out of the room. Then I heard her sobs. She was crying. *Crying for her child. Crying for herself as his mother.* In all the conversations we'd had she'd never once cried. She'd just repeated the same mantra. *It was for the best that I go. It wasn't even that big an event. I was only a phone call away. If I got homesick I could just hop on a flight.*

I stopped back-pedalling and walked over to her. I knelt in front of her and touched her shoulder. 'Mammy, are you all right?'

She lifted her head. Her face was soaked with black water and her eyes were puffy. She raised her hands to me and I wrapped my arms around her. I held her like a baby and rocked her there until my knees surrendered. We drank tea. *We always drank tea.* This was my last chance.

'Mammy, I don't want to go. I want to stay with you. I'm frightened you're going to have another heart attack. That you'll die and I won't be here. I don't have to go. I can stay. I can do my exams. I know I'll do well. I promise I'll work hard. I'll get a part-time job. Help out more around the house.'

She sat her tea on the floor and turned to face me. She raised her hands and cupped my face. I could feel my eyes well and a heavy tear dropped onto my cheek. She swiped it away with her thumbs and stared into my eyes. 'Now you listen to me. D'you think I want you to go? D'you think your daddy wants you to go? Of course we don't. I want you to stay more than you'll ever know. You're sixteen now but you're still my baby. I love you with all of my heart. I've prayed to God every night not to take me before I see you reared. You're not there yet so I'm going nowhere. Don't worry about me. Stop worrying about me and everything else you fret about. Geraldine will still be here if you both want that to be the case. If it's meant to be then it's meant to be. If it's not then it's not. Worrying about it won't change that. This life is short, son. I know that more than most. I've had my life. This is your turn. You can't make my heart better any more than the doctors can, but if anything happens to me I will still live as long as you have me in your heart. I will always be by your side for as long as you want me there. We are one and the same. You're me and I'm you. If I thought there was a better future for you here I'd put that case away and you'd be going nowhere. But there isn't, son. There is nothing here for you. This island is rotten to the core. Go to England and show them what you can do and who you are. Be kind to people and they will be kind to you. Never confuse being nice with being soft. No one can walk over you unless you let them. You'll meet good people, I'm sure, but there are plenty of the other sort too. Those that will try to put you down, hurt you, make you feel less than you are. Watch out for them. They come in many shapes and sizes but you'll know them when you meet them. Never shy away from them. Take them on. All of them. Every time. Have no time for braggers, liars, and cheats, and never ever be one yourself. Work hard at everything you do and you'll get your rewards. Be brave in everything you do. Commit fully to everything you do. Never give in and never give up. Staying the distance is half the battle in this life. Now go to England, chase your dreams. Don't let anyone or anything stop you. When you feel like you want to give up, when it all gets too much, just don't. Don't quit. Don't ever give up. I'm proud of you, not because you're a footballer – that will only get you so far in life. I'm proud of you because of the person I've watched you become. The world won't know what has happened to it if you have the courage and belief in yourself to go out there and show it. You can do anything you want, be anything you want. The only thing that will ever stop you is yourself.'

By the time she'd finished her thumbs were working like window wipers on my cheeks. But something had changed in me. My axis had shifted. I looked at the determination in her eyes and I was sorry for her that her body had failed her when she was so young. I was sorry that the world she was born into hadn't given her a real chance to unleash her spirit on it. I was going to England. I was going to show the world my talents. *I was going to do it, not just for myself but for her. She never had the chances I was being presented with. She never would. I would grab this opportunity and never let it go.*

I sat with her until the birds welcomed in my final day at home. We'd talked for hours about things I never knew or cared to ask about before but now urgently needed to know. I needed to commit them to memory, store them in my heart and in my head. She talked about her mother, her father, my father, her hopes and dreams as a girl and her fears and regrets that her illness had robbed me of the best of her. I'd never felt closer to her. Never loved her so much and never felt more loved by her. I felt a bond with her that not even death could break. I ached to make her proud of me. *I would make her proud of me.* I left her where I'd found her. I climbed the stairs in broad daylight as she sat in the middle of my possessions and began to place her youngest son's life neatly into a suitcase.

When I came down the stairs again it was time to go. I'd slept my way through my last day at home. Geraldine was already in the living room, fighting for seating space with my brothers and sisters and their growing families. All the confidence I'd got from last night's talk with my mother was gone. I could feel my legs weaken as I weaved my way through the bodies and perched on the end of the settee next to where Geraldine was occupying a patch of cushion, the rest of which was taken up by three of my excited nieces. She slipped her hand into mine. She looked pale. We hadn't even had the chance to speak when Denise came in and announced my departure.

'Right, kids. Give your Uncle Paul a hug. He has to go to the airport now.'

Fifteen minutes later, my weak knees were helping me carry the heavy suitcase to the front door. I hugged Denise and Elizabeth. The two surrogate mothers who'd stepped in countless times to help my mother when she wasn't well enough to take me places or cope with the demands of a lively boy growing up too fast. They whispered frantic last-minute words of encouragement and I was out of the door and dragging my belongings to my father's car. My mother was already in the passenger seat staring straight ahead. I climbed in the back seat next to Geraldine and the loud noise from the exhaust was my cue to wave goodbye to the familiar faces of my childhood and the only home I'd ever known. We sat in silence as my father navigated the mountain with a fully intact steering column. I willed the car to go slower but he regarded every journey as a race to the finish line. He got to the airport in record time. My hand was soaked with sweat from gripping Geraldine's for the whole journey. We were rushed through check-in and hurried along to the gate. My mother had to stop twice, which slowed us down, but everything was still happening far too fast. I could hardly move my legs as we reached the door behind which lay my future. I must have been hurting Geraldine's hand from gripping it as tightly as I could. My chest was so uncomfortable that I felt like asking my mother for one of her magic heart tablets that seemed to ease her pain so effectively.

And then it was time.

Just like that. No fanfare. No drum rolls. Just a moment. Like any other moment. Except this one felt like the most important one of my entire life. I didn't speak. I couldn't speak. I just hugged them one by one. First my father, then my mother, and then Geraldine. They felt small. Really small. I held on to each of them for as long as I could. I wanted them to feel, *really feel*, what my heart and my mouth couldn't say. There were no words and no grand gestures. No tears from my mother. She didn't look me in the eye. She just let go and asked me to ring when I got settled in my new home. Then they stepped back and left me with Geraldine. As soon as I felt her arms around me I could feel the first sting in my eyes. I could feel the moisture of her cheek against mine. I inhaled as deeply as I could to stop myself from crying and to gather as much of her as I could into me before I walked through the doors behind me. I promised to call her every day and write once a week. Then I walked away. I turned to wave but the uncaring door had already shut tight behind me. Everything and everyone I loved was now locked on the other side of it.

CHAPTER 15

I DON'T KNOW if it was because the door had shut too soon and took them from me before I was ready, but I felt a feeling that I'd never experienced before. As I started to walk towards one of the plastic chairs that lined either side of the empty hallway, I started shaking. It was in my legs at first. Like someone had removed my bones and I was still trying to stand without their support. By the time I felt for the seat the bones in my arms and shoulders had deserted me too. I sat down and tried to compose myself. I took some deep breaths and opened the *Belfast Telegraph* my father had just passed to me. I tried to focus on the writing on the page to calm myself, but my eyes were blurred. I couldn't read the first sentence. In spite of my best efforts to pull myself back, the first tear hit the page with a loud splash. It spread out quickly. In seconds it was joined by a downpour saturating the entire page. I tried to stop it but I was powerless. So I held the paper up over my face on either side and cried like the lost child I was until it was time to board the plane. A tall man with a kind smile tapped me on the shoulder as I was wobbling to my future and asked if I was all right. I lied and he left me alone.

I don't remember when I stopped crying, but it was sometime between take-off and landing. By the time I walked out of the Arrivals hall in Newcastle to meet Brian Watson I'd washed my face and found my missing bones. We left the airport terminal and the icy north-east rain hastened our footsteps to his car. I sat next to him while he talked me through the arrangements for my first day as a footballer. I listened but didn't hear any of it. Instead I closed my eyes and I was in the car with my parents and Geraldine.

They were taking me back home. My mother would make dinner for us and then I'd walk Geraldine to her house. I'd kiss her goodnight. I'd get home and climb into my bed. In the morning I'd awaken to the smell of fried potatoes and go off to school and play football with my friends after that.

He brought the car to an abrupt halt, throwing my head forward and all thoughts of home flew out of it. I looked up and could see I was sitting outside a three-storey red-brick building. It was in a stranger's house and not my home where I'd be laying my head tonight.

'You'll have to eat something.'

I was sitting at a long kitchen table that could easily accommodate twelve people. Brian had left and Mrs Nicholson had just about exhausted her offerings. She had a thick county Mayo accent and had arrived in Newcastle twenty years previously in search of a new life. Her husband subsequently died, leaving her to bring up her young family on her own. Mac, who was a quiet, but pleasant presence sitting to the right of me, had stepped in and helped shoulder the burden. The house was vast compared to our end-link council house. I'd walked along the never-ending hallway past the payphone on the wall. I'd left my suitcase at the foot of the steep dark staircase, before entering the kitchen I now sat in. Beyond the door to my left was a pantry leading to yet another passageway. I'd stayed here for two nights when I was on my trial and I'd already met the family. Mrs Nicholson had five children – the oldest had already left home and the youngest was my age. In addition, the house was occupied by three students, who shared a room on the middle floor, and one young footballer, Scott Snyder, who'd been here as a guest for almost two years. I'd met him briefly a month ago and liked him. He was from Ayrshire, and looked like the child that Bruce Lee and Cliff Richard would have had if they'd been a couple and managed to defy the laws of reproduction. I'd been looking forward to meeting him again. He was confident but not arrogant and I'd found him to be very open and friendly with me in my short time with him. He of all people would at least understand how I felt tonight, having made the same journey himself not too long ago. I was disappointed when Mrs Nicholson told me he was in Scotland visiting his parents.

She gave up trying to feed me somewhere between a ham and cheese toastie and a ham salad sandwich and was now going through the house rules. *No entering the kitchen after 9 p.m., no hogging the payphone in the hall, pay 5p if you want a shower, no need to visit the shop on the corner as there was one in the front room. Mac ran a mobile general store.* I listened and didn't speak or ask a question, in the hope that I'd be excused so that I could go and speak with Geraldine and my mother. After she finished talking, she brought me into the small living room, where her youngest son, Kevin, still in his school uniform, was sprawled on the couch watching TV. She slapped his foot and he sat to attention. *No lying on the couch* was added to my list. With a lot of persuasion and eye movement from his mother, Kevin was tasked with showing me to my room. He ascended the stairs in front of me, while I bumped my suitcase up one steep step at a time. As we rose further into the darkness I could feel a chill biting into my bones. The higher we got, the colder it got. The more stairs we climbed, the darker it got. The last few steps I navigated by feeling my way with my spare hand. We reached my room at the top of three flights, just as my arms were about to give in to the concrete my mother had packed in my case. He pushed the door open, mumbled something, and quickly descended into the light. I peered into the narrow darkness. I felt the wall with my left hand. I lit the room and it was framed in a dull yellow glow. It had two single beds. One to my right, which ran the length of the wall and had been slept in recently; the other stood along the back wall at the end of the room. They were joined by a short fat wardrobe that acted as a buffer between the head of one bed and the foot of the other. I pulled my case over to the tidy bed and left it there. I felt for the change in my pocket and headed for the warmth and light of the hallway and the payphone that was to become my best friend.

I thought for a moment no one was going to answer at all, but she picked up on the fifth ring. My mother's voice resonated in my chest. She sounded tired. We spoke about food, personal hygiene, and how quickly Christmas would come around, but most of all about how there was nothing at all to be upset about. We spoke for too long so that when I phoned Geraldine everything would be rushed and the phone would die after the pips and before we'd said goodbye. Geraldine picked up on the first ring. We talked hurriedly, about phoning, writing, visiting, about how there was everything to be upset about. I told her we were being silly and that my mother was right. We just had to get on with it. I was proud of the maturity of the lie. Then she told me what had happened on the other side of the airport doors.

As soon as they had closed behind me, my mother's mask had slipped and her tears had replaced it. She sat in a chair and wept for me while I sat on the other side of the door and ruined my newspaper. She had chest pains. Her magic pills didn't help. Geraldine and my father had to help her to the car.

The pips interrupted her but I'd run out of change. We were cut off before saying goodnight.

I looked at the door to the living room in front of me. Perhaps I could go in and get to know Kevin better? Ask him about his school, his hobbies, and if he liked football? I looked at the frosted glass door of the kitchen and could see Mac still seated on the long bench. Mrs Nicholson was flitting in and out of view. Maybe I could go back in and let her make me the sandwich my rumbling stomach clearly needed? I looked at my watch. Ten past nine. I wasn't sure how strict the rules were, so instead I slipped out of the front door, turned left, and walked the short distance to the corner shop, with my face buried in my coat to shelter me from the freezing rain. The bell rang me through the front door of the shop. The place was an alien world to me. So different from MacFarlane's at the bottom of my street at home. It was dimly lit, like my new bedroom, and I wondered if the bulbs in England were all programmed to be duller than Ireland. The shop was teeming with boxes – they covered the walls and windows from the floor to the ceiling. It seemed to sell everything and anything – things you didn't even know you needed until you entered. I knew exactly what I wanted and found them on a rack below the counter.

I crept back through the front door and climbed to the roof of the house. I lit the room in dull yellow and poured the contents of my bag onto the bed. I lay down, wrapped my coat around me and unwrapped my first Curly Wurly of the night. I had another. Then another. I didn't stop until I'd finished all six of them. The man in the shop had given me a quizzical look when I'd placed them one by one on his counter. *He thought I'd stopped buying at two Mars Bars, a Twix, and a Fry's Chocolate Cream.* I hadn't intended to eat them all in one go, but I wasn't getting comfort from any of them, so just kept going in the hope that the next one would do the trick. But the only thing they did was give me a sore jaw and an aching stomach. I looked at the Mars Bars and thought about making a start but felt it was best to wait for the pain in my belly to ease. I slipped my hand into the top pocket of my new coat for going to England, and pulled out the long strip that it held. I lay staring at the only photos I possessed of Geraldine. They had been taken in Woolworth's on Saturday. There were four black and white images in a row and none of them looked anything like her. I thought about us lying on her floor with the cassette tape unravelled between us. I sat up and nearly brought the knot of Curly Wurlys back up my throat.

I managed to get the suitcase open after sitting on it and taking the skin off my finger. I sucked my blood to stop it dripping on the floor, and it mingled with the sugar in my mouth. It wasn't a taste I was familiar with and I didn't like it. My stomach liked it less. I only just made it to the bathroom and had my head hovering over the toilet before the sticky mess navigated my throat and turned the toilet water dark brown. When I had nothing left to donate to the toilet and was safely back in my room, I lifted the top flap of the case. I was looking for my cassette player. I found it wrapped inside three shirts. I had four cassettes: Simon and Garfunkel's *Bridge over Troubled Water*, Queen's *Greatest Hits*, Dire Straits' *Making Movies* and the one I was looking for – the one I'd made at Geraldine's house and nearly lost, until my pencil-rolling skills had redeemed all of it, with the exception of 'Miss You Nights', which started off all right but sounded like someone was strangling Cliff at the chorus. I opened the cassette recorder to put my tape in and a folded note fell out of it and on to the floor. I opened it and there was a handwritten barely legible scrawl across the page. It read:

Dear Son,

I wanted to let you know that I'm very proud of you. I know this isn't easy for you but please promise me you will give it your best efforts. Take one day at a time and if you ever feel that you want to come home then we are always here for you. Please try not to fret too much about me or about home. We will all be here when you come home for Christmas. I know tonight will be difficult for you but it will get better I promise. Now try and get some sleep and know that even though you can't see me, I am always there and always thinking of you. You are loved more than you'll ever know.

Good Night and God Bless,

Your Loving Mother

If her intention was to comfort me it didn't work. I could feel the room begin to spin. I think that for the first time in my life I was experiencing loneliness – hopeless, fear-filled, abject loneliness. I looked around the cold room and thought about the strangers downstairs. They were probably good people, a nice family, but they weren't my people, my family. My family were living their lives without me across the water. And I was here and wished with all my heart and soul that I could turn back the clock and be there. I lay on my back on top of the bed so that the earphones of my cassette player wouldn't bore into my head. I held her note in one hand and Geraldine's photo in the other. I listened to familiar songs with an unfamiliar sensation. Saltwater ran in a steady stream and pooled in my headphones. I thought it would never stop but fell asleep when no more tears would come.

The cassette ending jolted me awake. For a moment I thought I was at home in my bed, until I felt the squashed Mars Bar pressed against my back. I heard the door open. I didn't move my head but opened my eyes just enough to see a figure approach the other bed.

He didn't look towards me. He was a couple of years older than me and wore strong aftershave. He was unsteady on his feet and nearly fell over as he fought to get his trousers off. He stood in his underpants and, gathering all of the contents of his nose deep into his throat, gave a loud snort. The sort of snort that is usually accompanied by moving the contents of the throat into the mouth, ready for a giant green spit. He ignored the last two steps in the process and instead gulped the slimy contents down his throat and into his belly. Not happy with the results of his first attempt, he repeated the snort and followed the process through twice more. He staggered to the light switch and back to the bed. I lay there listening to his snoring and comforted myself that I wouldn't be staying. I'd ring home in the morning and catch the next flight to Belfast on Thursday. I kicked the Mars Bars out of bed, zipped my coat up as far as it would go, and thought about how excited Geraldine would be when I told her I was coming home. Even *I* could cope with two nights away from home.

CHAPTER 16

T HERE WAS a large group of them congregated just outside Central Station. I thought I recognised some of their faces from my trial game but wasn't sure. I stood a little way from the bus stop to make sure they didn't see me. There was loud laughter and lots of pushing and shoving. They looked bigger than me. Everything about the place looked bigger. The people, the buses, the giant train station, the imposing hotel opposite. I suppose Belfast was just as big but I didn't really know. Because of the Troubles I hadn't really spent much time in the city that was only 8 miles from my home in Lisburn. When I did go, it was always with my parents or my sisters. Certainly never on my own. Lisburn was my only real measure in terms of size and Newcastle dwarfed it. I felt very small, insignificant almost. I wished I was going to school instead of standing in this strange city. I'd have breakfast with my father, wash myself in the cold bathroom with water that was liquid ice, meet my friends in the yard, and wait for the assembly bell and one of Noddy's red-faced sermons. I'd speak with teachers who knew me, friends who liked me, and then go home to my mother's baking.

I leaned back against the wall and buried my face deep into my coat. I was wearing the same clothes as yesterday. *So much for the personal hygiene conversation with my mother.* I'd sneaked out of the house without washing or eating breakfast to ensure I avoided any contact or conversation. On the bus from Gosforth to Central Station I'd eaten a Twix and a squashed Mars Bar. I was glad the night was finally over – I thought the darkness would never end and only fell asleep as the early morning sunshine cast its shadow across my snoring neighbour. I didn't feel as anxious this morning. Mainly because I was going to speak with Brian Watson as soon as I got to the training ground and ask him to book me on the first plane home on Thursday. I waited for the group to board and then jumped on at the last minute. They were filling the back seats so I climbed the stairs and had my choice of the top floor. The bus pulled away from the stop and took me through new territory towards the training ground in Benwell. I noticed the stickers as soon as I sat down. They were small and round and written on them in black ink one read:

PADDY GO HOME.

Another one beside it proclaimed:

NO IRISH HERE.

They were both accompanied by an NF logo. The bombings and murders committed by the IRA had convinced the National Front that frightened sixteen-year-olds, who cried themselves to sleep, avoided washing and all conversation should be sent back to Ireland immediately. I agreed with them.

I followed the throng through the gates and into the training ground. There were three pitches, all covered in a white blanket of freezing fog. A small car park stood in front of what looked like an old cricket pavilion. Opposite that was a big red-brick building with a corrugated iron roof that I presumed housed the indoor pitch and gym area. I'd been inside the pavilion on my trial and followed the boys through its thick blue door. There was nothing much to the place. To the right and left were the first team and reserve team changing rooms with a boot room attached to the first team's room. Immediately in front of me was a communal area about the size of my living room and front room combined. A door to a room on the left of this space had a black sign informing me that it housed the manager. Next to that in the left corner was the coaches' room, which in turn led into the physio's room. To the bottom right was a tiny kitchen that fed into a laundry room. The boys disappeared through the kitchen while I sat in the communal area waiting for Brian. The blue door opened and closed and the building filled up rapidly. The boys were busying themselves like worker ants in and out of the laundry room with arms filled with training kit. They were well drilled and very efficient. Occasionally a half-dressed senior player would poke his head round the corner and shout some orders and immediately someone would appear with apologies and his missing garment. I sat in silence opposite the manager's office, with my chin on my chest for thirty minutes – like a naughty school-boy outside the headmaster's office. I watched the door for Brian but it had long since stopped opening and shutting. Everybody who was meant to be here was here. I peered at the coaches' door in the corner. There were a couple of people in there that I recognised from my trial. I was just building up the courage to get up and make my way to the door when the manager's door opened. I looked up just as he caught my eye.

'Aye aye . . . who do we have here then?'

He had an accent that I couldn't place. He wasn't Geordie. It reminded me of the Crossroads Motel.

He walked towards me fully dressed in his kit and ready for train-ing. He was tanned and had a gleaming white smile. His black hair was a perfectly trimmed crewcut. He looked a bit like Action Man, only with more wrinkles. He walked like he knew he was in charge and everybody else knew he was in charge.

'I'm Paul Ferris, the new apprentice.'

He leaned into me as he offered his hand. 'Speak up, son.'

He gripped my hand in his vice. Let go and then shook his head. 'Call that a bloody handshake, son. That's a wet fish. If you're going to shake hands, shake hands.' He smiled as he said it. He had kind eyes behind the bluster.

'I'm Arthur. Arthur Cox, son.'

He looked around the room and boomed to no one and everyone.

'Who's looking after our young Paulie here?'

Paulie?

A tall wiry boy who'd stepped straight from the pages of a Dickens novel appeared from the kitchen and was standing to attention next to him.

'Me, Gaffer. I . . .'

'Well, don't just stand there. Get the boy some kit and introduce him to the others. Poor lad's been sitting there for the whole bloody morning. That's no way to introduce him to Newcastle United. His bloody parents will have my guts for garters and they'd be right. How are your parents, son? Are they good people? That's the important thing, son. Be a good person. I wish you well.'

He offered his hand again. I squeezed with all my might. He laughed as he let go. 'Good boy, Paulie. That's the spirit. I love a quick learner.'

With that he disappeared into the first team changing room and I could still hear his voice echoing as I followed the tall boy through the kitchen and into the laundry. There was something about him that certainly terrified the life out of me but there was honesty about him too. I had no evidence to support my feelings but I believed that he'd be a fair man. That he was a good man.

'This is Irish, our new apprentice. Is there a set of spare kit for him?'

THE BOY ON THE SHED   111
THE BOY ON THE SHED   111

The Charles Dickens boy was introducing me to the group from the bus stop. On a closer look I didn't recognise any of them from my trial game. These boys were older. There were ten of them sharing a space for five. I could barely see them hidden in behind two huge dryers that were whirling noisily in front of them. From behind two voices shouted in perfect harmony. 'Number 39 is available. Give him that one.'

The Dickens boy grabbed a bundle from a shelf above where the boys were changing.

'I'm Chris. The head apprentice. Do what I say and we will all be all right. Don't do things properly and we're all in the shit. Hurry up and get changed. You can do the nets with John.'

I could smell the kit as soon as he handed it to me. I couldn't be expected to wear it surely? I handed it back to him.

'It stinks.'

He raised an eyebrow. 'And your point is?'

'My point is it stinks and I'm not wearing it. Is there no clean stuff I can put on?'

A loud voice from behind the kitchen had them all scurrying out the door before I'd settled the argument. Chris shouted as he left in a hurry with the others. 'Get it on and meet John at the first pitch behind the gym or we're all fucked, Irish.'

I got changed behind the dryers and left my clothes in a bundle on the floor. The kit was a yellow shirt and thick blue shorts that were three sizes too big. An oversized purple sweat top and one blue sock and one yellow sock completed my new uniform. I pulled on my shiny new boots for going to England and held my breath until I got to the front door and out into the freezing air. I rounded the gym and could see a solitary figure blowing into his hands and jumping from one leg to the other and back again. When I reached him I could see his legs were red from the cold.

He was a little taller than me, stocky in build and had a face that looked like he liked a fight and might have had a few. He reached out his hand.

'I'm John Carver, but everyone calls me JC.'

I clamped his hand firmly as was my new custom. He yelped. 'Fuckin' hell. Steady on. You nearly took me fuckin' fingers off, man.'

I loosened my grip. He looked at his fingers and then at me like he might head-butt me in retribution. Then he laughed. 'The gaffer gave you the handshake, didn't he?'

'Sorry, John . . . I . . .'

He backed away. 'Fuckin' hell, man. What's that smell? Have you shat yourself?'

'Not today. But I think somebody shat in my kit last week and left it there.'

He was laughing again. 'What's your name again? And where do you play?'

He was very excited when I told him I was a left winger. He was a left back. He was from the West End of the city. His school, St Cuthbert's, had just won the Schools Cup. We chatted like old mates while he showed me how to put the nets up. It was all going well until my fingers stuck to the freezing metal of the goal frame.

'Don't be fuckin' daft. You cannot be stuck, man?'

He was laughing again. I wasn't. 'Stop laughing, man. Me fingers are fuckin' stuck.'

I was learning the language.

On his advice I spat my way off the freezing crossbar. When we were done he put his arm around my shoulder. 'Stick with me, son. I'll look after you.'

I'd just made my first friend in Newcastle.

We jogged over to meet the others as they came round the back of the gym. There was going to be a full-scale practice match. The 'first' team would play against the reserves and juniors. The coach threw me a bib. 'You're playing left wing, Paddy.'

I could feel a little tremble in my legs. John was beside me.

'Divvent worry aboot it, son. I'll keep you reet.'

We warmed up separately from the senior team and then there I was standing on the halfway line about to play against a team that had been playing at St James' Park on Saturday, the day after I'd just left school. Before I'd had time to think and be nervous, the tall central midfielder looked up and drilled a pass hard at me. I was on the left side of the 18-yard box. As it approached I leaned forward as if to take it in front of the first team full back. He leaned with me. I opened my body as he lunged forward. Me and the ball were around the back of him in an instant. I hit it early with my left foot before the keeper had a chance to readjust his feet. It flew across him as he dived and nestled into the corner of the net I'd just constructed with John.

'Aye aye, what have we here?'

The manager's voiced echoed across the training ground. 'Paulie's got a trick. Paulie's got a trick.'

I forgot where I was for the next hour and a half. I was a boy playing with his mates in the park, I was Lisburn Youth's best player, and I was showing off for my father and Geraldine. Towards the end of the game the full back got tired of chasing me and began kicking me. I loved it when that happened. I kept thinking about the manager shouting 'Paulie's got a trick' and I was getting more excited as the game wore on. I was excited because I did have a trick. The manager was right in his assertion. I had a trick all right but I hadn't shown them it yet. Now I felt the time was right. I got the ball and as the tired full back approached me I knocked it past him and down the left wing. I knew I was faster than him and so did he. I got to the ball just in front of him, running as hard and as fast as my legs would carry me. I made an exaggerated movement as if to cross it but as he desperately slid to stop me – they always did that – I wrapped my left foot around the ball, twisted my left knee as far as my straining ligaments would permit, flicked the ball over him and watched him slide along the ground and off the pitch. I'd been perfecting that movement since I'd been Kevin Keegan in the park. It never failed then, it never failed at school, or at Lisburn Youth, and now it worked on professional footballers too!

I listened for the manager's shout. He didn't let me down. 'Paulie's got a trick. Paulie's got a trick.'

The final whistle blew. The full back came over to shake my hand. I gave him the 'wet fish'.

'How old are you, Paddy?'

'I'm sixteen.'

He slapped the back of my head. 'Fuck me. I hope I don't have to play against you when you grow up. Well played today, son.'

It was late in the afternoon and all the senior players had long ago left for home. I was sweeping the communal area next to the manager's room, when Arthur Cox came out and walked right past without looking at me. I felt a pang of disappointment that he hadn't acknowledged me. After my performance surely an honest man, a fair man, would have said something? Maybe he wasn't what I thought he was after all? I continued brushing the carpet as he opened the blue door behind me.

'Paulie.'

I turned. He was rolling his car keys around his finger. 'Well done today, son. Phone your parents tonight and tell them I said you did them proud. Stay honest. Keep your feet on the ground. Work hard. You've got a real chance here, son.'

I raised my head to thank him but the door was already closing behind him. I felt like I was floating momentarily across the floor. The long dark night was forgotten. I decided to postpone my conversation with Brian.

CHAPTER 17

THE NEWCASTLE United I joined in November 1981 was mired in second division mediocrity. Jackie Milburn's glory days of the 1950s were a distant memory. Apart from a Fairs Cup win in 1969, there was only the brief flourish of the Malcom Macdonald led team that I'd watched Kevin Keegan destroy when playing for Liverpool in the 1974 FA cup final at Wembley. Relegation and years in the wilderness had led the scout who sent me for my trial to describe it as a 'small club'. The team was a cobbled-together patchwork of ageing old pros, journeymen, and local non-league players.

The first game I watched from the half-empty paddock next to the home dugout was a soulless draw with Rotherham United, notable only for the abuse the people around me were giving Bobby Shinton, their own centre forward. Their language was colourful, their veins bulging, but their passion undeniable. There was something special about this place and these people, even then. I found the atmosphere inside the old stand intoxicating. I stood on the terrace behind the forbidding fence and imagined myself running through on goal in front of the packed hordes of the Gallowgate. I'd smash the ball and bulge the net and then wait for a split second until they would erupt in celebration of their new hero. I'd get a shiver down my spine every time I thought about it. I'd watch the players I trained with play in front of 20,000 people and I was desperate to do the same. I loved playing against the first team in practice matches. It gave me an opportunity to show everyone that I was good enough to be in the team. I loved the training; running around in five-a-side games, shooting sessions afterwards, and extra sessions in the afternoons with the juniors. I found it hard to comprehend that I was actually getting paid just to play football. I would have happily paid to do that. I was happy on the training pitch and happy playing games for the junior team on Saturdays. But when I wasn't training or playing? That was a whole different ballgame.

When the other boys would leave the training ground for home, I'd hang around as long as I could. Then, when it was time to go, I'd get the bus into the city. The city was a mirror image of the football team. It had seen better days, it was tired around the edges, and the loss of its traditional industries had seen unemployment rates spiralling out of control. The whole country was in a dark depression, with rioting in inner cities dominating the nightly news. The rioting never reached Newcastle but the mood of the day certainly did. In spite of that, I could feel there was something about this place and its funny-speaking people. Underneath all of the doom and gloom, it had a big beating heart and a vibrant soul. The people were warm and friendly; even if strangers did look at me quizzically when I said hello to them as I approached them in the street. *I established that this custom was unique to Ireland and so I quickly dropped it.* I'd wander around Eldon Square and end up in one of the many record shops there. I could occupy myself for hours flicking through albums and cassettes I never intended nor could afford to buy. I'd get to my digs just in time for dinner. *Chicken and chocolate biscuits on a Thursday.* Scott had a girlfriend and wasn't around much. So after dinner I would pass Mac's shop in the front room on my way to buy my stash from the better one on the corner. With my spare change I'd hog the payphone in the hall and tell my mother everything was OK and my father how I was better than the first team's left winger. Chris Waddle was a big loping, lazy-looking lad with a languid running style, who'd been spotted playing non-league for Tow Law Town FC. He would develop into one of the great players of his generation, but in my first few months and long before he boarded his rocket ship, he was firmly in my sights.

The rest of my evening would be spent writing letters to Geraldine, listening to my music, eating my Curly Wurlys, and living with the dull ache of loneliness that just wouldn't leave me alone. It was there in the morning when I opened my eyes and again at night when it wouldn't let me sleep without taking me to the depths of despair. It was there when I sat at the back of the bus with my new team-mates, instead of upstairs on my own, or when having dinner with the others in my digs. I took it to Mass every Sunday for the first three weeks in the hope that the familiar ritual would rid me of it. Nothing I did could shift it . . . apart from playing football. When I was training and playing it would completely disappear. My mind was filled with being a footballer. Being better than my opponent. Being the best that I could be. Sometimes I could cope with it better than others, just accept that it was there as an emptiness within me. But at other times it crushed my spirit, drove me to my bed, and forced its way out through my eyes. Events could bring it to the fore when I was least expecting it.

We were on a coach travelling to the coast to train on the beach, the only part of the North East that wasn't under a thick blanket of snow that day. I was collecting plastic cups from the cup holders on the tables.

'Take my cup, young'un?'

He was part of a group of four first teamers at the table. I'd never really spoken to them in my three weeks as a footballer. I removed the first three cups, which were sunk into the holes on the table that housed them. The fourth cup was turned upside down. As I bent over to pick it up the others were already laughing. When I looked down to where the cup had been, his penis was poking through the hole, standing to attention, and staring me in the face.

'Sort this out for me, young'un?'

I retreated to my seat with the howls of laughter still ringing in my ears. I felt like I wanted to throw up at first. Then I could feel the anger building. I was annoyed with myself that I didn't have a response. Didn't have the tools to deal with it. I wanted to go back and reply to the conversation. He would say, 'Sort this out for me, young'un' and then I would do just that. I would pull my arm back, thrust it forward and punch him as hard as I could right on the top of his disgusting shiny dome. Smash him right on the tip of it so it disappeared back down the hole like Whac-A Mole. Instead, I sat in silence for the rest of the trip. I didn't train well that day. *I felt a very long way from home.* I was wary of him and his group after that. It wasn't the last time I saw him produce his erection for their entertainment. He jumped out of a kit basket one day completely naked like a pornographic jack in the box. He chased Scott around the packed changing room with it flapping wildly back and forward off his stomach. He caught him and bent him over the skip and pretended to have sex with him, telling him how smooth his skin was and how much he'd always wanted to fuck him. The club chaplain was welcomed every Friday by the sight of him and his little friend. He'd flick his hand across it and bounce it up and down while standing on the changing room bench.

'Ever seen one of these, Rev?'

The poor man would just give a weak grin in response and then squirm all over again the next time he visited. When he wasn't getting his penis hard for the pleasure of the rest of the group, he would regale them with sordid tales of 'shagging me missus with the bairn on me back' or 'wanking the dog off'. At sixteen years old and out of school a year before my time, I couldn't fathom what he and the others found so funny about it all. I felt lonelier than ever at times like this. But I did have an escape. I could always find respite by playing. Just playing football for football's sake gave me momentary relief. So I did that with all the intensity and passion I could muster.

I was selected to play for the reserves within weeks of my arrival. They played at St James' Park on Saturday afternoons when the first team were away. I felt like a real footballer getting changed in the home changing room; running out onto the famous old turf; looking at the imposing main stand; taking in the empty Gallowgate where I dreamed of scoring my first goal; smelling the hops from the nearby brewery; playing against real footballers in a competitive match. All of it gave me a buzz of excitement that I'd never experienced before. I didn't touch the ball much in the entire first half of my debut appearance for the reserves. In fact, I'd touched it so little I was beginning to think there wouldn't be a second half for me. Then, just before the referee blew the half-time whistle, our right winger beat his man and lofted a ball to the back post. As he crossed it I was on my way ahead of the sleeping full back. I watched it float over the flapping keeper and got there just as it was flying past the far post. I wasn't going to make it . . . unless. Unless I dived full length and head first at it. So that's what I did. I threw myself forward and off my feet. I strained my neck as far as it would go. I connected with it and saw it fly into the net just before my lights went out. I awoke in the changing room with the reserve team manager, Willie McFaul, standing over me and telling me I was either very brave or very stupid. I didn't care one bit. I'd scored a goal at St James' Park for Newcastle United; albeit for the reserve team. I couldn't wait to get to my digs to hog the payphone. Three days later I played my first Youth Cup game. The manager and his staff all travelled to watch us at Doncaster on a wet and windy November evening. After the game he came into the changing room and turned the air blue with his criticism of every player one by one as he prowled the room. I was dreading the moment he would inevitably reach me. When he did get to me there was no acid tongue, no cutting remarks. He just walked over to me and patted me on the shoulder. 'Youngest boy in the team. Best player on the park.'

He told me to keep doing what I was doing. If I did that then good things would happen for me.

The following day I entered the hut that acted as the club's administration and ticket office. It sat at the edge of the car park opposite the main stand. I had to go there to collect my wages; £20 for me and £30 for Mrs Nicholson. There was a tall man standing at the hatch. He was talking to Linda and the other two staff that comprised the entire administration staff of Newcastle United. He was in no hurry to move and was clearly on very friendly terms with them all. It was Thursday and I was impatient to get to Gosforth for my chicken and chocolate biscuits. I waited and waited but he clearly liked being there and showed no sign of leaving. I accidentally on purpose dropped my bag on to the floor. It landed with a clank from my studs inside and did its job to perfection. He stopped talking and turned.

'So sorry, son, I didn't hear you come in.'

He stepped away from the hatch and Linda was already getting me my money. She asked me how I was settling in and how I had got the bump on my head. I told her about my meeting with the goalpost and lied about how well I was adjusting to my new life. The tall man interrupted. 'Whereabouts in Ireland are you from, Paul?'

He knew my name?

I looked up from my envelopes. He was smiling at me. His grey hair made me think he would be around sixty. *A kind old uncle.*

'I'm from Lisburn. It's just outside Belfast, but you won't have heard of it.'

He spoke through his smile. 'Oh . . . I know Lisburn. Where the army barracks are. Isn't that right?'

I got it now. He was an old soldier – probably served in Thiepval Barracks, the giant British army garrison stationed in the town during the Troubles. Retired now, no doubt, and back home safely to his family. I was glad for him. He had a good aura about him, and spoke to the staff with a gentleness and warmth that couldn't be forced but came only from being a decent human being. He continued. 'I used to live in Ireland for a short while. It's a lovely place with great people. I wish I could've stayed longer but things didn't work out for me there.'

I congratulated myself on my accurate analysis of him and his army past.

'I watched you play on Saturday for the reserves. You were very brave for the goal. Not many players would've attempted the header knowing they were going to hit the post. Keep up the good work and you'll be in the team sooner than you think. Anyway must be off. Lovely to meet you, Paul. I'll keep an eye out for you.'

I thanked him and proudly showed him my war wound. He shook my hand and left me there with Linda and the others. I turned to thank her for my money. She was shaking her head and gesticulating to the others. I looked at Tony and Ken sitting behind her. They were laughing at me too. I could feel my neck bristle.

'What's so funny?'

Tony got up from his desk and came to the hatch. He wore thick glasses and looked like he'd left school the week before I had.

'You've no idea, have you?'

I was getting annoyed now. 'About what?'

'Who that was?'

He was right. I didn't, but I had a fair idea. 'An old soldier who served in my town?'

He stopped laughing just long enough to tell me how wrong I was. 'That was Wor Jackie.'

That didn't help. 'Wor who?'

Now he was annoyed. 'WOR BLOODY JACKIE, MAN. Jackie Milburn. Wor Jackie Milburn.'

I turned to the closed door. *Jesus. Jackie Milburn. And he knew my name? And he told me I was brave. And he knew my name!*

I couldn't wait to tell my father, Kieran Moran, anybody I knew, or who I would ever know. Jackie Milburn spoke to me. He knew my name. *And he was really nice too.* I strolled to the bus stop and bought the *Evening Chronicle* for my journey. I bought it every night from the same bloke whose only two teeth were strangers to each other, and who pronounced Chronicle nothing like it was spelled. The newspaper was the bible for fans desperate for information on their local team. I turned to the back page and had to read the headline twice to make sure my Jackie Milburn moment hadn't scrambled my brain entirely. I'd been right the first time. There, in big black letters, the headline read:

UNITED KIDS ARE GREAT: AND FERRIS PROVES IT.

The story below it was an interview with the manager singing my praises after my performance the night before. I took it home and read it out over the phone to Geraldine and my mother; after I told them that Jackie Milburn knew my name. After my chicken and chocolate biscuits, I skipped my nightly visit to the shop and instead sat the newspaper against the wall at the side of my bed. I must've read it ten times that night. I could've recited it word for word. I knew at that moment that if I kept doing what I was doing that one day in the future – maybe not this year, or even next year, but one day – I was destined to play for Newcastle United. One day the goal I scored in the Gallowgate end wouldn't be met with empty silence but with a roar from the crowd that would echo all the way to my family back home in Ireland. The chest-crushing emptiness of my nights, and my constant yearning for home were simply the price I would have to pay if I was ever going to achieve my dreams.

CHAPTER 18

As the weeks progressed, 'Irish' and 'Paddy' were replaced by 'Ferra' and I made more friends at the club. My Christian name was obsolete. The only person who came anywhere close to using it was Arthur Cox, the manager. He would pass me every day as I was sweeping the floor. Most days he wouldn't stop, but he never passed without acknowledging my presence. It would be 'Afternoon, Paulie.' 'Well done today, Paulie.' 'You've missed a bit, Paulie.' Or his favourite – 'How are your parents, Paulie?' I'd sometimes look up to answer but he'd already be gone. Out through the blue door and halfway to the car park. Even if he didn't stop to wait for my reply, I appreciated the gesture. Asking about my parents made him a decent man in my eyes.

I'd seen enough of him now to know that he was a very tough taskmaster. Senior players would lower their heads and scurry past when he walked into the room. There was no doubt I was a little frightened of him. He was a big character and a strong personality. A born leader. He commanded respect from everyone in the building. I thought he must have served in the military – as a sergeant major, maybe? But he hadn't. He'd suffered a serious leg break as a young footballer making his way in the professional game. With his leg and his dreams shattered, he moved into coaching and held senior positions in his twenties, when he coached and barked orders to players who were sometimes several years older than him. He was a great example to me and any young player of how to behave and conduct yourself as a professional footballer. I could tell he loved managing Newcastle United. He loved the history and he recognised the potential of the club. He had regular meetings with Joe Harvey, the legendary captain of the 1950s Milburn era and the last manager to lift a trophy, who now acted as his chief scout. His coaching staff carried out his orders to the letter. Coxy was the Boss. Even the Boss had a nickname. There were stereotypes that were impossible to shift. *All cockneys were loud. All Jocks were tight with money. All Welsh people had sexual relations with sheep. All Makems were inbred and all the Irish were thick.* So after fighting to stay at school because I thought I was clever enough to get myself to university, my role at the football club was to play the part of the thick Irishman. I got told I was thick so often that I started to wonder if maybe I was. That was until I overheard two senior players chatting while warming up for training one day. They were gently jogging just in front of me. One turned to the other.

'What does your wife do for a living?'

They jogged on.

'Oh . . . she's an estate agent.'

A long pause followed while the questioner digested the information he'd been supplied with. Then he replied with a knowing nod. 'You'll be all right for your holidays then, won't you?'

Maybe I wasn't so dumb after all.

Even away from the club, the assumption was that because I was Irish, I was somehow thicker than the thickest brick in Thickville. If someone found out that I was a footballer too? *Irish and a footballer?* Well, that was irrefutable proof that I was indeed the single most stupid person walking around the north of England. I spoke to Brian Watson about it. Not about people calling me thick. About the promise I was made that I could continue my O levels on day release. I pointed out that every Saturday there were boys playing in the youth team who were doing their A levels full time and were still affiliated with the club. They'd been offered apprenticeships but instead they'd stayed at school, trained with us during the holidays and played all the games in the evenings and at weekends. He mumbled something about A levels being different from O levels and there being nowhere I could do O levels on a day release scheme. He assured me that ensuring all the apprentices had worthwhile qualifications was a top priority for the club. I'd no reason to doubt the sincerity of the sentiments.

He was true to his word, in a sense. Two weeks later we were all enrolled on a course at Newcastle College. We would spend one day a week learning skills that would help us get jobs should our football careers not progress as we all hoped. Three weeks later I was running around an arc welding workshop in the college, trying to get away from our drunken centre forward who was chasing us with a lighted blowtorch turned up full blast with a foot-long blue flame protruding from it. Four weeks later I was putting up wallpaper very badly and building walls that wouldn't withstand a light summer breeze. Fixing plugs and hammering nails into planks of wood were new skills I mastered too. Well, when I say mastered, we weren't allowed near the hammers again after I mistook John's thumb for the top of a nail. He got told off for his language that day as well.

As part of the course we went orienteering in the dark around Lake Windermere. We left the creepy old guesthouse one by one in alphabetical order and into the pitch-dark night, armed with a map and torch. *Carver first . . . wait five minutes . . . Ferris next . . . wait five minutes.* I left the lights of the house behind me and stepped deeper and deeper into the black night and along the narrow lane into nothingness. The wind was howling and the water was crashing against the rocks and jetty in the distance. The moon was peeping out from behind the thick clouds just enough to cast dancing shadows though the gnarled branches of the twisted trees. I quickened my step from a walk into a half jog. Something moved at the foot of the hedge next to my right foot and I progressed to a full jog, just as a bat swooped and squeaked and brushed the top of my head.

That did it. I screamed 'Fuckin' hell' to no one and started running as fast as my boots would let me. I yelled for John. He was a tough lad from the West End. He was probably halfway round the course now: *kicking the monsters in the hedges and biting the heads off the bats as he went along.* I'd be a little embarrassed about being scared of the dark but he was my new mate and I'd swear him to secrecy. After the rustling I'd heard in the bushes, and my brush with the vampire bat, he could tell the *Evening Chronicle* for all I cared. I was sprinting now. I could feel my hamstrings tighten from pulling my heavy boots through the mud. I shouted his name. I looked up ahead. No sign of him. No torch light swaying as he eased his way around the course. I could hear something behind me. It might have just been the wind or the waves crashing. I ran even faster. My heart was thumping loudly in my chest. Then I smacked straight into a five- bar gate that knocked my torch forward and me in the other direction. I was just getting to my feet when something grabbed my shoulder. I screamed the first thing that came into my head.

'MAMMY, MAMMY, MAMMY!'

John screamed back. 'Fuck's sake, man. Slow down, will ya? I've been chasin' ya for about a mile. I'm fucked now. Are you deaf? Did you not hear me calling ya?'

He was doubled over now gasping for breath.

'You're supposed to be in front of me.'

He stood up now and took a long drink from his flask. He handed it to me.

'I was in front of you but I was shittin meself, so I hid in the hedge to wait for you so we could go round together. I was just about to speak to you and then you fucked off like Alan Wells.'

Not so tough after all.

We waited for the others and navigated the course as a team. We then staggered our entry into our accommodation. John grabbed my arm as I was taking my wet boots off.

'MAMMY, MAMMY, MAMMY. What the fuck was all that about?'

I'd forgotten about that bit. I sat up and leaned back against the cold wall. 'You won't tell anyone, will you? It's a bit embarrassing.'

He put his arm around my shoulder. 'Divvent be daft, man. We're mates, aren't we? I'll look after you, son. Divvent ye worry aboot that.'

He never did tell. I'd made a good friend.

I'd made a few in fact. Scott broke up with his girlfriend, which was bad news for him but great for me as he was around all the time in the evenings. He encouraged me out of my room and rid me of my Curly Wurly fixation. He encouraged me to mix with the Nicholson family and that made my stay much more tolerable – I even ventured into the living room. He also introduced me to Derek Bell, a very talented and highly regarded midfielder at the club. Derek was two years older than me but we quickly became friends, and he regularly invited me to his home to have Sunday lunch with his mother and father and older brother, Alan. His parents were originally from East Kilbride in Scotland and had settled in Newcastle when the boys were young. His mother Yvonne began phoning my mother when I was there and also gave her progress reports on a regular basis throughout the week. That one simple act of phoning my mother and connecting both my worlds gave me an enormous boost. Suddenly home didn't seem so far away. I looked forward to my Sundays with the Bell family. Their extended family would visit and I loved their Uncle Jim. He had a strong Glaswegian brogue and an irreverent sense of humour. As a committed Glasgow Rangers fan he would tease me mercilessly and I eventually plucked up enough courage to give him as good as I got. They made me feel part of their family and I felt like they genuinely cared for me and for my wellbeing. I began staying at the Bells' every Thursday night. I swapped my chicken and chocolate biscuits for pizza and a game of pool at the Denton pub at the end of their road. I got great comfort from that. It took me back to Donegal and the pub with the great jukebox and the warm glow of my parents.

My new-found friendships and regular visits to the Bells definitely eased the ache in my chest. It didn't stop me counting the days until I could spend Christmas at home, however. Brian Watson gave me my train tickets and the timetable for the boat from Stranraer to Larne. The club weren't prepared to pay the air fare from Newcastle to Belfast. I didn't really care – I would have walked home. The snow started falling as I sat in the station. By the time my train to Edinburgh set off it was blanketing down. The train before had been cancelled so I found a space in the passage-way between carriages, and was jammed against students and families laden with bags and presents, all on the same journey home for Christmas. The thought of seeing my family again and spending Christmas with Geraldine helped me tolerate the stench of stale sweat. The beer-burping student blowing hot air in my face bothered me a little, but nothing could dampen my excitement at the thought of going home. That was until the train ground to a stuttering halt. By the time it started again, I knew I'd missed my connection from Edinburgh to Stranraer. I'd missed the last boat home. The burping student's breath suddenly made me feel very queasy. I tried to move my nose and mouth away from his but there was nowhere to go. My relief when we finally rolled into Edinburgh was offset by the confirmation that my connecting train had gone. I climbed onto the next one but knew that the last boat would be gone before I reached Stranraer. I'd phone my mother when I got there and try and find a cheap place to spend the night.

The longing to get home and the realisation that it wouldn't be today manifested itself in a tight knot in the centre of my chest. I couldn't believe it when I got to the port and saw the boat still standing at the dock. I was going to get home tonight after all. I ran to it dragging my suitcase through the snow. I climbed on board and searched for a seat. I found one in a quiet area between two decks. Ten minutes later I was surrounded by a group of twenty or thirty Glasgow Rangers fans. A fat man draped in a Union Jack squeezed in beside me and offered me a beer. I told him I was sixteen and he agreed I'd better not. He asked me where I was from. Lisburn satisfied him that I was definitely a Protestant and he shared his corned beef sandwiches with me. I was elated to be on the boat and to be going home. Then an announcer with a broad Scottish accent told us we weren't sailing that night as the waters were too rough. I wanted to go and find him, stop him talking. Shut him up. I wanted to tell him to just get on with it. Set sail and take our chances. I just wanted to go home. I'd left Newcastle ten hours ago. My family would be waiting. Worried. I looked around for somewhere to lay my head for the night. I settled for the floor underneath the row of chairs the Rangers fans were bouncing on. They serenaded me to sleep.

> Hullo, Hullo
> We are the Billy Boys
> Hullo, Hullo
> You'll know us by our noise
> We're up to our knees in Fenian blood
> Surrender or you'll die
> For we are
> The Brigton Derry Boys

The boat shuddering against the dock in Belfast woke me. My Billy Boys had gone and only their beer cans rolling and spilling their contents over the dirty floor evidenced that they'd ever existed. I crawled out from under the chairs, trying to avoid the river of alcohol that flowed past my head and ran down the stairs. I saw his Union Jack first. He was lying on the chairs directly above me.

'Morning, son.' He sat up as quickly as his huge belly would let him.

'Morning. I thought you'd all gone.'

He stood up and took my case from me. 'A wee boy like you shouldn't be travelling alone. Now come with me so I can make sure I get you to your parents.'

I will never forget the look on my father's face as me and my new friend, clad from head to toe in red white and blue and wearing a Union Jack cape, stepped off the boat together. They shook hands warmly and I was on my way home for Christmas.

CHAPTER 19

M Y WELCOMING party was similar to the one that had seen me off eight weeks before. My whole family was in the house when I arrived. *Eight weeks?* It felt more like eight months. There were times when I had felt I would never be here again, in this familiar place, with these smiling faces and in the arms of my mother. I held her as tightly as I could for as long as she would let me before she let go. I lay on my bed. I lay on the settee. I pushed the buttons on the TV. I made myself a sandwich. I lay on the bed and the settee again. I walked to Geraldine's house, my tight chest now replaced by a churning stomach. *What if she'd decided she didn't want to be with me anymore? To have a boyfriend who didn't even live in the same country as her?* But when she opened her front door and threw her arms around my neck I knew nothing had changed. If anything she looked more beautiful than when I'd left. I spent the entire Christmas holidays with her. Then in the evenings, when everyone had gone to bed, I sat with my mother. We just sat. Sometimes we'd talk, and I'd tell her my hopes and fears, but most times we just sat, drinking tea, and being with each other. And then it was over. Time to go back. My chest tightened again. I talked to my mother. She told me if I really wanted to then I could stay but then she asked me not to give in, but to give it my best shot.

Leaving them at the dock was as difficult as the first time but once I was on the boat it was different. A big part of me would always be there with them, the people I loved most in the world. Another part of me was excited by the start I'd made already and

I was determined to see where I could get to if I carried on the same way. Seeing them all again and realising that nothing had changed – my mother was still there, Geraldine was still there – gave me enormous strength to carry on. When I got back to Newcastle there were smiling faces there too. The Nicholsons, the Bells, my team-mates. My homesickness didn't disappear but it wasn't the all-consuming force it had been when I first arrived. I could live with it. I was living in a different country from my family and friends but I was being given the opportunity of a lifetime and I was determined to take it. I became a regular in the reserve team, was constantly picked to train with the first team, and got selected for the Northern Ireland Under-18s team. I scored the winning goal as we beat the Republic of Ireland 1–0 in Belfast in front of all of my family. This prompted the manager, Arthur Cox, to tell the local press that I was 'two years ahead of my time'. My first season was coming to an end. The first team had struggled in mid table all season. There were only three games left and then I'd be home for the whole summer. It was the end of April and I was walking off the training pitch. The night before I'd scored twice for the reserves as we'd beaten Blackpool away from home. I was thinking about my friends sitting in the classroom at school frantically preparing for their O levels and here I was scoring goals for Newcastle reserves and holding my own in training against the first team regulars.

'Coxy wants to see you in his office.'

John was standing at the door of the changing hut and pushing me towards the manager's office. Derek Bell was sitting nervously outside. I sat down beside him.

'What do you think he wants?' I'd barely sat down before I was quizzing him.

He casually shrugged his shoulders. 'Soon find out.'

The door opened and Arthur stood with his hands on his hips. The sunlight from the window behind cast a shadow so I couldn't see his face. Just his sergeant major silhouette.

'Come in, Derek.'

They disappeared through the door. It had no sooner closed than it opened again and Derek was out and past me with not so much as a glance.

Arthur beckoned me. 'Come in, son. And don't look so worried.'

He moved around behind his desk and motioned for me to sit on the wooden bench opposite. 'How'd'you think you've done since you've been here, Paulie?'

I hated questions like that. Questions that demanded an answer, which if I answered truthfully might make me appear conceited or big-headed. I knew how I'd done. I was sixteen years old and should still be in school, but I was regularly training with the first team and wasn't out of place. I was scoring goals in the reserves and had been man of the match in the youth team several times over. I wanted to say that I'd done really well, that I thought I was the best young player at the club and that I should be playing for the first team. Instead I mumbled something about my right foot not being good enough and promised to practise harder to make it better. He let out a loud burst of laughter and clapped his hands. 'Jesus Christ, Paulie. Don't be so hard on yourself, son. You've been bloody fantastic since the day you arrived here. You've got some rough edges but we can knock them off you. I brought you in 'cos I wanted to say keep it up, son. You have a big future here.'

I stood up and said thank you. Relieved that soon I'd be out the door.

'Sit down, son, I'm not finished. What's your hurry? I've got some good news for you. I'm bringing you with the team to Blackburn on Saturday. You won't start but depending on how things go I'll play you in some part of the game. You deserve it. Well done, Paulie. Now go and let your parents know. Tell them I was asking.'

The sudden weakness in my knees forced me back onto the bench. *A year ago I was still wetting the bed; six months ago I was playing for my boys' club; five months ago I was crying myself to sleep, my friends were in school today doing history and geography and kicking a tennis ball around the playground at lunchtime and now I was going to play for Newcastle United?*

I was sixteen years old.

My heart was wrestling to escape my ribcage. I wanted to jump up, run around the desk and kiss him. I wanted to run outside and shout to anyone who would listen, but most of all I wanted to ring my family. I wanted to talk to my mother, to Geraldine. I floated out of his office.

When I'd eventually calmed down I walked home with Derek. His mother hugged him when he told her he'd be playing for the first team on Saturday. Then I told her my news too.

'You'd better ring your mam then.'

She sat the phone in my lap and they left me in the living room. My mother said two words then cried for the rest of the call.

The evening newspaper told me in late April 1982 something I didn't know and hadn't thought about. On Saturday, if I played, I would become the youngest player in Newcastle United's history. The next two days crawled by but eventually I walked proudly into Ewood Park with my team-mates; there were a pile of telegrams on the treatment table. To my embarrassment they were all for me. None of my family made the journey over, a combination of the short notice and affordability. But I knew they were there with me. The game itself was a disaster for Newcastle. We had a man sent off in the first half and were 3–1 down with 10 minutes to play. I could feel my spirits sink as the minutes ticked by. Then Arthur Cox grabbed me by the scruff of the neck and threw me out of the dugout.

'Get warmed up, son, you are going on.'

I ran towards where the Newcastle United fans were congregated behind the goal. Just as I ran towards them they let out an enormous roar. I turned to see if I'd missed us scoring a goal but I hadn't. They started chanting. I heard a familiar sound. The sound of my name being sung over and over again. *The whole Newcastle United end singing my name when yesterday they didn't even know it.* I replaced Chris Waddle and took up my position on the left wing. The Newcastle away fans, who'd had very little to cheer about, roared on my every touch. Even a fourth goal for Blackburn didn't stop them chanting my name. I'd never experienced a feeling quite like I felt that day. I felt elation, joy, drunk, high; all of those and more and I wanted to feel it again and again and again. After the game I carried the kit and placed it in the bowels of the bus. As I was about to step on for the journey home, a small group approached. They thrust their hands towards me. I signed their shirts, their cards, their books. I posed for pictures with old men, young men and children. When I was done I sat on the bus and waved out of the window and wondered what they would be like if I actually did something worthwhile like scored a goal or the team did something worth shouting about like win a game? I was officially the youngest player ever to play for the team since its inception in 1892. I was sixteen years and 294 days old, so the newspapers informed me. I played once more before the end of the season, for 10 minutes at St James' Park. We lost 4–0 against Terry Venables' QPR in front of 11,000 fans at the dilapidated old stadium. People recognised me on the Metro train home from the game. I was crowned the club's Most Exciting Young Player at the end of season supporters' club awards night. I went home that summer confident in the belief that I was going to be a footballer. Not just an ordinary footballer. I was going to be a great footballer. True, I felt a pang of envy when my friends were sitting their O levels and I was waiting at the school gates to hear how they got on. But this was offset by the pride I felt that I had already played for Newcastle United when I should still have been in the classroom with them. Nearly everyone I met in Lisburn wanted to congratulate me on making my debut. To tell me how proud they were of me. I walked home from Geraldine's house late one evening. I approached my childhood tormentors still standing by the same back lane. I raised my head with my new-found confidence and nodded in a friendly gesture as I passed them.

'What the fuck you looking at, you Fenian cunt?'

The tallest one of the group of four was walking towards me. His friends pulled him back. I didn't look up again until I got to my back gate. Everything had changed but nothing had changed. I smiled as I got into the house. *I might be a Fenian cunt but I'm a Fenian cunt who's just played for Newcastle United and you're still standing on the same back lane.* I loved the long summer at home but was happy to go back for pre-season training. I played in a game at Workington with a mixture of first team and reserve team players. Everything I did came off. We won 6–1 and I had the game of my life. Some fans carried me on their shoulders from the changing room to the players' lounge. By the time we reached Newcastle the local newspaper was screaming my name on its headline.

FERRIS WHEELS IN

I'd continued right where I left off and was selected to travel with the first team on a trip to Madeira. Arthur Cox didn't go with us.

There were rumours he was making a big signing. We played Maritimo and were sitting in the hotel after the game when the coach, Tommy Cavanagh, came into the lounge. He was shouting and waving his hands in the air.

'We've got him. We've got him. We've bloody got him.'

Kevin Carr, our goalkeeper, spoke for all of us. 'Got who, Tom? Got who?'

'Kevin Keegan. We've signed Kevin Keegan.'

And we had. Second division Newcastle United had just signed twice European footballer of the year and current England captain Kevin Keegan. I went back to my room, which I was sharing with Kenny Wharton. We just looked at each other. He spoke first. 'Kevin Keegan. We've signed Kevin Keegan?'

I lay awake in my bed and thought of all the times I'd pretended to be him in the park. All the goals I'd watched him score for Liverpool and England. All the goals he'd just scored for Southampton. And now he was going to be my team-mate? I whispered to myself as Kenny slept. *Kevin Keegan. We've signed Kevin Keegan.*

CHAPTER 20

B Y T H E time we got back from Madeira the city was in a frenzy. The *Evening Chronicle* was devoting front, back, and middle pages to 'KK', 'King Kev', 'Special K', and any other K they could conjure up. The dreary hut where we trained didn't feel so drab anymore. The world's press descended upon it. The car park was crammed with TV crews from across the globe. The anticipation and excitement extended into the dressing room also. A team full of older pros, journeymen, and ex non-league footballers, that had struggled to maintain its position in mid-table of the second tier of English football, was not where you would expect one of the greatest footballers in the world to choose as his next destination. The fact that Terry McDermott, another Liverpool legend, had chosen to join us as well was almost completely overshadowed by Kevin's arrival. As I walked past the throng of journalists huddled by the front door I knew that everything about the place was about to change. I felt a mixture of excitement and a little fear. Excitement that I was to get the opportunity to play with someone I'd idolised all of my life. There was no one to match Kevin Keegan in my affections – no one. Never in my wildest dreams did I think it would be possible for someone like me to meet him, never mind play football with him. The fear came from the thought that maybe I wasn't good enough to be in the same team as him? It was all very well winning man of the match awards in the youth team and twisting and turning my way past ageing old pros in training. But Kevin Keegan was different. He was a world-class footballer. I was a sixteen-year-old boy who should still be at school. One thing I knew for certain was that my pathway into the first team had just got a lot more difficult. Fears aside I couldn't wait for him to walk through the door, to meet him, to play football with him.

He'd been in the building for an hour and I still hadn't met him. Arthur Cox ushered him through the front door in a flurry of activity and flashing cameras, and whisked him past me and into his office as I was sweeping the floor in the hall outside. I looked up briefly to see him disappear behind the door. I only saw the back of him but his profile was unmistakable. His thick curly hair flowed across his broad shoulders. *It was him*. I continued brushing outside the door until John came and told me to get a move on. I didn't see him again until our coach gathered all of the apprentices in the changing room. Arthur came through the door first and had the smile of a proud grandfather welcoming his first grandchild. Kevin followed him. He was already in his training kit, minus his left sock. He hopped on one leg as he pulled the missing sock over his foot and then stood in front of us. My heart was thumping with excitement. He smiled warmly and then spoke to us all in a voice I'd heard many times through our old TV in the living room at home.

'Very nice to meet you all. I'm Kevin. The gaffer tells me there is a player or two amongst you? Ability will get you so far but attitude is just as important. I wasn't blessed with the greatest ability in the world but I worked hard with what I had. Never shirked a training session. Practised on areas where I was weak and I got my rewards. I hope in the time I'm here I can help some of you achieve your potential too.'

His smile was warm and genuine. He had an aura about him, a presence that I'd never experienced before. He looked like he came from another planet to the rest of us. We looked like runts. He was built differently. He looked like a block of solid muscle to me. He walked around the room shaking hands with each of us individually. Before I knew it he was standing right in front of me. Looking intently at me. I struggled to maintain eye contact with him and could feel my palms moisten with sweat as I reached out my hand to shake his. Arthur introduced us.

'And this is Paulie. The one I was telling you about.'

The one I was telling you about?

'Keep an eye on him. He's going to be a player.'

Jesus. He's telling Kevin Keegan I'm going to be a player?

He shook my hand. I gave him the 'wet fish'. I couldn't help it. The moment was too much for me.

'Great to meet you, Paul. Arthur speaks very highly of you. Looking forward to seeing you play.'

With that the manager ushered him out through the door.

I sat on the bench and looked at my hand. I'd just shaken Kevin Keegan's hand. He'd said he was looking forward to seeing me play. Kevin Keegan was looking forward to seeing me play?

Fuck me twice over.

Everything changed after his arrival. Our training kit was cleaner. The food we ate was better. The whole place felt more professional. Players trained with more intensity. It was as if everyone wanted to show they were worthy to be on the same pitch as him. He didn't disappoint either. From the minute he stepped onto the training pitch he trained and played like his life depended on it. But he was much more than someone who had just worked his way to the top on limited ability. He was clearly a great footballer. His first touch was brilliant, he could pass equally well with both feet. He was perpetual motion when he moved. Quick, strong and brave, he could score goals – every type of goal; headers, tap-ins, great goals. He was the perfect player. The consummate professional. A great role model. Everyone raised their game when he trained with us. He would accept nothing less. But there was something else about him. His personality. He was full of charisma but very down to earth. He treated everyone the same from the senior pros to Bill who made the tea. He was mobbed every day on his short walk from the changing hut to his car. He never refused an autograph or a photograph and had a natural warmth with any fan who spoke with him. The manager moved me into the first team changing room. By chance or by design I got changed right next to him. He took the time to ask me about my ambitions, my hopes for the future. Encouraged me when I trained well, stayed behind after training with me and tried to pass on his knowledge. I was desperate to impress him. To show I was worthy. He was quick to praise me when he thought I'd played well and not afraid to be critical when I hadn't. I played well more than I didn't. I was training with the first team regularly now. I got called into the full Irish squad for the first training camp after its 1982 World Cup heroics in Spain when they beat the host nation to reach the second round. I left the camp early to travel to Belfast to play for the Under-18s team against Wales. I scored our goal; one of the best I'd ever scored in a 1–1 draw. These were heady times for me. I felt like I could do anything. Like I could be whatever I wanted to be. I woke up one morning to a telephone call from my mother.

'Go and buy the *Daily Mirror*.'

I asked her to tell me why but she told me to call her when I'd bought it and hung up. I dragged myself to the corner shop. I sat on the wall and read the front and back pages. Nothing. I opened it and read the inside front and back page. Nothing. I stood up to throw it in the bin when I noticed a thin column on the top left corner of the page. I sat back down and read the headline. And read it again and again. It said:

KEEGAN: FERRIS THE BEST
I'VE EVER SEEN AT HIS AGE

I read it on the Metro and on the bus on the way to training. I waited for him to come into the changing room.

'Thank you for what you said.'

He raised his eyebrow. 'What did I say?'

I was a bit embarrassed at mentioning it now. Maybe he hadn't even said it and it was some kind of journalistic mistake or exaggeration?

'The stuff about me being the best young player and all that.'

He smiled. 'Oh, that. Yeah. Now go and prove me right. You can be Manchester United or Crewe United. It's all up to you.'

With that he was out of the door. I made my way to the boot room. Picked up the brush and polish and prepared the senior pros' boots for training. I hated cleaning the boots – the hard wire brush would regularly take the skin off my fingers as I daydreamed about anything else but cleaning the boots. Come to think of it, I wasn't much of a fan of scrubbing the floor, sticking my freezing hands to goalposts, sweeping snow from the stands in the stadium, cleaning the rancid baths, or mopping the floor. But they were my duties as an apprentice. I would train with the first team, play for the first team, but before and after training and games I was an apprentice. And I would be one for another year, as I wouldn't sign my first professional contract until I was eighteen.

That afternoon I was called to a meeting with the manager at the stadium. It was two months past my seventeenth birthday. Neil McDonald, my new friend at the club, was also there. We'd both been training regularly with the first team. He'd also made his debut as a sixteen-year-old but was a little older than me when he did it. We regularly roomed together on first team trips. Two kids in a man's world. He was a local lad so his father was with him for his meeting. I was first in, and sat opposite the manager. He was seated high behind a giant desk. The room had no windows and was made up of dark mahogany and beige leather. It was inadequately lit by a single lamp on the manager's desk. My chair felt like the legs had been cut off and as I sank into it my bum was nearly touching the floor. I had to sit forward just to see over the desk where the manager was perched on his chair with its legs obviously intact.

'Don't look so worried, son. I'm not going to bloody bite you.'

Looking worried was my default facial expression. I did it very well. I shouldn't have worried. Today was not a day for worry. Today was a day to be happy.

'You are a part of my squad for this season, son. You won't play very often but you will travel with us for every game. I will ease you into it here and there when I feel it's appropriate. You've done well here. I couldn't be happier with your progress. With that in mind I want you to sign professional forms a year early. I don't want you training and travelling with us and then doing all of the other chores. I want you to concentrate on your football. You have a big chance here, son, and I want to give you every opportunity to take it.'

I felt like I was hovering above the chair as he continued. 'You know I'll look after you. I want you to sign a three-year contract. I'll pay you £120 a week.'

£120 a week? Fuck me.

I could hardly breathe. I was earning £20 a week and knew the other young pros' starting salary was £65 a week. £120 a week sounded like a lot of money to me.

He wasn't finished. 'Oh . . . I'd like you to have £50 appearance money if you are in the first team squad.'

My mind was racing.

Hadn't he just told me I would be in the squad all of this year? That was £170 a week. Add win bonus £50 a point to that. Win two or three games in a month. Add £400 more. Jesus Christ, I was rich.

'You OK, son?' He was around the front of his desk now and standing in front of me.

I stood up. 'I don't know what to say. Thank you. Thank you so much. I won't let you down.'

He put his hand on my shoulder. 'Don't thank me, son. You deserve it. That's only the start. I'll review it if you are playing regularly. Get you to the same level as the senior boys. If you work hard the rewards will come. Now don't be silly with it. Don't go spending it all on crap clothes and silly haircuts. Save some.'

'I won't. I promise.' I turned towards the door.

'Oh, and son, I've thrown in six free return plane tickets a year to Belfast for you too. Important you get to see your parents regularly.'

My day couldn't have got any better.

No doubt I was frightened of him. I wasn't alone in that. No doubt he wanted it that way. But I knew he was decent, he was honest and had my interests at heart. I was in the right place with the right manager to help me become the player I hoped to be.

Neil and his father seemed to be in there for hours. I waited in the hallway for him as promised when all I wanted to do was find the nearest payphone and tell my parents I was a footballer. A proper footballer. A professional footballer getting paid lots of money for doing something I would have done for nothing. Neil's father left us in the car park and we walked past the Gallowgate and Stowell Street, towards our favourite coffee shop in Newgate Street. Every day after training we'd order a microwaved bacon and tomato sandwich, which regularly scorched the skin off the roof of my mouth. We'd follow that with a huge slice of strawberry cheesecake smothered in some air filled foam cream. We got all the way to the table with our food without either of us asking the other the question we were dying to ask. I held my nerve longer than him. I was just about to rip my mouth off with the steaming hot tomatoes in my sandwich when he could wait no longer.

'Go on, then, what did you get?'

I'd played twice in the first team and he'd played once so I was pretty confident I'd have gotten more than him. I let my sandwich cool to roasting rather than scorching hot. '£120 a week.'

He spat his tomato out. 'Bastard.'

I wasn't sure if it was because he'd burnt his mouth but suspected it was the news that I was getting paid more that caused it.

'£110. Bastard.'

I felt a surge of satisfaction and addressed my steaming sandwich again. I wrapped a napkin around it to stop it burning my fingers. Bad enough my mouth. Not my hands too.

He was still probing. 'What about appearance money?'

I prepared to take a triumphant bite. '50 quid.'

'Same.' He took a bite of his sandwich.

'And six return plane tickets to Belfast.'

He choked a little, recovered his composure, swallowed, and scalded his throat.

That was it then. We'd got almost identical deals. I took great pleasure in the fact that I'd got a little more. £10 extra on my salary and six tickets home were a reflection of my seniority and the fact that I'd played in two games and he'd only played in one. I finished my sandwich and was fighting my way through the foamy stuff on top of my cheesecake when he spoke.

'What about a signing-on fee?'

I stopped poking my cake. 'A what?'

He knew he had me. *I knew he had me.*

'You did ask him for a signing on fee, didn't you?'

He knew I hadn't.

'I didn't ask him for anything.'

He scooped up the biggest bit of cheesecake he could get onto his fork. He leaned across the table so no one could hear but me.

'I didn't ask for anything either.'

My relief was palpable. He was just messing with my head. He hadn't asked for one either. I'd still got the better deal. I picked a bigger bit of cheesecake up with my fork. I brought it to my mouth.

'My da' asked him.'

I paused the foam at my lips. 'Your da' did?'

'Aye, that's why I brought him in. To act as my representative in case I was too shy.'

I sat my cheesecake and foam down. 'How much did your da ask for?'

'Fifteen grand.'

I nearly spewed my bacon and tomato mush back out of my stomach and all over him.

'FIFTEEN GRAND?'

He shushed me. 'Quieten down. I didn't get it. I only said he'd asked for it. Right at the end, when we were going out the door. He wasn't meant to do it. He just said it to chance his arm a bit.'

I was relieved. 'What did Coxy say? I bet he was furious?'

'He said no. No way. The club weren't prepared to pay someone as young as me that sort of money.'

I could just imagine the manager's anger at the cheek of it. I was glad that I hadn't been so stupid, so greedy. I picked up my melting foam and cake. I shoved it in my mouth. And then spat it all over him when he spoke.

'He gave me ten grand instead. Five this week and five this time next year.'

I pushed my plate away and handed him a napkin to wipe my cheesecake off his face.

Ten grand just for being cheeky enough to ask? I cursed my upbringing for making me too shy to ask for anything, never mind £10,000. I couldn't even imagine what that amount of money looked like. Or what a person would do with it. I found out soon enough. Three months later Neil was charging me £1 to take me to training in his brand new Mini Metro. Me? – I was wearing crap clothes, had a silly new haircut, and had no savings in the bank.

CHAPTER 21

THE MANAGER was as good as his word. I trained and played with the first team all of the 1982–1983 season. I didn't play often but was substitute or thirteenth man in most of our games. When I did play it was for ten or fifteen minutes at the end of games. He was getting me accustomed to first team football. I was still playing mostly on instinct and youthful enthusiasm. The coaches would work on making my right foot better and getting my head up to pass to my team-mates more. Trying to get me to be more consistent. But I was best when instinct took over and there was a flurry of legs in front of me. I was incredibly fast and could jink and twist and turn my way out of most situations. It meant that sometimes I could be frustrating for my team-mates but at other times I was capable of doing things and scoring goals that others couldn't.

I played on confidence. If it was high I was unstoppable. If it was low I was unwatchable. But I was confident and the more I played with the first team the more I felt like I belonged there. I was no longer in awe of the senior players. I wanted to be better than them. I was playing well enough to be in the team. My route was blocked by Chris Waddle. Since Kevin's arrival something had changed in him. He was blossoming into something entirely different to what he had been the season before. I loved watching him lazily approach a defender before bamboozling him with a drop of his shoulder or a step over. It was going to be difficult, but not impossible, to make my way past him, but I felt part of the team, part of the future, and was dreaming of the day when I would bring the whole stadium to its feet with a great goal to win an important game. The more I played the more I wanted to play. My brief appearances in the first team led to more and more people recognising me in the street, at the shops, and on the bus. It was quite unnerving having a complete stranger stopping me to ask if I was 'Paul Ferris who played for the Toon?' I got such a shock at first that I'd deny that I was in fact Paul Ferris and instead tell them that they were somehow mistaken. I'd walk off leaving the person as confused as I was as to why I'd just lied about my identity.

Off the pitch my life was settling into a routine that I was content with. I'd moved digs and now lived in Gosforth with Ted and Vi Hughes, a kind and gentle couple who treated me as if I was their own child. Mid-week, I would play an away game and not get back to the house until 2 a.m., but there'd always be a supper left on the kitchen table for me with a flask of hot chocolate. No matter how many times I told Vi I didn't need her to leave me anything cos we got fed on the team coach, she paid no attention, and made me supper anyway. I'd sit down in the early hours in her kitchen and hear her bedroom door open. She'd be down beside me sharing the chocolate and asking me how I'd played and what else was happening in my life. When you're seventeen and living away from your family, small gestures mean so much.

I developed a passion for buying clothes and changing my hairstyle every week. It was 1983. The afternoons were long and I didn't play golf or snooker. So instead I gave my money to the city's retailers, and hairdressing salons. *Especially the ones that did the great perms.* Music shops got the rest of my money. Van Morrison got most of it, much to the bemusement of John, Derek and my other friends. He was singing about Belfast and Ireland and his music soothed me. I'd lie on my bed and listen to it for hours. I'd rewind 'Madame George' until it rocked me to sleep. Van Morrison brought my home to me. That still didn't stop U2 taking some of my money from him – I was easy prey for any Irish artist.

But something else was happening. The football club – its history, its heritage, what it meant to the people – was seeping into my bones. I was proud of it and of its traditions and I was acutely aware of the privilege I was being granted in playing for it. I was growing to love the city as well. The two were intertwined. The club was the city and the city was the club. If the city was an entity then the club was its heartbeat. I'd never really spent any time in Belfast as a child because I wasn't allowed to go there. But after training I would spend hours walking the streets of Newcastle, gradually falling in love with the place and its people. I was born in Ireland and was fiercely proud of that, but I was growing up in Newcastle. The city was shaping me. I was still lonely at times, painfully so on many occasions, but I loved the city and its people. It had a unique 'soul' and the people had great warmth. I felt they were very much like the Irish people I'd grown up with. Not the ones who were bombing the life out of innocent people, or the bigots in my home town, but the decent people, the family and friends who meant so much to me.

Geraldine had been to visit me and that had united both my worlds. I could see they didn't have to be separate but could both be a part of me.

While I loved the city, it never fully replaced my affection for the country of my birth. Newcastle wasn't my home. Ireland was my home. Yet even that was different now. When I did go home it never really felt the same as it had before I left. I was caught somewhere between both worlds. Never fully belonging in either but I was making a life where I was at least content with that. The freedom from the bigotry of my hometown was something that I grew to cherish. I wasn't seen as a 'Fenian' in Newcastle. Nobody asked what religion I was. Nobody cared. People dying in IRA bombings and UDA reprisals were no longer dominating my existence. I never fully escaped it as my family were still living it every day and it was there every time I'd go home for a visit. I stopped going to Mass and lied to my mother about that. The lie was necessary. She would have felt she'd failed me if she knew I was committing a mortal sin every Sunday. Once I'd missed a couple of weeks and hadn't been struck by a thunderbolt I just never felt the urge to go back. I didn't miss anything about the Catholic Church; the ritual chanting of the Mass, accompanied by the incoherent sermons of the priests and the squirming embarrassment of regular confession. I'd never felt comfortable sitting in a cupboard in the dark and telling a stranger how badly I was failing to live up to laws laid down to Moses aeons ago by a particularly wrathful and vengeful Almighty.

The 'don't do anything remotely enjoyable or you will be damned to hell forever' mind-set had cast a shadow over my childhood and I was glad to be rid of it. I regarded it as controlling nonsense and wanted to be released from its grip on me. I initially felt liberated to be free from it. That was until I realised that I could never really escape it. The 'feel guilty about everything' part of my Catholic upbringing stayed with me long after I stopped practising its antiquated rituals. I just couldn't shake it off. No matter how hard I tried.

With Kevin Keegan in the team there was an expectation that Newcastle were guaranteed promotion. In the early part of the season it looked like that would be the case. Keegan had been joined by Terry McDermott, David McCreery, Jeff Clarke and John Craggs as the manager's team-building revolution gathered momentum.

Imre Varadi provided the goal-scoring threat and Chris Waddle was beginning to emerge as a supremely talented left winger capable of winning games on his own. At seventeen, with my newly signed three-year contract, and regular substitute appearances making me feel more and more a part of things, I was happy with my progress. St James' Park was filled to noisy capacity every game, a far cry from the half-empty hopelessness of the season before. There was expectation and excitement in the stadium and in the city. Unemployment and the death of the traditional industries that had been the city's lifeblood for decades still cast a dark cloud, but from the first home game when Kevin scored on his debut against QPR the team provided a burst of sunlight and a ray of hope. It seemed to me that everybody in Newcastle owned a black and white shirt and they wore it with great pride. I'd get the Metro or the bus to the games on Saturdays and walk with the congregation on their way to worship their new Messiah in the cathedral on the hill. He didn't let them down and he was better than anyone could've hoped for. Any thoughts that this was just a last payday before one of the greatest footballers of his generation hung up his boots were dispelled in his first game and banished forever by his complete dominance on the field and by the way he immersed himself in the city and embraced its people off it. He covered every blade of grass, cursed and cajoled his team-mates through every game and charmed his way through a series of talk-ins in the city's pubs and clubs. If they wanted a hero, someone to represent them and what they stood for, then he was up for the challenge. It was as if he wanted to carry the entire city on his shoulders. I'm convinced we would have been promoted in his first season but for a 'poke in the eye'.

A 'poke' in Kevin's eye while playing in a testimonial match saw him miss some vital games and our results dipped in his absence. His blurred vision meant that after several appearances as a substitute I finally made my full debut. It was on 4 December 1982 we played Charlton Athletic at the Valley in a game that was billed as a shootout between two 'European Footballers of the Year'. Alan Simonsen, the Danish superstar, versus Kevin Keegan, his English counterpart. At seventeen I was already impatient to be in the team but my crippling shyness meant I would never be one to knock on the manager's door and demand to be there. I would have loved to have had the courage to do it and watched with envy as others with less ability did just that. But I couldn't seem to find my 'voice'. Part of me, deep down, didn't have the belief that I was worthy of playing. No matter how many times others would tell me how well I was playing and what a great future I had in front of me, I was racked with self-doubt. I was driven by a fear of failure much more than any desire to succeed. Every day I buried my fears as deeply as they would let me, and just trained and played to the best of my ability, hoping that doing so would be enough to catch the eye of the coaches or Arthur himself.

'Paulie plays instead of Kevin. He won't let anybody down.'

The Friday night team meeting had come to an end. I'd spent most of it staring out of the window at Tower Bridge from my half-hidden chair at the back of the room. I was getting used to being named as substitute at best, but more often than not I was there for the experience of travelling with the team. Arthur's finishing flourish brought me back into the room.

The game itself passed me and the team by in a blur. I wore Kevin's number 7 shirt and started on the left wing. It weighed heavily on my back. Chris Waddle played centre forward alongside Howard Gayle, who was on loan from Liverpool. We were under pressure from the first minute and I barely touched the ball before they scored just before half-time. Arthur tore into the team at the interval. He spared me.

'There is a young boy out there making his debut and you lot are letting him down. Show some passion for the shirt, for Christ's sake. At least get the thing dirty. We're losing the game and some of you haven't broken sweat. There are people behind that goal who've spent every penny they have just to get here and watch you lot produce a performance like that. They can't even feed their bloody kids. Jesus Christ Almighty. It's a bloody embarrassment.'

He reserved most of his anger for Chris. 'I played you centre forward. You're bloody 6 feet 2 inches. The young boy Elliott has won every header against you. Come on, son. At least challenge him.'

Chris had obviously found his voice. 'D'you think I'm not trying to win fuckin' headers? Have you seen the size of him? Who d'you think I am, fuckin ET?'

A glare from Arthur finished the exchange.

We were 2–0 down five minutes after half-time. Alan Simonsen had scored and the ancient old ground was rocking. Our role today was to be extras in the Simonsen show. I stood on the left wing and spectated. I saw our sub getting warmed up and realised my debut was coming to an end and it had largely been a non-event. We had a rare break down the right. I moved off my wing and towards the back post more in hope than expectation. I saw Terry McDermott wrap his foot around the ball and float it into the box. I was 5 yards behind the full back and saw him ready himself to jump and head the ball clear. I realised from the flight of the ball that he was going to be underneath it. As it passed over his head I jumped and connected fully with it. I headed it firmly back past the flailing arm of the goalkeeper and watched it fly towards the inside of the far post. Time slowed to a stop. I saw the Newcastle fans behind the goal jump in the air as one. I realised the ball was going to bounce once and settle in the far corner of the net.

I'd scored on my debut.

I'd fuckin' scored on my debut.

I'd risen like ET and scored for Newcastle United on my full debut.

Everything that had gone before wouldn't matter. I raised my left arm to celebrate the greatest moment in my short life to date. I could feel a surge in my chest and my head was exploding. Then the ball landed on a divot and shot off almost at a right angle and instead of following its natural path, hit the inside of the post and was cleared to safety. I watched the TV replays ten times and still couldn't understand how I hadn't scored. If I had scored maybe I'd have started the next game at St James' and really been on my way. As it was, I'd have to content myself with being a perennial sub for the time being. At seventeen I knew there would be other opportunities. I also knew that I wanted more than anything else in the world to feel that feeling again. The one that I'd felt for a fleeting moment when I'd seen the ball head toward the goal, certain that I'd scored. It was like nothing I'd ever experienced. My whole body had tingled from head to toe. I'd felt more alive than ever before. Time had stood still and for a brief moment all of my senses had gone into overdrive. But it was gone all too soon and I couldn't get it back. The only way to do that was to score an actual goal. I was desperate for the day I would experience that.

CHAPTER 22

As the season petered out and after months of begging on my part, my mother and father finally came to a game. My mother was frightened of flying and her health was getting poorer. The only other time she'd left Ireland was when Bolton Wanderers had paid for her and my father to travel with me the day I signed schoolboy forms for them. On that trip we'd stayed in a pretty run-down hotel/B and B. This time they got the boat and a bus to Newcastle with my coaches from Lisburn Youth and two teams of boys, some of them not much younger than me. I was in the squad to play Blackburn Rovers at home the following day. The club paid for my parents to stay in the Swallow Hotel in Jesmond. On the Friday evening I went there to meet them.

As I approached the front entrance, I caught a glimpse of their familiar figures in the window of the dining room to the right of the door. I walked back and sat on the wall outside and watched them talking and laughing with each other. She was wearing a red dress I'd never seen before and her hair was freshly cut. Her perfect make-up couldn't hide the fact she was older than her years. He was wearing a light grey suit and a red and grey tie. His Brylcreem box must have been empty as I could see his hair glistening brightly from my vantage point on the wall. He reached across the table and took her hand. He got up, walked around to her, leaned down and kissed her. He sat down again just before dinner was served. The waiter poured her some wine. I'd never seen her drink wine before. I don't know that she ever had. A pint of Guinness sat half-drunk by my father's left hand. The rain started to fall lightly on my jacket. I didn't move. I never wanted to move. I just wanted to keep them there – safe, happy, framed in the glow of that window. I wished they could have this life all of the time. I knew they could. All I had to do was play football and I could give them that. A life they'd never had the chance to have. Theirs was a life of struggle, of trying to make ends meet, raising seven children, in a country damned to Hell. Maybe I could change that for them? I couldn't bring her health back, I knew that. But I could give them a life they could only dream of. That was within my grasp. I felt a rush of excitement just contemplating it. I saw her anxiously look at her watch and take a long draw on her cigarette and knew that the moment was gone. She was worrying about where I was. I had one last look at them and imprinted the image on my brain for the days when I would pass by that window and they would be just a memory. I left the cold wall and made my way in to finish off their desserts.

The following day I stood on the touchline at St James' Park. Behind me the old stand cast a giant shadow over half the pitch. We were attacking the Gallowgate end. As I ran across the pitch to take up my position I looked up to the place where I knew they were sitting. I saw them. It wasn't difficult. They were standing and wildly clapping my entrance, while the people around them were a little more restrained in their welcome. I waved and she waved back. She was wearing the red dress I'd seen only once before. He was wearing the grey suit with a newly purchased Newcastle United tie. I turned my attention to the game. I could feel my eyes sting as the ball came towards me. That my parents were actually there in the stands watching me play at St James' for Newcastle United was almost too much for me to comprehend.

My chest was thumping long before I embarked on my first run of the afternoon.

I was on the same pitch three days later playing a reserve game. I chased a pass in the dying minutes. The full back was the favourite to get there. I liked it like that. In my short career as a professional footballer one thing I was certain of was that I was quick, very quick. I was faster than anyone else at the club and I hadn't yet come up against a full back that I couldn't out-run in a sprint. I loved the moment a midfield player would slip a pass inside my opponent. I would be off. Even if I started 5 yards behind the scrambling defender I would always get there before him. What I did after that wasn't always as productive as it should have been. I could be erratic with my 'end product'. A great cross could be followed by a failure to clear the first defender. A great individual goal by a weak effort against the keeper's legs, but at seventeen I was happy that I was learning and I was getting better. Out-sprinting my opponent was never in doubt. I loved the feeling of racing past my opponents. When I was at full speed I was travelling so fast that I felt like my feet were barely making contact with the floor.

This occasion was no different. As soon as the ball was played I was off – my studs biting into the turf to give me some traction, before I really got into my stride. The ball raced towards the by-line. I sped after it determined to catch it before it drifted out of play. I sensed the full back disappearing in my slipstream and put in one last push to reach it. Then someone shot me in the back of the leg. Shot me with an exploding bullet. I crumpled in agony to the floor. The pain was excruciating. I lay there chewing the grass for a second trying to work out what had just happened. I heard the physio's voice. I tried to walk but the burning sensation in the back of my left leg increased with every step I took. I sat down and waited for a stretcher.

'Will he be fit enough to take to Japan?'

I lay on the couch in the treatment room as the manager and physio spoke.

'He probably won't be fit for the first couple of games but should be fine for the last three.'

We were due to travel to Malaysia, Thailand and Japan for a month at the end of the season. The trip was three weeks away. Because of Kevin there was a new-found interest in Newcastle United from all over the world. I didn't know much about hamstring injuries, or any injuries for that matter, but the pain in the back of my leg suggested to me that the physio was being very optimistic. I needed crutches to get home and walked with a limp for the next week, but in spite of that I was named in the squad to travel to the Far East. Part of me would rather have gone home instead – to spend a long summer in Ireland rather than a month on the other side of the world. But I was also determined to stay in the first team picture. So I was happy when the decision was made to take me.

We got off the plane in Kuala Lumpur and were met with 40-degree heat and a 50-foot poster of Kevin Keegan. Everywhere we went he was mobbed by throngs of well-wishers and autograph hunters. He dealt with it in his usual manner and we got used to waiting on sweltering coaches while he posed for hundreds of photographs and signed thousands of autographs. The entire trip was arranged around him. That had its advantages for the rest of us too. We checked into our first hotel in the middle of Kuala Lumpur. It was nothing special but pleasant enough. Another giant billboard of Kevin adorned the wall opposite the room I was sharing with Neil. We'd barely opened the Toblerone from the mini-bar when the phone rang. It was Russell Cushing, the club secretary. We weren't staying. Kevin thought the hotel wasn't good enough for us. My initial frustrations at having to pack my things up and leave were completely gone by the time we arrived at the replacement hotel on the outskirts of the city. It was like nothing I'd ever seen before. Giant marble halls lined with designer shops and a huge atrium stretching to the sky above the reception area. Our room had two enormous beds with enough pillows to supply a whole house, a lounge with a giant TV and a balcony overlooking the swimming pools below. Well, not pools as such, but one giant pool that was subdivided by several bars in the middle of the water. It looked like it stretched for miles. It was too tempting for Neil and me. We didn't even unpack before we were in it and swimming from bar to bar; stopping for a coke in one, a fresh juice in another and some nibbles at the next. We were just ordering club sandwiches at the fourth when a head popped out of the water next to our stools.

'This good enough for you two?'

It was Kevin. He was smiling at us. 'Stick with me, boys. I'll look after you.'

With that he swam off and did just that. He had a meeting with the representatives from Malaysia and club officials. We were entitled to £7 a day expenses on official overseas club trips. That was the figure proposed by the club. By the time it was communicated to us, and after Kevin's intervention, we were to be paid £30 a day. I didn't spend a penny of it. By the end of the trip I couldn't close my wallet and had to store some of the money in my suitcase. The tour was a long one with game after game coming thick and fast. Every player in the eighteen-man squad played his part. Everybody except me. I spent most of my time with the physio. Initially I would train and have treatment twice a day. My progress was painfully slow and so the physio began treating me in the evenings as well. I'm sure the last thing he wanted to be doing was spending his evenings with a seventeen year old boy with a badly damaged hamstring. Nevertheless, every night he'd be in my room, ultrasound at the ready, before heading off with the coaches to sample the culture of Malaysia, Thailand, and Japan. If the smell of his aftershave helped cure hamstring injuries I'd have been fit before the second week was out. The lack of fitness aside, I found the whole trip to be a magical experience. I relished sampling new cultures and foods and speaking with people whose lives were so very different from mine. In Thailand and Malaysia, in particular, I loved the gentleness of their spirit, their kindness and warmth. Everywhere we visited we stayed in the best hotels and were treated like visiting royalty. Well, nearly everywhere. We arrived in one hotel in Thailand after a four-hour journey through jungle terrain. It was early afternoon and according to our itinerary we were booked into the Holiday Inn for an afternoon nap before facing the Thai national team in a town 20 miles further through the jungle. As the coach pulled up outside our destination, and we caught our first glimpse of the one-storey ramshackle building we were to sleep in everyone on the coach looked at Kevin. He talked with the officials at the front of the bus and then addressed us on the microphone.

'Sorry, boys, this is all there is in these parts. We're only here for three hours so let's get in, get some sleep and make the most of it.'

The officials handed us our keys as we got off the bus. There was no one to greet us in the cramped reception area. A door was opened and we made our way, single file, down a dimly lit narrow hallway. All the doors to the rooms were on the left and on the right was a damp wall losing its plaster in the suffocating heat. There was a dull yellow lightbulb at the far end of the passageway, providing just enough illumination to identify our room number.

Neil opened the door and I followed him into blackness. He fumbled around and switched on the light. The room was bathed in a deep purple glow. I could barely see him, apart from his teeth, which were illuminated and gleaming at me in the fluorescent light. There was a small desk in the corner and an enormous bed that dominated most of the space. It was draped in purple velvet and had black satin pillows at the head of it. Or, rather, in the place where the head of it should have been. It was the first round bed I'd ever seen.

Neil looked at me. 'This is all a bit weird, isn't it?

I nodded.

He walked around one side and I climbed on the other. We lay on our backs side by side. And burst out laughing as soon as we saw ourselves mirrored in the ceiling. He sat upright. 'Fuck me. It's a brothel, man. I'm not sleeping in this thing.'

He jumped to his feet and began frantically brushing his hands across his tracksuit – cleaning the bed off him. He banged his leg on the table and knocked a bottle of oil onto the floor. He bent down to retrieve it but instead came up with a leather whip in his hand. He just stood there, whip in hand, while I lay looking at my teeth shining back at me from the mirrored ceiling. It was the strangest room I'd ever seen in my short life. So far removed from anything I'd ever experienced. Then 'Sad Movies' began playing through the tannoy system and into the room. I'd never heard that song played by or sung by anyone else apart from my mother. It was her song. The one she hummed when she was making my tea, or doing the housework; she sang it at parties when she'd had a little too much to drink. Now it was playing softly to me while I lay in a brothel in the jungle in Thailand.

'Everybody out. It's a brothel. Everybody out.'

Our door nearly came off its hinges. I leapt off the bed. Neil sat his whip on the table. We peeped out. Arthur was marching up the hall, banging on every door. I opened our door and stepped out. I could see the entire team standing in the hall, all in various stages of undress and confusion. Kevin and Terry McDermott were last out of their room. They were in their underpants and looked like they'd been wakened from a deep sleep. Kevin spoke with Arthur.

'What's the fuss?'

Arthur was indignant. 'Jesus Christ, man. What's the fuss? It's a bloody brothel, son.'

It was like he was convinced that if we stayed there we'd all end up as pimps or, worse still, prostitutes. Kevin turned to go back into his boudoir. 'Yeah, I know it's a brothel but we're not customers and there's nobody here but us. Now can we get some sleep?'

With that he was back in the room and all the others followed. I looked along the hall just before closing my door and could still see Arthur standing to attention outside his room. We slept there all afternoon. In our tracksuits, just in case. When I opened my door to go and find a bathroom the sentry was still on duty at the end of the hall.

The flight to Heathrow was long and bumpy, and I was relieved to be off it. I was laughing with Neil as we approached the customs desk. Then I felt a sharp whack across my ear. I spun round as Arthur walked alongside me.

'You've nothing to be laughing about, son. I've just taken you halfway round the world and you haven't kicked a ball for me. You were meant to be fit for the second week. What's that all about? Make sure you come back fit and raring to go.'

I felt sick. It was the first time I'd disappointed him and I didn't want to do it again. I was determined to come back for pre-season fitter than ever. It was the first injury I'd had as a professional footballer. The first hamstring injury I'd had in my whole life. I vowed it would be my last. But I was wrong.

CHAPTER 23

ARTHUR'S WORDS were all the motivation I needed to make sure I came back to pre-season training fit and healthy. I trained all summer in Ireland and then suffered through the gruelling double sessions of pre-season. I played in all the warm-up games and travelled to Hamburg for our pre-season tour – then pulled my hamstring again. Not as badly as the first time, but in the exact same place as before. One minute I was sprinting after the ball and the next I was on the floor in agony. I got used to arriving before everyone else, spending my day with the physio and leaving long after the others had gone home. This time I only missed three weeks' training. I'd come back and play a few reserve games and get myself in contention and then it would happen again . . . and again. It would be three weeks here, a month there, six weeks on another occasion. The cumulative effect was that I moved further away from the first team picture as the team was going from strength to strength. I was suddenly 'injury-prone'. I did everything that was asked of me and was desperate to be rid of this recurring nightmare. I lost faith in my own body. I became a sprinter who was frightened to sprint. But no matter how hard I tried to protect my delicate hamstring it would let me down time and time again.

'What are you crying for? And what happened to your head?'

I was sitting on the grass leaning my back against the wall of the indoor training pitch. It was late afternoon and I'd listened to the players' cars disappearing one by one until I was sure they were all gone. I'd pulled my hamstring yet again that morning and knew I was facing another month on the side-lines. Another month where I'd be first in, and last out, another month where the team would continue winning, another month where I would move further and further away from achieving my dream of scoring a goal at St James' and playing in the team regularly. Being injured gave me too much time to think, to worry, and to miss home. John Carver slid down the wall and sat beside me. My eyes were red and sore and I was bleeding from a cut on my forehead.

'I need to go home, John. I need to go home today. I've had enough. This isn't working. I can't stay fit for a minute. Everybody thinks I'm injury-prone. I'm further away than ever from the first team.'

I turned to look at him. He was shaking his head. 'Have you finished? I don't know whether to play me violin or hit you over the head with it. What d'you mean you're going home? Don't be so stupid, man. You're seventeen and you've already played in the first team. The manager loves you. So what that you're having a few injuries? Just pick yourself up and get on with it. Train harder to get fit and try harder to stay fit. That's all you have to do, man. Fuckin' pick yourself up and get back in the team. That's why you're here. Now get up and make your family proud. Come on, man. I'll look after you. Get up and get changed and let's fuck off for the day.'

He stood up and reached out his hand. I grabbed it. He pulled me into him and hugged me for a split second. He quickly stepped back. 'Fuck me, you're turning me as soft as you, man.'

He was staring at my head. 'How'd you cut your head?'

I pointed at the gym wall. 'I head-butted that in frustration.'

He shook his head. 'You stupid Irish bastard. How'd you think that was gonna turn out?' He started to laugh.

'I don't know but I did it twice.'

We made our way into the deserted changing rooms. That afternoon he walked around town with me and later met me in the evening for a pizza in town.

While I was caught in a cycle of injury, rehab, re-injury, it wasn't all plain sailing for the team either. But despite a few hiccups it was clear from early in the season that Newcastle would be mounting a strong push for promotion. Imre Varadi had left and was replaced by Peter Beardsley, who arrived just before the season commenced. Off the field he was the most unlikely footballer. A family man with no interest in the bright lights of fame and fortune, he came in to work, trained hard, and went home again. No fuss, no fanfare. But on match days he came alive. The forward line of Keegan, Waddle and Beardsley was a sight to behold for any young footballer making his way in the game. Keegan was coming to the end of his career but was still exceptional on his day. Waddle was developing so rapidly that I'd never again dream of telling my parents I should be in the team ahead of him. But for me, Beardsley was the real star of the team. Of all the players I played with he had the most natural talent. Gazza was coming through the ranks, Keegan was still there, and Waddle was unplayable at times, but Beardsley took my breath away. He could pass, dribble, dummy, tackle, create, and score great goals. In that season, in the second division in 1983–1984, he was mesmerising. Every game he would run at defenders. I knew what he was going to do, the defenders knew what he was going to do, and everyone in the stadium knew what he was going to do. And then he would do it. He'd approach his marker, lift his leg, shimmy to move, pause . . . and then go. Every time. The same approach, the same shimmy, the same result. He was undoubtedly the most naturally gifted footballer I ever played with. The team were promoted that season. Keegan was influential, inspirational at times; Waddle was enigmatic, majestic on occasions; but Beardsley was consistent and brilliant – a footballing genius in my eyes.

I was standing in the paddock next to the home dug-out as the helicopter carried Kevin Keegan into the night sky. My star had fallen so far in my injury-ravaged season that I didn't even make the squad for that end of season party against Liverpool. I left for Ireland the following day, dejected and confused as to how I could get my career back on track. I was eighteen, but because I'd played in the first team at sixteen I felt so much pressure to live up to the expectation of the 'wonder boy' tag thrown at me and I was failing miserably. I struggled to find perspective for the situation I found myself in. Most of my friends at the club hadn't been anywhere near the first team. Most young players my age at other clubs were the same. They were still making their way steadily in the reserves, hoping to make their breakthrough when they were mentally and physically ready to do so. I'd been thrown into the team when I was so young. I just wasn't ready for it – mentally or physically. My mind was in turmoil every time I picked up an injury or played badly, and my body wasn't ready for the demands placed on it week in and week out. I don't know what caused my first hamstring strain but I do know that rushing back too quickly time and time again in a vain attempt to get back into the frame for selection was hugely detrimental to my long-term ability to stay fit. Scar tissue had built up on scar tissue to the point where I barely had any flexibility when stretching my hamstrings.

More importantly, I was mentally drained. Going home for the summer, back to my family and Geraldine, was exactly what I needed. The prolonged period of rest with no pressure on my body and the love and support of people who were always rooting for me was like someone releasing the pressure valve. I spent the summer at home and in Donegal. I spent the time really getting to know my older brothers who were now living back home with their own families. I'd missed that when they were forced to move away. Parties, where my brother-in-law Tom would bring his guitar and we'd sing late into the night, were the perfect antidote to the traumas of the previous months. The familiar songs and stories seeped into me and nourished a sense of belonging and an identity that I needed to cling on to and never wanted to lose. These times would see me through the lonely nights to come when I'd go back to Newcastle and leave them all behind again. I could feel my mind clearing and my spirits rising the longer I spent with my family. I felt rejuvenated by those times. Geraldine was by my side all summer and when she was then everything was OK in my world. Every time I went home she would have changed a little. She was growing into a woman – a beautiful woman. When she greeted me at the airport she would take my breath way. When we were together I'd steal glances at her and know with certainty that I would sacrifice anything to keep her in my life. We spent that summer making plans. Plans for when we could be together all of the time. Not just for stolen summers and an occasional few days. I was still living in digs with Ted and Vi. She had only just left school and begun her first job. We agreed we couldn't do it yet. We were too young and our parents wouldn't allow it but we knew if we were to have a chance of staying together then we couldn't do that with her living in Ireland and me in Newcastle. If our love was to survive then we needed to be together.

My mother's failing health cast a dark shadow. Even in the midst of the liveliest party or in the brilliant sunshine of a summer's day, I was always painfully aware of her struggling for breath and of the fragility of her existence. Even the most mundane of tasks was now a challenge for her. Any exertion and she would be slipping tablets under her tongue like they were sweets. She could barely walk from our back door to the gate without having to stop for air. Or sit down till the pain in her chest subsided. I was no longer the frightened boy sitting on the shed watching her through the kitchen window but I still had the same dread deep in my gut that she would one day just give up and be gone from my world forever. I would feel physically sick as I stood helplessly beside her while she held my arm and we waited for the debilitating pains to leave her. Then we'd repeat the process 10 yards further up the road.

'Don't worry about me. I'm going nowhere until you're old enough to look after yourself. God will spare me till then.'

It was her stock answer every time I vocalised my fears to her. I used to get comfort from it when I was a child but now it had a hollow ring to it. I was already old enough to look after myself and, as for the God bit? I'd long since stopped believing in her God.

I sat with Marty Crossey as he talked excitedly about studying law at Queen's and was filled with admiration for him. He'd got the best A level results in Northern Ireland and had been awarded a scholarship to go there. I met some of his friends from school who were all heading off to university. As the night wore on I had less and less to contribute. They were living in a different universe from me. When they spoke to me they talked as if I was George Best. 'Saw you on the TV.' 'You lucky bastard.' 'What's Keegan like?' 'You must be loaded.' 'What car d'you drive?' I wanted to tell them how jealous I was of them all preparing to go to university but all they wanted to do was talk about football and the fact that I was a footballer. After two years of living away from home I was more confident than before but was still nauseatingly shy. I was afraid to join in their debates in case they discovered how stupid I was. Even when someone made a ridiculous observation about the current state of affairs in Ireland, or the inadequacy of government policy on education, I still couldn't find my voice. I would feel the urge to join in and correct the error but I never found the courage to do so. Instead I played the part of the footballer and left the intellectual debates to them.

I trained five days a week through the summer of 1984. Marty joined me on occasions, my brother Joseph on others. I was determined to go back fitter and stronger than ever. I'd a good incentive to do so. Arthur Cox had followed Kevin Keegan out of the club and had been replaced by Jack Charlton. I was sorry to see Arthur go – he'd played me in the first team at sixteen and I was always confident he had my best interests at heart. Even after the wasted year I'd just had I never doubted he believed that I could one day be a regular in the team. Now that a new manager was coming in I was desperate to be fit and to impress him. I didn't want to meet him in the treatment room. First impressions matter. Mentally I was re invigorated by the love and support of a long summer with my family and Geraldine. Physically I could see my body changing. I was building muscle and becoming a man. We were now a first division team. There was a new manager in place, players would be coming to join him, and others would no doubt be leaving. I hated the uncertainty of it but I was confident that if I could stay fit then I still had a big future at Newcastle United.

CHAPTER 24

Striking a ball accurately over 50 yards is an impressive skill to master. Doing it while nursing a cup of coffee in one hand, a cigar in the other, and wearing a pair of suede loafers is something else altogether. That was our introduction to Jack Charlton. I met him on the first day and found him warm and affable. He was a giant with a big personality and a clear vision of how he wanted his team to play. He wanted the ball in the opposition's box as quickly and as often as possible. He had his quirks. 'No half volleys. I hate half volleys.'

He stopped a training session once to tell me that after I'd smashed a half volley off the crossbar. 'Half volleys are for crowd pleasers. Always rising, never score. Volleys are always dipping so you always score.'

'Flick it up and volley it, man.'

Steve Carney was staring blankly at him. It was the first afternoon of pre-season training. Jack was standing at the side of the pitch puffing his cigar and sipping his coffee. He was dressed for hunting, shooting or fishing. He wore a flat cap on his famous head and was dressed in green and khaki from head to toe. He strode onto the pitch and took up the position he'd played over 700 times for Leeds United and from where he'd watched Geoff Hurst create immortality for him in 1966.

'Here, pass it to me.'

The coach rolled the ball towards him. He hooked his loafer underneath it and lifted it into the air. Then in one fluid movement he launched it 50 yards and on to the chest of the centre forward at the other end of the pitch. He turned to Steve. 'Now you do it.'

With that he was striding off into the distance and into his car and away to his engagement with the country life he adored so much. Steve and the other centre halves spent the next hour getting caught in possession as they tried to replicate Jack's technique to no avail.

I trained and played in every session and in all of the games and had no problems from my hamstring. I was glad of that as our physio had moved on and we operated with a part-time sponge-man from a local non-league team. We were a first division club without a qualified physiotherapist. I think that scenario scared me into staying fit. The situation was rectified when a player's delegation insisted we needed proper medical support. Derek Wright arrived from Fulham, fully qualified and dedicated to his profession. My hope was that I wouldn't get to know him too well even though I warmed to him immediately. He was an honest and decent man and wanted to do his job to the best of his abilities and with the minimum of fuss.

Jack recruited Gary Megson, Pat Heard, and later George Reilly and Tony Cunningham – all good professionals who fitted into the squad very well and added to the atmosphere in the dressing room. They didn't have the star quality of Kevin Keegan and were received underwhelmingly by the Geordie public, though Tony did get a terrace song dedicated to him:

He's black. He's broon. He plays for the Toon. Cunningham!

George's and Tony's signings in particular were a sign of how Jack was going to play. It was a big change of direction from the previous season. My good form and more significantly my ability to stay fit meant that I was brought back into the first team group. I thought I'd a chance of starting our first game but just missed out in the end. I didn't have to wait long to get my first taste of first division football however. I was back to being a regular sub and my troubles from the year before were fading further with every appearance.

I was getting a bit frustrated at always being a sub. I trained hard and played well in the reserves. I was a different player to the boy who'd made his debut when he should've been in school. I wasn't overawed by the new players in the way I was when I trained and played with Kevin Keegan. I was more consistent. I still had my pace and trickery but I was learning how to use those qualities better. My touch was improving and my belief in my right to be playing was strengthening. I still didn't have the courage to knock on the manager's door and demand to be in the team, but my performances would do that for me. We were playing Bradford in the league cup on a cold night in October when the manager sent me on.

'Go on and have a run at Trevor Cherry, Ferrisie. He's older than me and he'll never catch you.'

The score was 1–1 and the second leg was to be played at Valley Parade in a week's time. I took up my position on the left wing opposite Trevor Cherry, the former England full back, as instructed by Jack. We were attacking the Gallowgate end. I barely had time to settle myself into the game when John Anderson lofted the ball high into the night sky. I saw Chris Waddle challenge the centre half and took a chance that he'd win the header. I started to sprint off my wing as he jumped. I was on the full back's shoulder as Chris won the header. I was 10 yards past him by the time the ball bounced off the turf in front of me. I saw the goalkeeper rushing towards the corner of the box that I was sprinting into.

And then it happened again. Time slowed down. Everything seemed to stop for a split second. The ball sat up. The goalkeeper was too far away to get to it. I put my head down and hit it as hard as I could with my left boot. I didn't even feel it connect. I watched it move through the air. I saw the goalkeeper dive after it was past him. I watched it head toward the far corner of the net. I didn't take my eye off it this time. I didn't raise my hand too soon in celebration. I watched it fly into the corner. I heard the net ripple. There was a moment of silence. Then the Gallowgate end behind the goal erupted. From the very first day I'd arrived in Newcastle as a tearful and timid sixteen-year-old boy I'd dreamed of this moment. I had wondered how I would feel scoring a goal at the Gallowgate end for Newcastle United. Now I'd done it and it felt like nothing I'd ever experienced in my life. My whole body came alive like never before. It was as if I'd suddenly been plugged into a socket. My heart was pounding, my head was buzzing and my arms and legs tingled. I tried to take some deep breaths to calm myself but I couldn't get enough air in to fill my lungs. I jogged back to the halfway line shallow breathing and trying to relax my mind and body. Then the crowd in the East Stand next to me started to bang on the metal hoardings. The noise was deafening. I looked around the old stadium. It was awash with activity, dancing, singing, hugging, screaming. I wanted more of this. I wanted to feel this feeling again and again.

'You all right?'

It was Neil. He'd come across from his position on the right wing.

'Not really. I can't catch my breath. Fuck me, I've just scored for Newcastle United.'

He laughed. 'Some of us have scored a few. Good feelin', innit? Now fuckin' snap out of it. We have a game to win, man.'

We did win the game. 3–1 in the end. Jack Charlton sought me out.

'Well done, Ferrisie. I told you he wouldn't catch you.' He slapped my back as he spoke.

I sat in the giant round bath with a layer of other players' scum nestling on my chest. My team-mates had gone off to their families in the players' lounge. I was in no hurry, my family weren't here. I thought about my mother and father at home. They'd know by now that I'd scored. They'd have heard it on the radio or seen it on Ceefax. They could watch it on the TV in an hour's time. I was living in a flat in Jesmond with John Carver and Gary Kelly. John was out with Angie tonight and Gary was in Preston visiting his family. I was in no hurry to go home. I wanted to stay in the filthy bath all night. I knew when I got out and left the changing room that the moment would be gone. I didn't want that. I wanted the moment to last forever. I got thrown out by the cleaner in the end. An hour after the game had finished I finally left the changing room through the back door. I didn't bother going to the players' lounge but instead wanted to go and phone my parents. I slipped out into the darkness and was just about to make my way down the stairs towards the Metro when someone pulled on my sleeve.

'Paul, can I have a quick word?'

Alan Oliver, the *Evening Chronicle* reporter, was pushing his Dictaphone into my face. I stopped and in seconds there were ten others having a quick word too. When they were done I got the Metro and phoned my parents from a call box outside the flat. I ate two Curly Wurlys and watched myself score a goal on TV. I slept in the living room with the light on until John came home.

I felt like everything would change after that. The manager would surely put me in the team and give me a run of games to establish myself. He showered me with compliments in the press for 'doing exactly as I was instructed to do'. I felt my time was coming. I was on the coach on the way to Bradford for the return leg when I got my wish.

'Manager says you're starting tonight, son. You deserve it.'

Willie McFaul, our coach, was smiling next to me. He'd been Arthur's coach as well. I felt like he'd always looked out for me. I had an affinity with him and his wife Eileen – they were from Northern Ireland and Willie was a legendary goalkeeper at the club. I'd pack my case with soda bread when I was home and bring it into training for him on my return. When my parents had visited he'd taken them to his home and tried to outdrink my father in Guinness. The result had been very messy for them both.

I was pulling the number 11 shirt on in the changing room at Valley Parade. The timing was right. My confidence was at an all-time high. I was fit and strong and felt ready to take on the world. To show it what I could do.

'Take that off, son. I'm playing Pat instead. I've just seen their team and I want him on the left side of midfield rather than you on the wing.'

Jack was pulling the shirt off my back as he spoke. He threw it to Pat Heard who gave me his number 12 shirt instead. The manager was nothing else if not thorough. The team came first and my feelings a distant second. In a way I admired him for it. Nothing would get in the way of his desire to win the game. Especially not the sulking of a nineteen-year-old whose name he didn't know. *Ferrisie would have to wait a little longer.*

The disappointment of not starting games was tempered by the fact that I was a firm fixture in the first team squad. Peter Beardsley and Chris Waddle were the stardust in the team. Gazza was beginning to blossom into something entirely different from the chubby boy with blotchy legs who wouldn't pass to me on my trial. But I felt like I belonged now. I always suffered from a lack of self-belief and confidence in myself but it never held me back once training or games commenced. I knew enough to know I was good enough to be there and was steadily becoming a better professional. My professionalism ended when I left the training ground. We got fed every day at Newcastle Brewery next to the stadium. The whole team would go there after training and eat with the brewery staff at the canteen. It was the only decent food my body was getting on a regular basis. We started off with the best of intentions in the flat but it all too soon became an untidy squalid mess. We lived on takeaway food, beer and sweets. The only home cooked meals we had were when John's sister would arrive with a mince pie his father had cooked for us. Our ground floor flat had a window that never locked. Gazza found out and I'd regularly come home to find him sleeping in one of our beds after making his way past the broken latch. I liked him. He was a bundle of nervous energy but had a big heart, a ready smile, and a prank for every occasion.

One downside of being a first team squad member was that as Christmas approached I knew I wouldn't be going home as I would be required for the festive fixtures. The thought of spending Christmas alone in our rancid flat was preying heavily on my mind. John would go home, Gary would go to Preston. Mrs Bell had invited me to her house but her son Derek's career had finished prematurely a year before when he ruptured his cruciate ligament. I felt a little uneasy about going there and preparing for a Boxing Day game when his future was now his past. Geraldine's parents were keen on her spending the big day with them. I put my fears to one side and attended our Christmas party after a reserve game at St James'. We made our way to the Eldon pub in the town. My side was hurting a little from an accidental knee, which had caused me to come off late in the second half. John got the drinks in while I went to the bathroom. I was standing at the long silver trough when I could sense the man next to me staring. I didn't have the courage to tell him to stop but concentrated on finishing quickly so that I could get back to the safety of my group. He tapped me on the shoulder. I felt my legs weaken. I looked at him. He was still staring at me. *Down there.* Anger overcame my fear.

'Have you got a problem, mate?'

He never took his eyes off my private parts. 'No, mate. But I think you have.'

He nodded for me to follow his eyes. I looked down. I wished I hadn't. I saw a thick stream of dark red blood pouring out of me and joining the huge pool that was now covering half of the urinal.

He washed his hands and left me blaspheming at my willy.

I found John perched on a stool, pint in hand in the centre of the group.

'I need to go to the hospital. I'm pissing blood. I think I'm dying.'

He sat his drink down. 'You can't be. Come and show me.'

We hurried back into the toilet and I showed him my party piece. Thick, sticky purple blood poured out of me. He lost all colour. 'Jesus. Fuck me. Jesus Christ. Fuckin' hell. Jesus fuckin' Christ.'

I zipped myself up. 'What do I do?'

He was already pulling me out the door. 'Fuck the party, man. You need to get to the hospital.'

I stayed in the private room off the main ward in the Royal Victoria Infirmary for nearly a week with a clot on my kidney. Not only was I not going home for Christmas but I was going to spend it in hospital. Every day the nurses would come in, raise my piss bottle to their faces and announce today's colour. It went from purple to dark red. Red to salmon. Salmon to pink. Pink to straw. I'd squirm as they would argue over the chosen colour. Two days before Christmas they told me I could go home. But I couldn't play for a month. Jack came in that night, opened my door, and threw a bag of sweets onto my testicles. I opened the bag and inside was a plane ticket to Belfast departing the following day. He stayed for five minutes talking to the nurses about the difference between pink and salmon. As he was closing the door he spoke.

'Go home and enjoy Christmas and New Year with your family. When you get back come and see me about a pay rise and sorting your contract out, Ferrisie. You've done well for me. Now I'm off.'

He shut the door as I nursed my plane ticket, sweets, and sore testicles.

I went home that Christmas with the promise of a new contract, a pay rise, and a question for Geraldine.

CHAPTER 25

LEO MCCAUGHERTY was pacing up and down our cramped living room. He rubbed his greying beard with one hand and ran his other through his red and grey flecked hair. I sat on the settee next to my mother. I needed her there for moral support. I didn't want to ask permission to marry his eldest daughter on my own. I wasn't sure how he'd react. He and Mary had provided a loving home for their daughters, Geraldine and Caroline. Caroline was still at school and Geraldine had just turned eighteen. I knew I was asking a lot of him and Mary and that I was too young to be doing so. But I wasn't asking permission to get married any time soon. In fact I promised him that was the last thing I would do. I liked them both and they liked me. I was always welcome in their home since the day I first met them as a spotty fifteen-year-old boy. It was the second question that was causing him to pace up and down. I wanted his daughter to move to Newcastle. Not immediately but in the summer.

'You want her to move to England? She's far too young, son. You're too young. Who's going to look after her all that way away? You? You're only a boy yourself. Give yourselves some time. You're just kids. You can't know what you really want. Things change. Feelings change. This will break her mother's heart.'

He was right. I was nineteen. She was eighteen. We were too young. Far too young. But we'd been living apart now for three years and with the offer of the new contract I couldn't contemplate the thought of two more without her. I could see by his face that her mother's heart wasn't the only one I'd be breaking. But I was lonely. I missed her. I knew I was breaking their hearts, but mine was breaking too. My mother spoke with him in private. After their meeting he shook my hand and gave me his blessing to take his eldest daughter away from her home and the love of her family. I just needed her to agree to it now. I knew she would. Not through arrogance or blind faith but because I was sure she loved me like I loved her. She had told me she would come to Newcastle as soon as she was old enough. Admittedly she'd said it during a frantic conversation in her house when I was leaving home for the first time. But I believed her. *I believed in her.* I was excited by the thought of her being with me in Newcastle. I wanted to share the journey with her. Whatever that journey entailed it wouldn't be complete without her by my side. I was as certain as I could be that I'd have a long career as a footballer at Newcastle, or if not there, then somewhere else.

Jack kept his promise. I signed my contract and got my pay rise. Geraldine kept hers too. She buried her fears about leaving home and agreed to come to Newcastle in the summer and to be my wife when we were old enough for the world not to care. My urine looked like urine again and I returned to playing on schedule. I lasted two training sessions before my troublesome hamstring ensured that I got to know Derek Wright better than anyone else at the club. My treatment was different this time. He was dedicated to his job and determined to get me fit. Not just this time – he was trying to prevent the next time from happening as well. I endured torturous sessions where his thick thumbs were buried so deeply in my tissues that it brought tears to my eyes and swear words to my lips that I didn't even know I knew. He examined my back and we discussed my summer job as a fourteen-year-old throwing heavy cow hides into crates for eight hours a day. I had ended up with a stiff back, pus spewing infections in three fingers and, in Derek's view, a predisposition to hamstring trouble.

John was injured too, with a thigh strain that would curtail any chances he had of making his way into the first team squad. We cut a miserable pair in our filthy flat, dining on takeaway food and chocolate, washed down with cans of Red Stripe beer. He was an avid fan as well as a player and would regularly travel on supporters' buses to watch the team play away from home. Several times we'd be in the team coach leaving a stadium and someone would shout 'There's JC.' I'd look out of the window and he would be in the middle of a column of Newcastle fans being marched by the police to the safety of their transport home.

I found the vitriol and bile exchanged between opposing fans intimidating even when I was in the relative safety of the team coach. I had good reason. I had been punched in the face as a seventeen-year-old on one short journey from our coach to the sanctuary of the Elland Road changing rooms at Leeds. One minute I was smiling and chatting with my team-mate and the next I felt a sharp sting in my mouth as my head rocked back. By the time I'd regained my senses the offending arm had disappeared into the baying throng. On more than one occasion bricks and bottles crashed against the windows of our team coach as we made our way out of away grounds.

'Come with us, man. What else are you gonna do? Sit around in your underpants all day? You'll love it. Divvent worry about anything. They're a great bunch of lads and anyway I'll look after you.'

I'd been injured for over a month. The first team was playing Nottingham Forest. John had asked me three times to go with him and his mates to watch the game. I was running out of excuses.

'What about the miners?'

He put his Red Stripe on the table and stabbed his sweet and sour ball.

'The miners? What the fuck do the miners have to do with you going to watch a match? Fuck me, man. I've heard it all now.'

He threw his fork down and took a swig from his can. I tried to explain.

'The miners. The miners' strike. The thing that's been dominating the news for the last six months. Maggie destroying them. Thousands losing their jobs, families ripped apart, picket lines, riots?'

He got up and stepped into the kitchen. He pushed his plate into the bin to stop his one remaining sweet and sour ball from popping back out and landing on the dirty floor.

'Whoa, whoa, whoa man. If I'd wanted a political debate I'd have watched fuckin' *Question Time* last night. It's like living with Robin Day. I know about the miners' strike man. Who doesn't? But what's it got to do with you not going to a match?'

I sat my empty plate in the sink on top of last week's plates. It rocked precariously on the edge of a mouldy pot before finding a resting place between it and the edge of the basin. A little trickle of bright orange sauce dripped slowly down the front of the cupboard.

'The Nottingham Miners – the UDM (Union of Democratic Mineworkers). They're not on strike. They don't support Scargill. There'll be trouble between the fans over that. Definitely.'

He opened the fridge and passed me a Red Stripe. 'You think about things too much. All that politics is fuckin' with your head. It's just a football match. A few pints. A bit of a laugh. Lighten up a bit, man.'

He was right. I was obsessed with politics – Irish politics mainly, but also what was happening to the city I lived in. I didn't talk about it at the training ground. People had other interests than that and I didn't want to stand out as the 'weirdo' in the corner. But I was living with John now so he could see it and had to listen to it. He did so with good grace mostly but I'd often watch his eyes glaze over in the middle of one of my angst-ridden monologues about the latest atrocity in Belfast, or anywhere else for that matter. I felt different to my team-mates but didn't want to be. I wanted to fit in. I wanted to be accepted.

That led to some interesting choices of clothes and a new-found love of a 'mullet' hairstyle. We all got our hair permed and dyed blonde. In my case more green than blonde. We'd stand at the mirror after training. Bend over and back blow our curly manes. Then compare whose was best. Gazza was adamant his ball of frizz was; I was sure my green effort was better; John claimed he was the inventor of it but the daddy of all mullets was Chris Waddle's. His brilliance on the field ensured his curly perm achieved worldwide fame. Away from the training ground I was obsessed with two things: music – U2 and Van Morrison in particular – and politics. After an upbringing in Northern Ireland in the 1970s, 'politics' was just in me. It was a part of my DNA. Politics meant life and death. Everything else just seemed unimportant. Meaningless even. The miners' strike was currently dominating my thinking. I watched every bit of news footage that I could. From the outset of the dispute I knew there'd only be one outcome. If Margaret Thatcher had watched ten men die on hunger strike – one of them an elected MP – rather than negotiate with them, and sent British soldiers to their deaths to maintain sovereignty of a lump of rock off the coast of Argentina, then she would think nothing of breaking the will of a group of working-class northerners led by their firebrand union leader. I knew she'd ruthlessly crush them, break their spirit and starve them into submission. I despised her, and her uncaring government. I'd walk through town, sign the petitions, put some money in the tins but hated the hopelessness of the miners' cause. They were doomed the moment her guns were pointed in their direction. John was right. All the politics was messing with my head. I decided to lighten up and agreed to go to the game with him and his mates.

Ten minutes into the journey from Central Station I felt a bit stupid about my comments to John. There were about forty of us squeezed into the coach. I think thirty had already come to my seat to welcome me on the trip. They were dressed for a night out rather than a football match; all smart shirts and LeBreve jeans. They each to a man promised to 'look after me'. *What was it with Geordies and looking after me?* They were a good-natured bunch and were delighted to have a Newcastle player on their coach with them. We pulled up outside a closed off-licence in Low Fell. The coach emptied. The off-licence wasn't closed. It emptied too. Our bus was overflowing with its contents. Thirty minutes later the coach was rocking as every terrace chant I'd ever heard, and some I hadn't, was echoing all around it. I nursed a can of Red Stripe until it was too warm to drink. A bloke in a crisp white shirt with bulging biceps and a shiny head came down to the back to ascertain as to whether or not I knew all of the words to the songs. When I satisfied him I did, he staggered back to the front to commence another one. We stopped off at a pub in Mansfield. I stayed close to John. He went off to the bathroom and a tall bloke with a prize mullet was standing in front of me. He was wearing jeans and a string vest. He had a mahogany tan, shiny white teeth and an earring in both ears. His string vest was no defence against his pointy nipples, however – they were poking through right in my eye line. I was transfixed by them for a split second – two bullets stabbing through the mesh. He was talking to me in a slurred Geordie accent. The bar was packed and he was talking in staccato. 'Hate these cunts. Wankers the lot of them. Fucking cowards. Fucking shithole.'

A mist rose up over his exposed nipples. I felt something on my leg. He just kept on talking. I looked down. His jeans were open and his willy was hanging out. He was pissing everywhere – on the bar, on the floor and on me. I looked up at him. He was still 'fucking this' and 'fucking that'. He didn't care that I and everybody else were getting soaked in his piss. I wanted to head-butt him. But before I could speak, John was back and dragging me onto the coach. I wanted the day to end there. I wanted to go home.

'Calm down, son. He's just a bit pissed. He meant no harm.' John was doing his best to defuse my anger.

'You can't go around pissing on people and on other people's property? It's disgusting. Where's the bloke running the trip? I want to speak with him.'

John pushed me back on the seat. 'Honestly, just let it go. Don't cause any bother. Do it for me please?'

He had a look in his eye I hadn't seen before. Fear maybe?

The coach moved off and I agreed to let it go. My jeans were still wet when we reached the stadium. We got off and headed for the Newcastle end. Half of our group set off in the other direction. My pisser among them. I'd been to Forest's ground before.

'They're going the wrong way, John.'

He just pulled my arm. 'Forget them. They're not here for the match. They're here for the fight. Just come this way.'

The game was five minutes old when a huge circle opened up in the Forest end. Our friends had started their fight. They were arrested and marched down the side of the pitch. We were in the bottom of the stand underneath the Forest fans. The mood darkened. I was the only one watching the game. The chants from the Newcastle fans were as predictable as they were antagonistic.

'Scabs, Scabs, Scabs . . . Scabs, Scabs, Scabs . . .'

The Forest fans didn't respond with a chant. Instead they threw coins. They lit newspapers and just as I looked up they pissed on us. They pissed on me. *What was it with football fans and piss?* I could see my team-mates only yards away from me and wanted to call out. Get someone's attention. Go back home with them. Instead I suffered in mortified silence. I was ecstatic when the game was over and we finally got back on the coach. That was until we stopped at a roundabout and a vote was taken on whether we should 'wreck Mansfield' on the way home. To my great relief the decision was in favour of going straight home. Four hours later we pulled into Newcastle. There were black bin liners filled with piss swinging from every skylight. I weaved my way around the leaking bags and turned down the request to go straight to Madison's nightclub. I also politely declined the offer to travel to the next away game.

CHAPTER 26

DESPITE DEREK Wright's best efforts to solve my persistent hamstring problems, I just couldn't stay fit for any length of time during the second half of the 1984–85 season. I spent most of my time with him and got to know him as a trusted friend. Derek became my agony aunt as well as my physio. He was a gentle and caring man and I appreciated the time he devoted to me in his quest to get me fit and keep me fit. I wasn't helping myself as much as I could have. I was doing everything asked of me in the treatment room and the gym but then going back to the flat and fuelling myself with takeaways and sweets. I rarely ate a sensible meal during that time. Sunday lunch was often Curly Wurlys and Wham Bars broken up on my plate. Our fridge should have been sponsored by Red Stripe. When the season was over, I embarked on another summer of rehab in Ireland. Pre-season was gruelling but I stayed fit. Jack Charlton walked out after a home game when a handful of disgruntled fans in the small crowd were chanting for his sacking. I was sitting behind him in the dug-out. He looked across to the half-empty Gallowgate where the heckling was coming from and spoke as he started to rise from his seat.

'Fuck this. I don't need this. I'm off.'

And then he got up and left and we never saw him again. Any managerial departure always causes great uncertainty. Will the next one like me? Will he rip up the blueprint and start again? You just never know. This occasion was different though. The club appointed our coach Willie McFaul to the role. It was a great honour for him and I was pleased for him and his family. He'd served the club with distinction as a player and had been a permanent fixture within the coaching team for many years. More importantly, I recognised the opportunity it presented for me. He'd been a fervent advocate for my abilities since I arrived. He'd told my parents I was destined for a great career. So when I reported for training on his first day as manager, I did so full of excited anticipation for what was to come. John had been released and moved to Cardiff, and I'd found a nice place in Lemington Rise that I'd agreed to rent for when Geraldine arrived in a week's time. Now Willie was to be my manager. I felt like everything was falling into place. The stars were aligning. I was certain that he would give me opportunities if I performed well.

I don't really know why I attempted the overhead kick in the first place. It could have been enthusiasm, a desire to impress, or just because instinctively it seemed the right thing to try. Our first session under Willie was coming to an end. We were playing an eight-a-side game. I'd moved across the front of the defender antic-ipating a cross from the right. As the ball was lofted towards me I realised I was too far underneath it. I turned and planted my left foot in the turf. I leaned back and swung my right leg forward to generate some momentum. I tried to move my left leg so that it would meet the ball at its full height but my studs got tangled in the long grass. My body continued to move forward and my ankle rotated until its ligaments prevented me from twisting it any further. My left knee was now taking up the fight. My full body weight trav-elling as fast as I could move it was now bearing down on this soli-tary joint. There was a brief moment when the structures of my knee held firm before a loud crack and a release of the tension signalled their surrender under the force of my entire body on top of them. The pain was instant and unbearable. I rolled onto my back. My knee felt like it had just been set on fire. I knew something was very wrong with it. My screams alerted everyone else to the problem. I tried to get up, but Glenn Roeder, our captain, placed his hand on my chest.

'Stay there. Don't move. You'll be all right. Derek's on his way.'

I tried to push his hand out of the way. I needed to get off my back. I needed to get up. To sit up. Quickly. He pushed me back. 'Paul, stay there. Try to relax.'

I pushed his arm away and managed to get up just as the vomit reached my throat.

Derek was thorough in his assessment. By the time I'd reached the treatment room my pain had eased but my knee was swollen. He pulled and prodded and pulled and prodded again. Players were popping in and out to assess the damage and offer their encouragement. I didn't need Derek to tell me that I was facing surgery and a long layoff. I just needed an estimate of how long. When he moved my left knee in certain directions and compared it to my right knee it was clearly lax where my ligaments had once been. He was talking to Willie, using words such as 'end feel', 'laxity', 'cruciate ligament', 'medial ligament', 'medial meniscus' – all terms I had heard before but none of which I understood and certainly none of which had been discussed while referring to me before. Willie shook his head and ran his hand across my knee. 'Sorry for you, son. You're not having much luck. Don't worry. Derek will take care of you.'

Peter Beardsley came in and sat on the other treatment couch. He asked the question I was too frightened to. 'What's he done, Derek? Looked a bad one when he did it.'

Derek addressed us both. 'First impressions are that the medial ligament is ruptured. Probably some associated meniscal damage. I think the anterior cruciate ligament is damaged too, but with the swelling it's difficult to say. I'll book an appointment with Mr Stainsby. I think we'll end up having an arthroscopy, where the surgeon looks inside and then he'll perform any surgery if he thinks it's necessary.'

Joe Harvey hobbled into the room on his ageing bow legs and decimated knees. His legendary efforts for the team in the 1950s had taken their toll and were all too painfully evident in the 1980s. He rubbed my head and tried to lighten the mood. 'Bloody kids these days, Derek. Soft as shit they are. In my day that sort of thing was just a bloody scratch. I'd be playing on Saturday.'

He turned and waddled and winced his way back through the door.

Derek booked my appointment with the surgeon for the same evening at the Nuffield private hospital in Jesmond. That afternoon, I hobbled on crutches onto St James' Park. I sat on a bench with my mangled knee extended as it wouldn't bend. Derek manoeuvred it into a position I was comfortable with. I posed with the other dyed blonde perms for our official team photo and Derek drove me to the hospital straight afterwards.

He was looking at me over his half-glasses in the dim light of his consultation room. Derek was at his shoulder. I was dreading the prognosis after his painful examination of my swollen knee.

'Well, young man, I think you've been rather lucky. I think you have a partial tear of your medial ligament. Everything else appears fine. We'll put you in a plaster for three weeks and you should be back playing in six.'

I couldn't have hoped for a better prognosis. 'So I don't need an arthroscopy then?'

Mr Stainsby was at the door and ushering us through it. He gave me a piece of paper. 'No, that won't be necessary. If you take this downstairs we'll get you in plaster.'

I pulled on my tracksuit bottoms, feeling relieved and embarrassed. Relieved that the club surgeon was telling me I hadn't hurt myself too badly after all. Embarrassed about my screaming, vomiting, hobbling onto the team photo and genuinely believing that I'd completely ruined my knee. Six weeks was nothing. I'd had hamstring strains that kept me out for longer.

The six weeks flew past like six days. So much happened that I didn't have time to dwell on my knee. I moved into my flat. Geraldine moved to Newcastle, and any lingering homesickness I felt was gone the minute she arrived. She connected both my worlds. My rehab had gone smoothly. I was a little tender when I was crossing the ball with my left foot but apart from that I felt ready to join in training with the team again. I flicked the ball over the defender's foot and chased it down the left wing. I got there just before him. I feigned to cross the ball before wrapping my left leg right around it. *My trick that never failed.* I didn't see him slide past. I didn't see him because I was crumpled in a heap on the floor. It was like someone had jabbed a red-hot poker through the inside of my knee and left it there.

'Stubborn scar tissue. That's all. Show me the exact spot where the pain is worst?'

I was back in the same dull consultation room. I manoeuvred my thumb into position on my knee and brought it to a stop where the red-hot poker was. He was standing in front of me with a syringe. Attached to it was a long thick needle. 'I'm going to inject a little bit of cortisone into your knee. It's not very pleasant and it might hurt a little for two or three days. When it settles you can go back to training.'

'Three days?'

'Yes, three days. This will take care of any inflammation you have. Your body produces cortisone naturally but we're giving it a little helping hand by supplying a concentrated dose to the affected area. Speeding up the healing process. The effects can be quite miraculous.'

He was right on all counts. It bloody hurt going in and ached like the worst toothache on the second day. But just four days later I was back on the training pitch. Five days later I was back in his office in excruciating pain. A result of the same attempted trick. I was OK up to the point where I really tried twisting my knee, then I was back to the same feeling I'd had when I originally made such a fuss over nothing. Three further breakdowns and three cortisone injections later I was no further forward and I could sense the surgeon was scratching his head.

'A little more rest. More work on your Vastus medialis. That should do the trick.'

I worked as hard as I could to get myself fit. I was desperate to get back playing and into the team. Six months had passed and I'd barely kicked a ball in anger. Derek must have been sick of the sight of me. I sensed a change in attitude towards me. It was nothing too obvious, but the coaches just didn't speak with me as much. Willie was concentrating on the team and on keeping his job. Neil was a regular in the team and racking up appearances. Younger players were making their way – Gazza was flying, Paul Stephenson, Joe Allon and Ian Bogie were all getting their opportunities. I was becoming last year's best toy – now broken and discarded for the shiny new versions. I'd lost my colour and was invisible at the training ground. What use is a footballer when he can't stay fit? He is a drain on resources. He takes a salary that could be spent more productively elsewhere. How can a manager rely on a broken player? Risk anything for him? I became paranoid. Were they whispering about me? *It's all in his head. Doc says he's fine. He's made of chocolate. Doesn't want to be fit. Isn't the player he was.*

Geraldine kept me sane. Going home to her, making plans and having a life away from the training ground were a daily escape from my predicament. Derek recommended a prolonged rest period to try and solve my problems once and for all. When I came back after another period of gruelling rehab I felt like I was finally getting somewhere. I trained for two or three weeks towards the end of the 1985–86 season and played in two reserve games. But something else was beginning to trouble me. My performances. The way I was training. The way I was playing. The combination of chronic hamstring problems and now my knee meant I not only lacked the explosive bursts of pace that were so much a part of how I played, but now I was also reluctant to get my body into the position where my knee was under too much strain. My 'trick' was a thing of the past and I couldn't bring myself to attempt to resurrect it. I was subconsciously trying to protect myself – I wanted to do it but my body just wouldn't let me. The result was that I was only half as effective as I'd been before. My efforts at protecting myself didn't work anyway. I would break down again regardless. The tricky winger who could 'catch pigeons', as my coach Colin Suggett used to describe me, was now a winged bird, fragile in body and mind. When the end came it happened so fast I didn't even see it coming.

My contract was up. I spoke with Willie. They couldn't offer me another one because I hadn't played all season. They also couldn't release me because they weren't allowed to do that to an injured player. I would instead move on to a month-to-month contract when I came back for pre-season at the start of the 1985–86 season and if I proved my fitness I would earn another longer-term one. I trained and played for the first two months of the season. There was interest from Port Vale. Willie thought it would be a good idea for me to go there and get some game time – the Newcastle scouts would monitor my progress. Port Vale would take over my month-to-month contract. I sensed he was as frustrated as I was by my inability to get fit and stay fit.

I travelled down with Geraldine and trained well for three days. I got excited on the fourth day, wrapped my left knee around the ball and felt a little twinge. Nothing more. But definitely something. *It still wasn't right after all this time?* The twinge in my knee set a volcano off in my head. How could my knee still not be right after all this time? *A whole year? A whole useless wasted year.*

I picked Geraldine up in a taxi on my way to the station. She tried to calm me down, bring me back to my senses. Told me to go and see the physio at Port Vale and he might help me. What was waiting for us back in Newcastle? We'd given up our rented flat that had swallowed up our money on a monthly basis. We'd nowhere to live and no money to live on. She was right, but I wasn't capable of rational thought. I could barely speak. I knew if I tried I'd make a fool of myself and break down and cry like a baby. I didn't want to do that in front of her. So instead I simply ran away from my troubles. Something I'd never done before. Something I didn't think I was capable of. It felt like a significant moment but I really didn't know why. We didn't speak on the journey to Newcastle. I saw the Tyne Bridge from the train and felt a surge of relief to be home – to my home that wasn't home and where I had no home. We arrived at Mrs Bell's house on Silver Lonnen in Fenham. When she'd got over the shock of seeing us, she agreed we could stay with her for a few days until we sorted out what we wanted to do and where we wanted to be. A night's sleep cleared my head. I trained on a patch of grass out the back of the house. I stopped and turned and felt the twinge again. My knee wasn't right. I went from calm to frantic. From blue sky to fog. I called Newcastle United. I didn't know what else to do or where else to turn. The receptionist answered. *She'd pass on my message.*

I waited.

I called again. *She'd passed the message on and someone would call me back.*

I waited.

I called again. She was irritated. *Yes, she had definitely passed the message on. Yes, she was sure.*

I waited.

It was over. I just hadn't realised it yet.

CHAPTER 27

O NLY A week ago I'd been a professional footballer at Newcastle United. I'd lived in a nice flat and had money in my pocket. When I'd managed to stay fit I was training with Peter Beardsley and Paul Gascoigne. Professional football was my universe. My daily routines revolved around it, my entire friendship groups were working in it, and my identity was shaped by it. Football was why I'd left Ireland and my family so reluctantly in the first place. It was why I'd tolerated too many empty nights when I was ill-equipped to cope with the gut-wrenching isolation from all those I loved most in the world.

I was a professional footballer. Now I had no job, no home, and faced a very uncertain future. I'd been yesterday's man for a long time in the eyes of some at the club. I recognised that now. I hadn't at the time. I was too busy trying to get fit and stay fit. The truth is I'd disappeared long before I left the building. I was frustrated and angry. Frustrated that I didn't have the courage to fight for myself and tell Newcastle United that I wasn't fit; that my knee wasn't right. Angry that I still needed help and deserved better than being shunted out of the back door. I considered contacting Derek Wright, the physio who had become my friend. He would help – I was sure of that. But my pride wouldn't let me. I still needed help from somewhere, anywhere. I contacted The Professional Footballers' Association. They had helped Mrs Bell's son Derek when his career had ended through injury – maybe they could do something? Get me some help to mend my knee? *Then I'd show them.* All those who'd written me off. Show them that I was worth more than that.

The PFA did help. They arranged an appointment with Sunderland AFC surgeon, Roger Checketts. He assessed my knee and felt there was some instability in it. He agreed to perform an arthroscopy and said that if he found anything then he would operate. He gave me a programme of strengthening exercises and would perform the surgery in six weeks. The PFA ensured that Newcastle United would pay the bill. It was early December and I was running out of money. I had just about enough for a boat journey home and I seriously considered it. Running away. Going home with my tail between my legs. A failed footballer who never quite made it. But I wasn't ready to give up on myself yet. Any thoughts of going home to live again were completely banished on 9 December 1986 when Paul Bradley, a Catholic man who was a former boyfriend of my sister Denise, was savagely beaten to death in a pub in Lisburn. Three men tortured him with an assortment of pool cues and pool balls; he was battered with them and had them forced down his throat. He was murdered in front of witnesses and the perpetrators then walked through another crowded bar covered in his blood. They were never charged with his murder . . . I definitely wasn't ready to go home just yet. But I *was* running out of money.

'Aren't you Paul Ferris the footballer? You play for the Toon.'

He'd caught me by surprise. But I'd had years of experience of denying my own existence. So that's what I did. I didn't convince him and he asked the man behind him if he thought I was Paul Ferris, the Irish lad who played for the Toon. I'd somehow thought that now that I no longer played, I would no longer be recognised.

Like the last five years hadn't happened. I didn't want to be there in this soulless holding pen in the first place. I really didn't want anyone else to know I was there. I'd walked a mile or two from Mrs Bell's house after she insisted I should make my way here sooner or later. I climbed the steep bank and just after I passed the crematorium a light drizzle became a downpour. I broke into a jog which reminded me of the many times I'd gasped my way up the same hill in torturous pre-season training runs. I dived into the sanctuary of the dry hallway and coughed my way past some wet smokers talking at the entrance to the main atrium. It was ugly and nondescript on the outside and grey and dirty on the inside. I joined the back of the long queue which ran the length of the hall towards a glass window behind which was a stony-faced fifty-something woman who'd either been doing her job too long or was suffering from a troublesome bout of constipation. She only seemed to know one word and she could only say it while exhaling and rolling her eyes at the same time. The two people behind me were still debating my identity when I reached the front of the line a yard from the window.

'Next.'

I walked forward when she shouted. I leant against the window and could smell the stale alcohol my predecessor had left behind.

'Name?'

I'd done her a disservice. She knew two words. I looked behind me. My new friend was leaning so far over the line and straining so hard to hear my response that he was nearly mounting me. I ducked down to speak into the tiny slot at the bottom of the perspex.

'Is there somewhere private I can speak? I'm a bit uncomfortable . . .'

She didn't let me finish. Her face was red and her bowels were definitely blocked. She barked at me. 'Speak up. I can't hear you. Name?'

I wanted to rise up and tell her not to be so rude. To have some compassion and to speak to me with a little respect. I could see by her rolling eyes it was pointless. I stood up straight and spoke loudly into the divider. 'Paul Ferris. My name is Paul Ferris. Is there somewhere private I can speak with someone on a delicate matter?'

There was a tap on my shoulder. I turned.

'I told you it was you, didn't I?'

'What?'

'I said you were Paul Ferris. You said you weren't but I was right. I knaa me Toon players, man. I knew it was ye. Irish accent gave it away. What you doin' here?'

She was shouting at me from behind her screen. 'What matter? You're holding up the queue, sir.'

I shouted back. 'I've no money. I've no job. I've no home and I am waiting for surgery on my knee so that I can go back to doing the job I was doing before. I don't know how any of this stuff works but I need help. Now can I please speak to someone in private?'

She didn't lift her head as she answered. 'You're in the wrong building. You need to go to St James'. Next?'

St James'?

My friend was pushing past me to get to the window. I stepped across him and blocked him with my elbow.

'St James' – as in the football stadium?'

She shook her head and rolled her eyes again. 'As in St James' Place – behind the football stadium. That's where the Welfare Office is. You need to go there. This is the Unemployment Benefits Office, where those fit for work come and make their claim. If you're not fit for work then you need to go to St James' and put your case. It'll be assessed on its merits by an officer there.'

She beckoned my inquisitor forward.

'Next?'

I ducked under his arm. I turned and he was pointing after me and excitedly telling the disinterested woman glaring at him that he knew I was me. I wished I wasn't.

I got off the bus at the stadium. Glenn Roeder was driving through the gates. I lowered my head and stopped to let his car go past. I walked down Barrack Road around behind the Gallowgate and turned left at the Strawberry pub. The Welfare Office was behind the East Stand. I didn't get my private meeting but instead I sat between partitions. I could hear everything being said on either side of me. To my right, a woman with three small children was begging for money. There was a young, 'old' man sleeping across four seats behind me. The contents of the Special Brew can on the floor were seeping into the front of his filthy jeans – I wasn't sure if they'd been through his body first or he'd spilled the beer as he slipped into his stupor. I told my sob story to a fat man with thick glasses and more humanity than the eye-roller in the dole office. An hour later I left with an emergency cheque for not very much, my name on a housing waiting list, and some valuable 'off the record' advice I should heed if I wanted to ensure I got my benefits regularly. I couldn't bring myself to walk back past the stadium. I turned left and made my way along Richardson Road and towards Mrs Bell's house. I applied for my first job that afternoon – as a sales assistant in a sports shop in Eldon Square in the city centre. Geraldine wrote the letter for me – *nicer handwriting to give me the best chance.* I put it all in; head boy, professional footballer, certificate in welding, wallpapering and changing plugs. And anything else I could think of. I was quite proud of our efforts. Three days later I got the reply:

Thank you very much for your application. I regret to inform you that you have not been successful on this occasion. We require a minimum of 5 Grade C O levels for the position. I wish you the best of luck in your job search.

Geraldine was more successful in her quest for work. Her eight months as an accounts clerk and eight O levels made her more attractive than me in the job market. She secured a part-time job at Northern Electric on the day I was rejected for mine. We were grateful for the money. We needed the money. We used it for the boat fare home for Christmas.

'What's happening with the football?'

That was the question I dreaded most and the one I was asked the most. I dreaded it because I didn't know the answer. I didn't know what was happening with the football because nothing was happening with the football. Not until I'd had my surgery at least. That was due for the end of January 1987 and provided me with some hope at least that I could begin to rebuild my shattered career. But my mother's rapidly deteriorating health took my mind fully off my minor problems. She was standing by the hearth when I walked into the living room. Her hair was almost white. She was bent over and this made her look even smaller than her 4 foot 11 inch frame. She wore no make-up and her smile was replaced by the haunted hollow look of someone who was in chronic pain. Her new teeth, *the ones she'd told me about on the phone,* looked too big for her mouth and her thin lips were losing their battle to keep them hidden. I felt a knot in my stomach and suppressed an urge to gasp when I entered the living room. I couldn't wait for everyone else to leave so that I could speak with her. I made her some tea after everyone had gone to bed and sat beside her on the settee.

'I'm really worried about you. Please don't tell me lies about the situation. I know it's bad – I only have to look at you to know that. You don't look like yourself. You're in pain. I feel helpless. I love you more than anything else in this world. You're special to me and you always have been and always will be. I need you to know that and never forget it. My heart is breaking to see you like this, son.'

I sat my cup on the floor. *She was worried about me?* I was more terrified than ever that I was going to lose her and I couldn't bear the thought of that. Especially not now. Not when everything was such a mess. It was typical of her. She looked like a walking corpse and twenty years older than she was. We talked long into the night and ignored the birds signalling the beginning of a new day. I told her the truth about my predicament and my hopes that my surgery would be a fresh start. All wasn't lost for me. It wasn't until we were getting ready to go to bed that I noticed.

'You haven't had a cigarette all night?'

She smiled and exposed her enormous teeth then put her hand over her mouth to hide them. 'I haven't smoked for a month. I'm seeing a new doctor. She's changed my tablets and says if I lose two stone I can have a bypass. She says I'll be much better than I am now. My heart is badly damaged but she'll clear my vessels and I should be able to walk better and I'll feel better. So it looks like surgery is going to sort us both out.'

It was like the clamp that'd been around my chest all night and for most of my life had been released. She was getting surgery after all these years. All my childhood sleepless nights and frantic prayers to her God begging him not to take her when deep down I was devoid of hope. And now He'd listened. Now He was going to let her stay. She was looking worse than I'd ever seen her and yet there was finally some hope. I enjoyed my Christmas at home in spite of the uncertainty about my career. It seemed insignificant now that I knew that she had a chance of a longer and better life. That she might still be here to see my children born and grow was the best Christmas present I could ever wish for. I spoilt the moment by asking her to put her old teeth in while I was at home. She was annoyed but she did it anyway.

When the holidays were over I hugged her in the tiny hall. It was the middle of the night and I held on in the darkness until Geraldine's father came to the door for the second time to say we were going to be late. I promised her it wasn't the end for me. Even if the surgery didn't work and my career was over. I promised I would fight. I would make her proud of me. She promised to never smoke again. To hang on. To be here and see my children grow.

I had my surgery at the end of January. I hadn't been mad after all. My medial ligament had been avulsed from the bone at the upper attachment on the first occasion and had been repeatedly doing so on all the other occasions. The surgeon drilled holes in my bone and reattached it as best he could. It would always be 'lax' but might be good enough for me to play at a high level. My cruciate ligament had also been fully or partially ruptured. He couldn't tell because scar tissue was now keeping it in place and would do the job of supporting my knee when twisting and turning.

My mother called me every night after the surgery. I was recuperating with my leg in plaster at Mrs Bell's. She called at six o' clock every night but tonight was different. She called late. After seven. She was upset. Really upset. She was crying and she never cried. Not to me anyway. My brother Tony was having problems in his marriage. It looked like it was over. I tried to calm her down but it was pointless. Catholic mothers are conditioned to believe they've failed their children if their children fail at marriage. She was adamant it was her fault. Something she'd done wrong. I told her to go and make a cup of tea and call me later when she'd calmed down. I hung up and walked my crutches through to the kitchen to make some tea of my own. My mother hung up and made herself a cup of tea too.

And then she died.

CHAPTER 28

RIGHT THERE in the middle of our conversation, her God came and took her from me. He didn't take her immediately. First He gave her a massive heart attack when she was upset and alone in her home. She called my sister Elizabeth to get help. Then she crawled along the hall floor and vomited at the front door. She unlocked it, lay on the floor and died shortly after Elizabeth and the paramedics got to her.

The phone rang. Mrs Bell answered. It was my father. I knew something was wrong – he never rang. It was a bad line and she hung up. I answered when he called back.

'Your mammy's dead, son. You need to come home.'

What do you do when your greatest fear becomes reality? What do you do when your whole world ends? I hung up. Geraldine hugged me but I couldn't feel her arms around me. Mrs Bell spoke to me but I didn't hear the words. How could she be dead? She was going to have surgery. She was going to see my kids grow up. She promised me that at Christmas. She promised me that.

She promised.

I needed to be alone. Away from the noise. I made it to the bedroom and the first tear came as I shut the door. I didn't make it to the bed. I slid to the floor and stayed there until no more tears would come. Then I felt totally calm. I needed to get home. I needed to be with her. I checked the flights. There weren't any until the morning. I checked the price. I couldn't afford it anyway. I phoned my brother Joseph. He told me not to be embarrassed. He understood. He'd sort it for me. I lay awake in Geraldine's arms till it was time. I bypassed airport security in my wheelchair. I was on the plane now. Someone was talking to me.

'Sorry I have to get you to do this, son.'

It was the tall stern-faced police officer who was stationed at the airport to monitor travel between Newcastle and Northern Ireland. He'd eyed me suspiciously as I travelled back and forward for five years and had never spoken a word to me. He handed me the Prevention of Terrorism card and I filled it in with Geraldine's help. Then he caught me by surprise.

He put his hand on the back of my neck. 'I'm so sorry for your loss, son. I know the pain of losing a mother. Take care of yourself.'

One small act. The touch of a stranger's hand broke through the wall I'd built the night before. He catapulted me out of my stupor and brought me painfully back to reality. I couldn't stop the surge. My shoulders began to heave. Geraldine wiped my cheek with her thumb and fought a losing battle all the way home. My father was at the front door as we pulled up outside. Geraldine passed me my crutches and I hobbled up the path to him. He was always a small man. 5 feet 2 inches in his prime. But in the cold darkness of this February morning he was way past that period of his life. His best days were behind him. His life lay on a mortuary slab in the Lagan Valley Hospital. He wrapped himself around me, jamming my arms and crutches to my side.

'Ah, son. It's good to have you home. Your mammy would've wanted you home. Come in. We're all here now.'

My brothers and sisters sat in silence in the living room. I took my place with them. My father came in.

'D'you want to see her, son?'

The look of surprise on my face forced him to elaborate. 'Your mammy? She's upstairs on her bed. The undertakers have just left.'

I wasn't sure. I didn't know if I did want to. To see the evidence that my life as I knew it was over and from this point onwards would never be the same again. I also didn't want my last memory of my mother to be of her lying in an open coffin on the bed she'd been sleeping in only a day before. I thought about saying no but was worried it would be misinterpreted. I followed him up the stairs. Her bedroom door was closed. He opened it and stepped to the side so that I could see her. I wished he hadn't. First of all, I saw the box she was in. Then, as I got closer, I saw her hands, white and interlocked. Her rosary beads were woven expertly between her fingers. Then I saw her face. It was her but it wasn't her. It looked like my mother, but it looked nothing like her. Her skin was thin and pale in places and purple and marked in others. She had an expression I'd never seen before. It looked like pain. Her lips were thin and parted. And then there were her teeth. *Those teeth.* They were staring me in the face and making my beautiful mother ugly. I leaned over and kissed her forehead. It was cold as stone. It wasn't her. It didn't look like her; feel like her, smell like her. The mother I knew was beautiful. She was warm. She smelled like my childhood. This was something else. It wasn't her. She was already gone.

'She loved you so much, son. You brought her so much joy. She was proud of you. She missed you. Every day she missed you. But she was so proud of you.'

My father's words broke the dam. I wept for her, for him, and for myself. Once I started I couldn't stop. I sat on the side of her bed. The one I'd climbed into on many occasions as a frightened boy after my latest nightmare. I rested against her coffin. It cut deep into my back, but I stayed there while a steady stream of friends and family came to pay their respects. *Doesn't she look peaceful? She's gone to a better place. No more pain now. She doesn't look like herself at all. She looks happy.*

It was too much for me. Denise was sitting beside me. I spoke too loudly to her. 'Of course she doesn't look like herself. What do they expect? How does she look happy? She's dead, for Christ's sake. How the fuck can she look like herself when there's no blood pumping through her, or look happy when she's dead?'

Denise calmed me down with an arm around my shoulder and the wisdom of someone much older than her twenty-eight years. She had children of her own now but had been a mother to me when she was still a child herself.

'This is what people do at a wake. They pay their respects. They tell stories. They eat and drink. They mean no harm. It's a mark of respect for her. Don't be upset by it. It just is what it is.'

I declined her offer to go downstairs and instead sat with my back against the casket until there was just me and my dead mother left in the dark room. My knee was throbbing and some blood had made its way through the plaster. I lifted it onto the bed and lay with my back to her. I'd climbed into this bed so many times before, exhausted and frightened after lying in my bedroom in the dead of night, imagining ghoulish hands crawling up from the abyss below my bed and ghostly shapes slipping out of creaking wardrobe doors and readying themselves to carry me off to Hell. I'd lie rigid with fear until my out-of-control imagination would get me to the point where I couldn't stay any longer. Then I'd jump out of bed, duck under the ghosts, and wriggle out of the grasping zombie hands that were grabbing my legs. I'd burst through her door, scaring her half to death in the process. Then I'd lie here, in this very spot, and wait for the warmth of her body to envelop me. I'd be asleep as soon as I felt her softness and the beat of her heart against my bony back.

Now I rested against the hard wood of her open coffin. The boy who was once so frightened of the dark and of imaginary ghosts lay there alone in the fading light with just her corpse for company. I felt no fear. How could I fear her? I loved her with all of my heart. I imagined her waking from her box. I tried to conjure her out of it. To make her come back to me. I closed my eyes and willed her back into this world again. So I could hear her voice and feel her warm arms around me once more. I whispered to her. With my back to her. I asked her to come back. I begged her not to leave me. If she had to go, I implored her to give me a sign she was still there, somewhere? That she hadn't just ended? That she wasn't gone forever? I talked to her with my back to her. I was angry with her. She'd told me she'd get better. She couldn't just leave, not now. I had no job, no home and now no mother. My biggest fear was now my reality and it was worse than I had ever imagined it would be. I was experiencing a feeling I'd never felt before. Emptiness. Just utter nothingness. It was deep inside of me and I couldn't shift it. I was completely alone there in the black hole of her bedroom. What was once my place of comfort was now my Hell on earth. Geraldine and my family were downstairs but I felt a hopelessness and a loneliness that even in my darkest days as a boy leaving home I'd never come anywhere close to feeling. It was all around me and all over me. Above me and inside of me. I wanted it to end. I needed it to end.

So there on her bed of death, and with my back to her, I begged her to take me with her; wherever she had gone. I pleaded with her again and again and again. I was still pleading with her in my despair when I finally fell asleep next to her. I awoke as the early morning light brought life into her dead room. I lay with my back to her. Her book of prayers lay open on the bedside table. I sat up and read the last prayer she'd read. I got no comfort from it. I sat up and lifted myself off her bed and onto my crutches. I got to the door and didn't look back as I spoke to her for the last time.

'Thank you, Mammy. Thank you for everything. For the love. For the strength. For teaching me right from wrong. For believing in me when I didn't believe in myself. I'll tell my children about you. What you mean to me. My children will know you. They'll hear your name every day. I'll never forget. I'm privileged I got to be your son. I love you and always will. You're in my heart and you always will be. You kept your promise in the end. Thank you for that. I know it wasn't easy for you. Thank you for staying until I was old enough to look after myself. I'm old enough now, Mammy. I'm old enough now.'

I spoke with my back to her and walked out of the bedroom without looking back at her. When I had to go back in that room I didn't look at her. I never looked at her again. Once was enough. I wanted my memories to be of her smiling, laughing, breathing. It wasn't her in there. The light in my life was extinguished. She was gone. A part of me left with her and I knew in that moment that my life would always be less than it was with her in it.

'How can they turn on the TV? Tell them to have some respect. Tell them to turn it off.'

Geraldine closed the living room door and blocked out the noise of a meaningless football match. We sat together in silence in the sitting room. It was three days after the funeral. People had been eating, drinking and laughing. *And now the fucking TV was on.* I didn't want it on. Didn't want them to drink, eat, or laugh. I wanted life to stand still. I didn't want to leave her behind. I'd held my father's hand as he walked behind her coffin from the chapel to Holy Trinity graveyard. I'd watched my brothers take turns in carrying her to her final rest. I was angry that I couldn't join them. I couldn't help to carry my own mother to her grave. Instead I'd sat

Above: The Newcastle United Physiotherapy team for 13 years (1993–2006). With Derek Wright, a great physiotherapist and an even better man. One of my closest friends to this day.

Right: Alan Shearer, the superstar who became my star patient, but most importantly my lifelong friend. The most single-minded and driven footballer I ever worked with. The best all round centre forward I've ever seen.

Above: Alan Shearer running for the first time since he suffered a fracture dislocation of his ankle. My most enjoyable and rewarding period as a physio at the club.

Left: Derek Wright pictured with Ruud Gullit. Ruud's tenure was the low point of all of my 18 years at the club. The wrong man, at the wrong club, at the wrong time in my opinion.

Left: Bobby Robson who completely transformed the club with his personality, enthusiasm, and ability as a manager. A truly great manager and an outstandingly good man.

Below: Bobby Robson with John Carver. Bobby oversaw a brilliantly exciting period in the club's modern history. John was the first person I spoke to when I arrived in Newcastle. We have remained firm friends ever since.

Above: Graeme Souness and Michael Owen. Graeme was one of my Liverpool heroes. I found him to be an intelligent and likeable man but he had a difficult time as the manager. I didn't enjoy his reign at the club. Michael's injury at the end of the 2008/09 campaign was a devastating blow to our chances of avoiding relegation.

Left: A proud day and the culmination of a lot of hard work. Being 'called to the bar' a Middle Temple in 2007.

ack for the third time as Head of the Medical Department in Alan Shearer's management team.

Joey Barton protests his innocence after his red card challenge on Xavi Alonso, despite the evidence on the floor in front of him. He continued to do so in the changing room afterwards after watching the incident in slow motion.

My friend and mentor Graham Wylie pictured with Ruby Walsh. A kind, patient, and encouraging presence in my life and someone I wish I'd met sooner.

With my brothers and sisters and my father Patrick in 1998. My father died a year later.

My 'shining stars'. My three boys Conor, Owen, and Ciaran, who have given me so many reasons to be proud of them. Watching and helping them grow has been the greatest joy of my life.

With Geraldine. It all makes sense to me when she is by my side. My Love. My life.

in a wheelchair and shook hands and nodded as familiar faces wished me well and told me what I already knew about her. Denise had gone home. After three days of making sure everyone else was all right she'd gone home to look after her own children. But not before stopping in the hallway and letting out a wail that was like nothing I'd ever heard before. I felt sick to hear her in such pain but I could do nothing to relieve it. I had my own and I couldn't ease that either. Her walls came down and my father held her up with a hug before she cried her way home. One by one they were leaving. The house that had been a buzz of activity was slowly settling to a state of resigned misery for those left behind. Only my father and three or four others remained. Now that the TV was on, I knew it was time for me to go.

It was time for us to go back. But back to what? I was grateful for the kindness of Mrs Bell but the last thing she needed were two waifs and strays overstaying their welcome. Especially now that one of them could no longer see the point of getting up in the morning, let alone make plans for any kind of future. I was facing another month in plaster and then the prospect of rehabbing myself for a further two months after that. Geraldine had her part-time job and that provided us with a little money. I'd no job, no money, and no prospects. I thought again about staying. I could live with my father. Keep him company in his hour of need. But the thought of living back in my childhood home with her not in it coupled with my fear of the increasingly brutal nature of the violence inflicted on often innocent people banished the notion as quickly as I'd entertained it. I was relieved when Denise and Kieran agreed to move their young family in with him.

I said goodbye to him in the same narrow hallway where I'd last hugged my mother and left him standing alone in the ruins of his life. He felt so small. I could smell Guinness on his breath. It was to become his new life partner. I looked back at the house as the car pulled away from the kerb. That's all it was to me now. *A house.* It was no longer my home. I didn't belong there anymore. Not now that she was gone. I didn't belong anywhere. Not now that she was gone. I didn't want to belong anywhere.

Not now that she was gone.

CHAPTER 29

WE WENT back and I fell into a familiar routine. Geraldine and the Bells would go off to work. I'd get up and be determined that today would be different from yesterday. Then I'd go and sit in silence in the living room with just my thoughts for company. Every day became the same day. The very thing I vowed not to do again, I'd just repeat over and over again. I was stuck. Trapped by what was happening inside my head. My own mind was dismantling me – slowly pulling me apart. I couldn't control it no matter how hard I tried. My thoughts were torturing me. Images of my mother swirled around my head. There was no room for anything else. Just her. I was tormented by her. Well, not her as such. Not my mother. Not my beautiful, warm mother. No. I was being persecuted by her corpse. I'd only seen it once, and even then I'd quickly turned my face away. Yet now a childhood of her smiles and laughter couldn't fight their way past the grotesque, distorted ugliness of her dead form.

I needed to move. I needed to get out of this prison I'd created for myself. I had to get up. To get outside. I climbed to my feet. Hopped on one leg to my crutches in the hallway. I opened the door on a bright February morning and stepped out into darkness. The sun was shining but its rays weren't penetrating my eyes nor reaching my brain. I walked on my crutches in the dull shadow of daylight. Her image haunted me with every step. I told it to go away. To leave me alone. I walked faster. As fast as my crutches would let me. I started to sweat. In trickles at first. Then torrents of salt stung my eyes shut but still the image was there. Burned into my skull. My dead mother. My poor, dead mother.

My mother was dead.

Tears married my sweat. My hands were hurting and they began to bleed from the blisters on my palms. My shirt was soaked and my chest heaved. My leg was burning – it wouldn't take me any further. When I could walk no more I finally slumped down, tormented, exhausted, bloodied and broken. I felt the familiar hardness of the bench underneath me. I heard someone speaking. I recognised the words. I knew some of them. *I knew all of them.* I spoke back without thinking. I felt the knot in my chest loosening. My mind was clearing. I was getting some relief. At last the image was fading. I felt totally calm. Like a gentle wave had washed over me. I was suddenly back in my childhood. I could see her again. Not her haunting corpse. It was gone. I could see her. *Really see her.* My mother. My living, breathing mother. She was standing at the kitchen sink, peeling potatoes and singing to herself. Lost in a fleeting moment of her life. I was on the shed. Watching her. Making sure she was still there. That she wasn't going to die today.

Someone brushed against my leg and stole my peace of mind. I was back to the pain of the present. I opened my eyes as the priest was giving his final blessing of the Mass. Mass? I was in Mass? Why was I in Mass? I hated Mass. I looked around the empty church. There wasn't much of a congregation. Just me and three old ladies with one good hip and two sets of teeth between them. I was at a weekday Mass somewhere in Fenham, a mile or two from Mrs Bell's house. I don't know how I got there or why I went there. I waited for the two bad hips to follow the one good one through the door behind me. They were using their two sets of good teeth to chatter loudly as they departed. My hands were sticky and sore as I made my way after them, curious to see where I was and work out how to make my way home with bleeding hands and a tired leg. The thin priest with a quiet voice caught me as I hobbled out of the gates of his car park.

'You're not my normal customer for a Tuesday morning in February? Is there anything troubling you? I'm always here if you'd like to talk.'

Me? Talk to a priest? Why would I talk to a priest? I didn't need a priest.

Two hours, four cups of tea, and too many tears later I was making my confession and promising to be back tomorrow. I did go back. Every day. I felt closer to her there. I could see her face and hear her voice when I was there. Maybe she wasn't really dead after all? Just gone to a better place. A place where I'd meet her again one day if I was good enough. She wouldn't be ill there. No one is. And then we would all live happily ever after. Mass took me back to my childhood. My mind needed to take me there. To find some peace there. To rest there.

While I was busy getting out of my mind and living in the next world in peace and harmony with all mankind, Geraldine was getting on with the practicalities of trying to ensure we survived in this one. Mrs Bell had found us a council flat to rent in Throckley, on the west of the city. Geraldine had been to see it and thought it would be a place where we could start to build a future for ourselves. I didn't bother looking at it. This world was too painful for me so I let her deal with it while I concentrated on the next and wished away my time until I could get there. I didn't visit the flat until the day we moved in. Geraldine was excited as we climbed the three flights of stairs, but the used syringe in the communal hallway as we entered the front door dampened my enthusiasm somewhat. I was glad I no longer needed crutches. We were on the top floor of the three-storey block. Two blue doors stood opposite each other across a narrow hallway. She slipped her key into one of them and pushed it open. It got stuck on a small mountain of junk mail but we were able to squeeze our way in. The flat had a long narrow hall, a bathroom to the immediate left, two bedrooms to the right and two doors at the end. The left door serviced a small kitchen and the one directly in front revealed a long living room that ran the length of the building.

It was the smell I noticed first. Like someone had died in it a while ago but the body hadn't been discovered yet. Then the colour of the walls and ceilings. They were yellow and brown from too many cigarettes over too many years. There was a sticky substance on most of the walls, like someone had poured chip fat on them instead of into the pan they were cooked in every day. Geraldine took me from room to room. She was going to paint this, strip that, furnish this and clean that. We reached the stinking kitchen. There was a decomposing sausage lying on the floor where the cooker had once stood and my feet stuck to the floor where the chip fat had made its way from the wall.

'The cooker will go here and we'll get a small table for the corner. Nothing too big. Just two seats or maybe we can get someone to put a bench along the wall there?'

I turned my back to her. I had stopped listening. 'I'm not living here. It stinks. It's covered in Christ knows what shit. How did you agree for us to come here? Are you mad? Let's go!'

I started to walk. My feet were sticking to the floor with every step. I got to the front door and turned. She wasn't there. I went back to the kitchen. She had her back to me. I was angry.

'Are you coming or what, Geraldine? Let's go.'

She didn't speak but I heard her sobs. It stopped me in my tracks.

I turned her around. Her dark eyes were filled with tears. I put my arms out but she pushed me away. I tried again but she wriggled free. And then she let it all go.

'I'm sick of this. All of it. I'm trying here. Every day I'm trying and every day you push me further and further away. I love you. I love you more than anything else in the world. I want to help you. It breaks my heart to see you like this. Not speaking to anyone. Moping around. Not looking after yourself. Your mammy wouldn't want to see you like this; she would slap your jaws if she was here. But she's not here. I am. I need you to let me in again. Let me help you get through this. I loved her too but she's gone and she's not coming back. Her life's over. We've ours to live. We've a life to look forward to. She'd want us to have that. I know this place is a dump but it's our dump. Mine and yours. What happened to our dreams? Why can't we start here? Why won't you let me show you what this can be? What we can be? We can do anything we want if we do it together. But if you don't let me in then I can't show you anything. I'll leave this place with you today. We'll go right now and never come back here. But when I do I'm going home to Ireland. I'm not staying if you don't want to build a life with me. It starts now or it ends now.'

I had never considered the possibility that she'd leave me. I'd never thought for a second that she wouldn't always be there for me. Even when I was ignoring her and drowning in my grief I'd always assumed that she would be there. I had taken her for granted. I was so wrapped up in my loss. So full of self-pity for my circumstances that I was destroying the most precious gift in my life – her love for me. Her words chilled me and jolted me sharply to my senses. I grasped her hand and knelt on the floor at her feet, begging her not to leave me. I rambled and pleaded and when I could implore no more I asked her to marry me.

I had asked her before, but that had been a request to get married in the future. I was asking her to marry me now. Right now. At the most inopportune time, when my mother was barely cold in her grave. We'd one part-time job between us and had agreed to live in a flat last occupied by a chain-smoking, serial chip pan user whose body had yet to be discovered somewhere in one of the rancid cupboards in the back of a dirty room. I wanted us to bring our plans forward. We were engaged so we could get married anytime. I wanted to marry her now. Not wait till we were old enough. I needed something to strive for in this life. Something to live for. I wanted that to be *her*. To be *us*. She didn't say yes immediately. Instead she made me promise to try. She wanted me to come back. Back to this life. My life with her. I promised her I'd build us a life beyond her wildest dreams. We'd start from here and see where life would take us. When she was satisfied, and just before my knees completely seized up, she knelt down on the sticky kitchen floor of our shithole and agreed to marry me as soon as we could possibly arrange it. The decomposing sausage bore witness to our commitment to each other on the bottom rung of our ladder.

In the weeks and months that followed she was true to her word and I kept mine. She turned our dump into a home. She did it with little money and a lot of hard work. She scrubbed, cleaned, painted and polished it into something I didn't think was possible. A place where I was happy to live and start to find a pathway back for us. We couldn't afford furniture and sat on two stools in the living room for a month until we got some through Angie Carver's Freeman's catalogue. We bought a second-hand cooker and cheap beds. She worked at Northern Electric and I shopped and cooked every day. I waited until 5.15 p.m. before going to the supermarket. Then I'd pounce on the cheap meat that had just been reduced by the

diligent staff. I rehabbed myself on the patch of grass at the front of
the flats, though I had to do it without my football boots. I had sat
them down one day while I jogged around the park and someone
climbed out of a third floor window, dropped onto the garages,
sprang onto my bag, and disappeared around the back and off into
the distance. I trained with Gateshead FC and they agreed to pay
me £20 a week to play. I was grateful for the money but horrified
by the realisation that my knee still wasn't right. Even after surgery.
It felt like it didn't want to move in the direction I wanted it to. So
I settled into a routine of playing half-fit, overweight and on one
leg. I buried my pride and took the money for being a fat shadow of
what I should have been. The upcoming wedding focused my mind.
I'd watch Geraldine go off to work every day. I was proud of her,
but ashamed of myself. An overweight one-legged footballer who
cooked cheap mince or sausages every night. I heard an advert on
the radio about courses at Newcastle College. *It's never too late to be
who you want to be.* I did nothing about it for weeks. Too frightened
in case I wasn't capable of passing the exams. I put it to the back of
my mind.

Four months after my mother's coffin lay at the altar of St
Patrick's Church in Lisburn I stood in the same spot with my heart
bursting out of my chest as I watched Geraldine's father walk her
down the aisle and into my arms. One month later I found the
courage to walk into Newcastle College to ask if I could enrol for
A levels. Ten minutes later I was dejected as I was told I needed O
levels in order to do that. I went home that day and surprised
Geraldine with my announcement. I was going to college to study
on a foundation course for a year. When I'd done that, I was going
to university to study physiotherapy. It seemed the obvious thing
to do after all of my injury troubles. I was going to be the first
person in my family to get a university degree. It wasn't the law

degree I had dreamed about as a boy – I didn't believe I was capable of that anymore – but it was a degree and it was a way out of our predicament.

'There is no doubt you'll get your degree. This is a brilliantly written essay. You can be anything you want to be.'

I couldn't wait to tell Geraldine what my English Language lecturer had said to me. My first assignment and she was telling me I could do anything? My confidence was coming back. *I could do this.* I was more than just yesterday's man. More than a fat, part-time footballer with a busted knee and a penchant for cheap meat. I was going to get a degree.

Football became a means to an end for me. I played for three or four non-league clubs and hated almost everything about it but I needed the money and I'd go wherever I could get it. Studying became my new focus and football was my old life. I played for Barrow AFC for one memorable season, which ended with us winning the FA Trophy at Wembley Stadium. My whole family came to the game and it was a great occasion. I played as well as I could in the circumstances and was enjoying the slaps on the back from friends and family afterwards. Sean Rickard, my old teacher and boys' club mentor was there. I found him in the corner of the bar at the after party.

'What did you think, Sean?'

He screwed up his face. He told me what I didn't want to hear. 'I found it a bit sad really. Watching you like that. It just wasn't the Paul I knew out there.'

I was angry with him. *How dare he come here as my guest and then insult me when everyone else was telling me I was one of the best players at Wembley that day?* I stewed on his words all night. In the morning

I was glad he'd said it. I was kidding myself. My football career had ended the day I twisted my knee in training four years before.

After Sean's words I wanted to retire immediately. I wanted to stop playing that day. It took me another year to finally do it. I joined Whitley Bay while on the first year of my physiotherapy degree. *I needed the money.* Then, one wet and windy night, on the same pitch where Gazza had once put his foot on the ball and refused to pass to me after I'd flown down the wing on my way to becoming a footballer ten years before, I decided that the time was up for me. I stood in the same place where I'd started my run for goal all those years ago. I watched my younger self, wriggling and spinning, twisting and turning, jinking my way to scoring my goal. I committed it to my memory.

I was twenty-five when I played football for the last time.

I was nineteen when I was last a footballer.

CHAPTER 30

THE WORDS of encouragement from my English lecturer ensured I threw myself into my studies with the same enthusiasm I'd once approached my football with. I loved the assignments, the lectures, the seminars, and the friendships. Meeting deadlines, preparing for exams and passing them, became a way of life for me. I sailed through my foundation course, was accepted onto my physiotherapy degree, albeit my offer was deferred for a year. I studied History and Politics A levels part-time over one year to fill the gap. I enjoyed them so much that I contemplated abandoning the physiotherapy route and resurrecting my boyhood dreams of studying law. I excelled at my A levels. Gaining an A grade though part-time study was solid evidence of that and was another boost to my ever fragile self-confidence. But it wasn't enough to make me believe I was really capable of studying law at university. Brilliantly intelligent people like Marty Crossey with the best A level grades in all of Northern Ireland studied law. Not former footballers who'd spent the last five years chasing balls and sitting on treatment tables. No matter how well I did in my exams, or how many times I was complimented on my academic prowess, I just couldn't silence the fears or dampen the destructive self-talk inside my head every time I stepped into a new room, or was given a fresh assignment to complete. The doubts would surface immediately. *They're all smarter that you, the last one was a fluke, you shouldn't be here, and you're going to get found out this time.* I was racked with self-doubt about my abilities. I'd left school with no O Levels and despite my obvious desire to stay on, no one else had seemed to share my enthusiasm for my potential as a student.

I'd discovered a way to cope with my insecurities that worked for me and I clung to it at all times. I had one mantra that I kept coming back to, over and over again. I repeated it to myself especially on those days when the doubts were crippling me and threatening to sabotage my dreams. I'd tell myself that nothing in life that was worth having ever comes easily. If I wanted it badly enough then I had to be willing to experience the fear and the doubts, take them into me, and just move forward with them there, gnawing away at me. No matter how insecure or unworthy I felt I was determined that I was going to keep going. Keep walking this path, stay the distance, and not look up until I was done with it all and I'd reached my goals.

I loved university life. I met and befriended people from different worlds to the one I'd been living in. I left football completely behind me. I had to. That part of my life was over now and there was no point in looking back. I had to move forward. I didn't watch a single Newcastle United game from the day I left, nor did I read the local paper with its blanket coverage of the day-to-day machinations of the city's biggest soap opera. It wasn't that I wasn't interested, it was more a case of it being too painful for me. What I'd lost. What might have been. I was on a long journey back from the death of my mother, the end of my career, and the loss of my home. I needed to bring all of my attention to building a future for me and Geraldine. I needed to make her proud of me. I was desperate to feel worthy again. I felt such a failure when my career ended that I couldn't even contemplate going home to Ireland to live, but I would have no such reservations doing so after getting my degree.

Even the Troubles held less trepidation for me. I knew that we'd be able to afford a home of our own well away from the violence.

Geraldine's parents owned theirs and while they lived in the same town as me they might as well have been in another universe. The murders occurred in the most socially deprived areas. We could live in Ireland in our own home and not be troubled by it all. By the middle of my second year at university that was our plan. We would finally go home to Ireland. That was our plan – until I received a phone call from Denise. Paul Moran had become the latest innocent Catholic victim to die at the hands of Loyalist terrorists in Lisburn. Kieran had been a brother to me since coming into my life when I was eight years old. Paul, his younger brother, was someone I looked up to. He always had a ready smile, loved his football, his music and his life. He married a Protestant girl and they had an infant son. His world was that of any young father trying to do what was best for his new family. He had no interest in the political violence that blighted the island of his birth. He just happened to live there. If ever there was a senseless killing of an innocent man then this was it. I knew in that moment that if they could kill someone like him then they could do the same to me, or, God forbid, my children, if I were ever to go back there. Geraldine was pregnant with our first child. Any lingering romantic notions I was harbouring about bringing that child up in Ireland died with Paul Moran. He was travelling to work in the early morning with my brother Patsy. They stopped at a shop and Paul got out of the car to buy cigarettes. Patsy saw a masked gunman emerge from the shadows. When he'd got over his shock, he got out of the car and followed him around the corner. He got there just in time to see the assassin standing on Paul before fatally shooting him in the chest and making his getaway.

I watched the news that evening and sat frozen, looking at familiar faces talking to me out of the small TV in our new flat in Denton Burn. We'd traded our council flat for a mortgaged one, in the hope of having somewhere to sell when I got my degree and first job as a physio. Kieran was talking, Denise was crying. They were pleading for no one to get hurt in reprisal for Paul's death. A grieving mother had lost her son, Kieran had lost a brother, a wife had lost her husband, and a child would never remember the father who had loved him so very much.

Within a week those terrified faces from the TV were sleeping on the floor of our living room in Denton Burn – Kieran and Denise, Patsy and Jennifer, Eamon and Dianne, and my father. They were all staying with us while viewing properties that they might be able to rent in Newcastle. Within the month Kieran, Denise, Patsy and Jennifer, all of their children and my father left their homes and moved to Newcastle. They were motivated by fear and revulsion at what had happened so close to home for all of them. I loved having them with me in Newcastle. They were there when Geraldine gave birth to our first child, Conor. Denise didn't last much longer than that in Newcastle. The pained expression she had when she arrived never left her until the day she took her family home again, my father with them. Patsy and Jennifer stayed and made their life in exile from the friends and family they grew up with.

The pain of Denise and Kieran going back home was lessened by the birth of Conor. His arrival, in April 1992, changed everything for me. It was not long after we brought him home that it happened. I don't remember when it happened but I remember clearly that it did happen. Every day I'd come home from university and lift him from his cot. I'd lie on the settee and place him on my chest. I'd watch his tiny body rise and fall in time with my breathing; the wetness from his mouth would trickle down my neck. I'd feel his heart beating next to mine. Then one day something changed in me. He just seeped into me. This tiny bundle climbed through my chest and filled a giant void in my heart that I had thought would be there forever after the death of my mother. Once he'd filled it then my world was no longer about me. It was about him. Making sure that he was safe and secure. That he was loved. Giving him the best that I could give him whatever that would be. Most of all protecting him. The fear that any harm would come to him was as strong as I'd ever felt as a child worrying about losing my mother all those years ago. Bringing him up in Ireland was not an option and never would be.

Denise, Kieran and my father, did come back to Newcastle to visit me. They came with the rest of my family to see me graduate. By that time I was already on to my second job as a physio. The first was at the Freeman Hospital in Newcastle, where my first day at work involved suctioning black and yellow mucus from a semi-conscious patient with tuberculosis. By the time I'd finished the black and yellow were joined by bright red as I nervously fumbled my way to doing more harm than good. At the end of my second month I was sitting in the nurses' station with a test tube between my knees and a cup half filled with freshly suctioned black and green sputum. No blood this time. My job was to get the contents of the cup into the test tube so that it could be sent to the lab for analysis. I turned the cup upside down and a thin watery liquid ran out over my hand instead of the test tube. The smell wafting into my nostrils was like nothing I'd ever smelled before and was making me retch. Nevertheless I persevered. I tapped the base harder and harder like I was trying to dislodge some stubborn ketchup from its bottle. Nothing happened except more trickling onto my hand from the cup and down my forehead from beads of sweat that were rapidly forming there.

One exasperated thump on the cup later and I was in the bath-room trying to get a dying man's diseased lungs off my trousers and the stains from my own efforts that had splashed back off the toilet bowl onto my pristine white tunic. By the end of my third month I was pretty sure that my future didn't lie in this area of physiotherapy. I was into my last week and looking forward to my next three months block, which would be in the Outpatients department. As a student this was the area I had felt most comfortable in. It was physiotherapy as I recognised it when I was a footballer. And now I was qualified I was sure it was the type of physiotherapy I wanted to practise. I'd only a week to go and it was dragging. I was in the rehab room working with an elderly lady who'd had a stroke. I was kneeling behind her. Her dead weight was putting pressure right through my useless knee. I was trying to relax so that she'd relax, but the pain shooting through my left leg ensured I was wasting my time and hers. A colleague peered around the door.

'There's a Derek Wright on the phone for you. He says you'll know what it's about?'

I nearly dropped my patient. Derek Wright? *Why was Newcastle United's physio calling me at work?*

I had liked Derek when I was a player but had lost touch with him when I left the club – mainly because of my own hurt pride that my career hadn't gone according to plan. I'd met him on one or two occasions when Newcastle United had sent a reserve team to play one of the non-league teams I was getting my money from. Apart from that I'd written to him when I was doing my final year dissertation on The Role of the Physiotherapist in Professional Football. It was my attempt to highlight that while clubs like Blackburn Rovers were prepared to pay over three million pounds for Alan Shearer, others wouldn't pay the money to ensure their prized assets had adequate medical care. Many were operating without qualified chartered physiotherapists and instead relied on 'sponge men'. Often an ex-player who had completed a six-week course and was now the front line of medical care as a new era of professionalism was supposedly dawning within the game. It earned me the highest marks in my year for a dissertation and also had me beginning to look longingly at the game I'd left behind and erased from my mind years before. I was starting to dream again. Maybe I could go back as a physio one day and make a difference to someone's career? Help them in their hour of need? Play a part in the game I'd known and loved all of my life? It was September 1993. Kevin Keegan had come back and steered Newcastle to promotion to the Premier League. The new season had only just commenced. If Derek was ringing to offer me a job, he couldn't have done so at a better time in my life. *He says you will know what it's about?* I didn't know what it was about. I hoped I knew what it was about. When I picked up the phone I was desperately hoping it was about what I hoped it was about.

I was lost. And I was going to be late. I really didn't want to be late. How could I get lost? *Follow the river.* The sweaty man at the station had taken ten minutes to make sure I'd gotten it. 'If in doubt just follow the river. Follow the river and you can't miss it. You'd better hurry, though. It's a fair old hike.'

I'd been following the river but felt like I was going around in circles. I came to a clearing. Some builders were on the roof of an old derelict cottage they were bringing back to life. I asked the closest one to me if he knew the way. He most certainly did. He had a strong Durham accent.

'Just follow the smell of the shite. You can't miss it.'

I could still hear their laughter when it came into view. I made my way through a five-bar gate and across a wide expanse of greenery. I'd been in Durham on many occasions but never visited these parts. The university playing fields stretched as far as the eye could see. I hurried breathlessly into the pebble-dashed pavilion. The receptionist pointed me down a narrow corridor to the left. The building was tired and in need of another colour other than grey. I heard laughter from behind the door on my right. The room was crammed with bodies. My knees were weak and my mouth was dry. I lifted my hand to knock but another burst of laughter scared it back down by my side. Someone was behind me.

'Bloody hell, son. They'll not bite. I'm Derek Fazackerley, but you can call me Faz.'

He pushed the door open. 'I found this fella outside. Does he belong to anyone?'

The room was packed with middle-aged men in various stages of undress. Some I didn't recognise, but one was unmistakable. Kevin Keegan was standing on the chairs 3 feet away from me. He was in the middle of his story-telling. He saw me. He stopped. Jumped down and shook my hand warmly.

'Ferra. Great to have you back. You couldn't have come at a better time. We're picking up a few injuries. Derek is desperate for the help. Welcome to the team. Let me introduce you to the rest of the backroom staff.'

Derek's call wasn't quite what I'd hoped for. It wasn't a job offer. It was an offer to meet with him and Dr Beveridge for an informal interview. Then the job offer followed and four long weeks later I was appointed assistant physiotherapist at Newcastle United.

My first day passed far too quickly. Something I hadn't dared to dream about had happened and it felt better than I ever imagined it would. Ray Thompson, the kit manager, who would become one of my closest friends, offered me a lift home that evening in his van. He lived near me in Denton Burn. He was in a hurry and gave me the perfect excuse not to get changed. I went home that night, lay on the settee and placed Conor over the Newcastle United crest on my kit. The boy who'd left dejected and broken was back again. I was part of the team again. Not in the way I'd dreamed of as a starry eyed teenager. Not the way it was meant to be. But I was back. Back where I belonged. After seven long years when so much had happened, the club I returned to was unrecognisable. As my young son lay sleeping on my chest, so was I.

CHAPTER 31

THE FIRST weeks and months of being back at the club were heady times for me. I wasn't earning a lot and had to supplement my income by staying behind in the evening and treating private patients – usually wealthy Durham University students whose parents ensured their monthly income dwarfed mine. It made for twelve-hour days. Days off were also at a premium. Players and coaches would have them but injured players were required to be there morning and afternoon, weekdays and weekends. But I didn't mind. Long days and working weekends were just a part of my new job and my new job was something I couldn't even have dreamed of during the previous seven years. In the early months I relied heavily on Derek Wright, who proved to be the gentleman I believed he was during my time as a young player at the club. He was generous with his time, patient with my incessant questioning and took great care in making sure I was accepted back into the closed world of professional football. I trusted him implicitly. We very quickly became a team with an unbreakable bond both professionally and personally.

The treatment room was very much the heartbeat of the training ground. Players would congregate there before training and the laughter and noise would bring Kevin out of his room to inquire if anyone fancied doing any work today. The atmosphere in the treatment room was no different to every other part of the club Kevin had built in his short time as a manager. Newcastle United in 1993 was an incredible place to be. It was a warm and friendly club.

Players and staff worked together and socialised together. There was a perfect mix of young local players making their way in the game for whom playing for their local club meant more than just football. Others like Robert Lee and John Beresford, who, although they had no previous affiliation with Newcastle United or the city, just seemed to 'get it'. It didn't surprise me that these players from other parts of the country would be describing Newcastle as the best place they'd played or the best city they'd lived in. The club, the city, and its people weave their way into your affections and once they get in they become a part of who you are.

Kevin Keegan had created something special when he was a player. He'd lifted the club on his broad shoulders and carried it from the doldrums of the second division to the bright lights of the first division. He retired before enjoying the fruits of his labours, but here he was as a manager creating something bigger and better than anyone could have imagined. His charisma and philosophy rubbed off on all those who came into contact with him. He was charming and affable but fiercely competitive. That belief system was instilled in all those who played or worked for him. His Newcastle United was the club of the people. The training ground was open to the public and they came in their hundreds and some-times thousands every day to catch a glimpse or get an autograph from one of their heroes. There were burger vans wafting fried onions into our treatment room – they smelt so nice that we'd often sneak one after the players and staff left for training.

While the club was a friendly and open place for everyone to enjoy, it was also an environment where winning was everything and competition was fierce . . . and that was before training. Kevin and Terry McDermott would challenge all comers at 'head tennis' and usually beat them. We had some badminton courts that became the scene of some epic battles and heated disputes and then there were the squash courts. I'd never played squash before but after a few late afternoon games against Derek I was getting quite good at it. Most games finished with an ice pack on my swollen knee but I didn't mind as long as I was winning. A few wins against some of the senior players soon had the big guns knocking on my door – or, rather, the biggest gun knocking on the treatment room door.

'Fancy yourself as a bit of a player, Ferra?'

I lifted my head from the groin I was examining. Kevin was at the door, two squash racquets in one hand and ball in the other.

'Come on. Derek can look after him. I've got a bit of a lesson to teach you.'

Fifteen minutes later I was running around chasing this stupid little ball as it came off the walls at impossible angles. When I wasn't doing that I was frantically trying to get around his stocky frame as he hogged the centre of the court. When I eventually did get in front of him, he just smacked the ball so hard at my arse that I had bruises for weeks. Every time he did it he followed it with two words and a grin.

'My point.'

My point? I didn't understand the rules initially and couldn't fathom how my sore arse could equate to his point. It didn't take me long to work out the angles and even less to work out how to hog the centre of the court. I had to stifle a belly laugh as I watched him drop his racquet to rub his arse after I smacked the ball off it. Instead I bit my lip and just asked if it was my point.

I'd started a fierce competition that regularly left me bloodied and bruised and sitting on my own treatment table with Derek treating my swollen knee and bloodied elbows. I beat Kevin regularly after that, but overall, in spite of his advancing years, he won more than he lost. So did his team. It was a juggernaut at times, and on some days I'd pinch myself that I was being paid to be a small cog in its giant wheel. Kevin was an impressive speaker and I looked forward to listening to his team talks before big games. Sometimes they were motivational, at other times emotional, but always inspirational. Some were longer than others but some of his shorter ones were his best. On one occasion he walked into the changing room five minutes before the kick-off of a crucial game with the opposition team sheet in his hand. He strolled into the middle of the dressing room and stood still until the chatter and clatter settled into respectful silence.

'I've read this several times, boys, and I want to tell you this. There's not one name on here that I would swap for anyone in this room. Now go out and prove me right.'

The pink slip was falling to the floor as he turned and his players rose as one, ready for battle, knowing that their general had complete faith in their ability to win at all costs. He signed great players and let lesser ones go. Foreign players with big reputations and big egos replaced the English old guard. Football was changing and he was leading the way. Philippe Albert, David Ginola, Tino Asprilla – world-class international footballers who came into the club and embraced the culture of the manager and the city. Philippe ruptured his cruciate ligaments and gave me my first opportunity to really contribute something worthwhile in my new role. We worked with him diligently until he returned to the team as good as new. I was happy in my new job. I never felt envious about what might have been. I really enjoyed being invisible but getting satisfaction from a job well done. I never commented on games or players' performances. That was for the manager and coaches. I was there to care for the wellbeing of my patients, who just happened to be footballers. When players understand you don't wish to judge them or break any confidence they share with you, then and only then can you really thrive as a physio in professional football. I was confident in my abilities when I arrived at the club. The more responsibility Derek gave me the more capable I proved to be. I was still very much the number two physio and I was happy with that while I established myself in the eyes of the staff and players. As the years rolled by I realised that my footballing background gave me a distinct advantage in certain areas of my chosen profession. When I rehabbed players, I knew instinctively what would make it enjoyable and relevant for them. I'd once been *them*. Often, just adding a competitive edge to their rehab sessions was all that was needed to elevate a boring session into something entirely different. I wanted them to forget their ailments and concentrate on trying to beat the physio at whatever drill we were doing. The last thing they wanted was the story of my victory embellished in great detail to the rest of the team in the treatment room the following morning. It could sometimes get a little too competitive.

'It was out.'

I was playing head tennis with the team captain, Robert Lee. He was almost fully recovered from an ankle injury and I wanted him to forget about it and get lost in the jumping twisting and turning of the game. He'd become one of my closest friends at the club – he was the same age as me and we shared the same sense of humour and enjoyed each other's company away from the club as well. I liked him as a player and as a man. He didn't agree that his match-winning effort was out, however. In fact he very much disagreed.

'It was in by a mile and you know it.'

I didn't know it. 'It was out. Play the point again.'

He didn't agree. 'Fuck off. It was in.'

I didn't concur. 'You fuck off. It was clearly out.'

He was walking towards the net. I was too.

'Don't tell me to fuck off. You fuck off.' I was in his face. He was shouting now.

The sound of the whistle-blowing snapped us out of our Fuckfest. When I looked up the whole first team squad were watching our shenanigans. We were playing just behind their pitch and had interrupted a particularly intricate coaching session with our blaspheming. I raised my hand sheepishly.

'Sorry. All good . . . Rob just doesn't like losing.'

I raised my other hand to Rob just as he was about to break the world record for saying the f word in one day.

'Only joking, man. You win.'

We laughed, shook hands and walked off towards the changing rooms. As we got to the door, I tapped him on the shoulder. 'How was your ankle, Rob?'

'What?'

'Your ankle? How was it out there?'

'Didn't feel it once.'

I smiled. He could have his victory.

For a Premier League club our facilities were fairly basic. The pitches at Maiden Castle were in excellent condition but the pavilion itself was rudimentary. The players changed in two rooms next to the students. There was a multipurpose indoor area that the students had priority over, a badminton court, squash courts and an ancient multi gym. Our treatment room consisted of two small rooms with the adjoining door removed. It was at the bottom of a narrow hallway next to the staff changing area. Upstairs was a canteen where the players had a choice of tea or powdered soup before Kevin introduced hot meals and insisted everyone stayed and ate them.

David Ginola was most distressed to discover we had no gym – judging by his impressive physique, he was used to better. In the absence of a decent gym he developed a habit of coming into the treatment room after training and exercising with dumbbells while he chatted to me and Derek. He was a very likeable, relaxed man who'd been brought up in the South of France and his upbringing was evident in how he conducted himself with us at all times. He was all flowing locks and Gallic charm and had a very positive outlook on everything in life. I enjoyed his visits to our room where we'd throw friendly insults back and forward and discuss the events of the day while he did his weights and perfected his English. He was intelligent and well-read with interests that ranged far and wide, and I enjoyed all aspects of his visits, apart from one – his torso. David was twenty-nine and the same age as me. He liked to take his shirt off while doing his weights, and every day I was forced to look at his washboard abs, impeccable pecs and bulging biceps. He was an impressive and demoralising sight. I found myself sucking in my stomach every time he was in the room. After many different approaches I finally got him to stop tormenting me with his physique.

'Teach me some English, my friend. Tell me some of your English jokes.'

He was in his usual spot, shirt off, dumbbells pumping, teeth glistening.

I lifted my head from the latest leg I was dealing with and sucked in my stomach. 'I'm Irish. I only do Irish jokes, David.'

He was working his pecs now. 'Oh, yes. I forgot. Forgive me, Paul. You Irish are supposed to be funny? Tell me something funny, my Irish friend.'

He was onto his sit-ups now. Sweat trickling, muscles rippling.

'I know one, David.'

He stopped mid sit-up. 'Tell me, my friend.'

'Did you know I speak a bit of French?'

His eyes narrowed. He was suddenly serious. 'No, I didn't know that. That's fantastic. What French do you speak?'

I had him. 'It's just a little. Nothing to get too excited about.'

He was up now and working his biceps again. 'A little is better than none my friend. Tell me some French.'

I walked over behind him, picked up his training top from the floor and lobbed it in the air. It landed on his perfectly formed shoulder. Then I gave him my best French. 'Fuck off out of here, would you? And put your shirt on. You're killing me. I can hardly fucking breathe from holding my breath in till you've finished your exercises every day.'

The smile on his face as he pulled on his top told me he was adapting to English football culture and he'd be here for a long time. He stopped at the door. 'You speak very good French, my friend. I like it.'

I could hear him laughing as he strutted up the hall.

Those early years were filled with big players with big reputations. One by one they came into the club and one by one they proved themselves to be great people as well as excellent footballers. Les Ferdinand arrived with a reputation for being injury-prone and left the club as a warrior who barely missed a game and became a legend on the pitch. Off it, he was just a thoroughly decent man who had a permanent smile on his face and was a pleasure to be around. I don't recall ever seeing him without an infectious grin from ear to ear. He developed a bond with the club and fans alike that maybe even surprised him. It was that type of individual – Les, Rob Lee, David Ginola and the rest – that came so tantalisingly close to glory in 1996. Great players with an unrivalled team spirit who bought into the philosophy of an outstanding manager in Kevin Keegan. It was intoxicating and a privilege to be a part of Newcastle United in those lofty days.

I wanted to be part of it forever but was beginning to get frustrated with the assistant physio role that I had agreed to three years before. I had come a long way in that time and was very assured of my abilities. If I was to stay at the club for any length of time I needed to be regarded as an equal to Derek, or my alternative was to leave and find a role at another club. I spoke with Geraldine about it and she agreed that if I had to move then that's what we would do. I loved the club and enjoyed so much being part of it that I resolved to put off any decision until after we got back for pre-season training. When we did report back I tried to pick the right moment to speak with Derek but we seemed to be busier than ever. He was off on one trip while I was on another. Before I knew it the season was upon me and the team embarked on its pre-season tour to the Far East. I was sitting alone in the staff room. All of the senior staff were on the plane apart from me and I was holding the fort at home and feeling a little sorry for myself. Then the phone rang. It was the chief executive Russell Cushing.

I had to be ready to travel in twenty minutes. I wouldn't be told where I was going. I was required to help conduct a medical. Three hours later I was in a private hospital in Manchester. The patient was behind the door directly in front of me and I was curious to know who it was. I was to pay particular attention to his groin and his left knee. I knocked on the door and opened it and found myself face to face with Alan Shearer – the man who'd spent his summer thrilling the entire nation with his exploits at Euro 96. I shook his hand, examined his knee and stuck my nervous finger up his scrotum.

Thirty minutes later, and after washing my hands, I was sharing tea and biscuits with him while his agent and Newcastle United thrashed out the remaining sticking points of his contract. After sitting with him for ten minutes I was no longer nervous. He seemed honest, sincere and determined to do well for the club. He asked me a hundred questions about everything and anything to do with the city of his birth. He asked me to drive his Jaguar to Newcastle so that he'd have it there when he came back from the tour to the Far East. I didn't have the courage to say no. To tell him I'd only passed my test two weeks previously. I drove it up the M6 without adjusting the seat settings or the radio from the Olympic Badminton followed by the Synchronised Diving. I crawled out of the car at Durham, my back in spasms, and climbed into Geraldine's car.

'What's he like?'

'Who?'

She rolled her eyes. 'Jesus Christ, Paul. It's all over the news. Alan Shearer. What's he like?'

CHAPTER **32**

H E WAS a force of nature. The best centre forward in the world in the prime of his career. He'd lit up the whole country throughout the summer of 1996. His goals had carried England to its best performance at a major championship since 1966. He could have gone to any club in the world but he'd chosen to come home. After sitting with him that afternoon, before the news of his record transfer reverberated around the world of football and beyond, I knew Newcastle United was getting more than just a footballer. He was no 'gun for hire' mercenary. This was a boy who had left home at fifteen and moved to the other end of the country to follow his dream. Now his dream had come true and he was coming home in triumph. I recognised that boy. I'd been that boy myself a long time ago. I knew the sacrifices he'd made to get to where he was. He was now at the very pinnacle of his career. The most sought-after footballer in the world. I often wondered what sort of person I'd have become if my own career hadn't been torn asunder by injury. Would I have stayed true to my upbringing, and to the principles my parents instilled in me from a young age? Or would the bright lights of fame and fortune have changed me somehow? Made me forget who I was and where I was from?

As I studied him over tea and biscuits in the sterile private hospital, I saw someone who'd remembered it all. The sacrifices of his parents, the dedication of his boys' club coaches, the uniqueness of his home town, the love he'd had for Newcastle United as a starry-eyed ball-boy watching the great Kevin Keegan score on his debut against QPR in 1982. We were getting the world's best centre forward – no doubt about that – but when I got into the car with Geraldine and she asked me what he was like, I already knew that someone very special had arrived at our club. We were getting the boy who'd left his home and family ten years before as an anonymous teenager now returning as a national hero desperate to make his own people proud of him. His desire to do well for his home-town club was palpable from the moment I met him. If he could have put his boots on in the hospital he'd have made his debut there and then. Newcastle United mattered to him. Newcastle as a city was home for him, being a proud Geordie defined him.

Alan's arrival had a profound effect on the club, the fans, and the city. His name echoed around the ground and every goal was met with thunderous applause in the cauldron on the hill. He proved to be the all-conquering hero we all hoped he'd be. Goals rained in as he formed an unstoppable partnership with Les Ferdinand. The mutual respect they had for each other on and off the field was obvious to all who witnessed it. The disappointment of Kevin Keegan leaving, which felt more like a bereavement than a manager resigning, was tempered by the arrival of another of my boyhood Liverpool heroes, Kenny Dalglish. Les and Alan continued to score goals at a phenomenal rate and we finished second in the table once again. Kenny was bright, articulate, funny, and was a character I liked and respected. He possessed values that were no doubt driven into him by his working-class Glasgow upbringing. Privately he was very different to the sometimes spikey persona that I'd seen interviewed countless times as he'd steered Liverpool and Blackburn to greatness.

My own role at the club was changing. When we discussed increasing my responsibilities, Derek was as accommodating as ever – he didn't want me to leave and I really didn't want to go. We began alternating games so that I'd do some of the on-field work. That simple act changed perceptions of me within the club. I was no longer the assistant physio and instead we were 'the physios'. We were joined by Roddy MacDonald, who became our first full-time doctor at the club, and we were now 'the medical department'. We'd come a long way since the days when the unqualified 'physio' with the dirty sponge used to limp on to the pitch to treat my injuries. Roddy, Derek, and Ray Thompson, the kit manager, were so much more than just work colleagues to me. They were my firm friends as well.

Maybe it was as a result of our very first meeting, or because he'd had a couple of niggling injuries that we'd helped him with, but we often had another friend regularly join us for a drink or a meal away from the club. Alan Shearer became someone we got to know as a person rather than the superstar England captain dominating our TV screens. He was great to be around; just a friend having a good time with his mates. Rob Lee and later Gary Speed would be part of our regular nights out. They were good people first and foremost who just happened to be famous footballers as well.

I was enjoying life again at the football club. My increased responsibilities and the team doing well made going to work a daily pleasure. My home life was a mirror of my work life. A pay rise had enabled us to move out of our mortgaged flat and into a small three-bedroomed house in the tiny Northumberland hamlet of Horsley. We even had a garden. Well, not a garden really, but more a yard or two of green between the back door and back gate. The local pub became one of our venues for our frequent nights out. The locals quickly got used to the 'superstar' in the corner having a pint with his mates. Our second child Owen was born in February 1997. He smiled at everyone and everything, slept when he was supposed to, and had eyes that were so much like my mother's that I could see her face staring back at me when I rocked him in my arms. Life was good on and off the pitch for all of us. Then Alan's world caved in. And mine changed forever.

He caught his studs in the turf in a pre-season game at Everton. It was the summer of 1997 and the beginning of his second season with the club. He fractured and dislocated his ankle, breaking bones and rupturing or damaging just about anything he could damage. It was a serious injury. His foot was rotated 180 degrees and was facing in the wrong direction. I met with him the following morning in the Washington Hospital outside Newcastle. He was pale and drawn after a night of pain and little sleep.

'I'll be all right, won't I?'

I could hear the fear in his voice. So I hid mine. 'Absolutely. The surgeon will have you as good as new and then you'll just have to put up with me and Derek for a while until you're back and raring to go.'

He wasn't convinced. He raised his eyebrows. 'You sure?'

I was more convincing the second time.

'Look. These surgeons do this all the time. We rehab people all the time. I guarantee you it'll all be fine and you'll be back in no time.'

The surgeon was Rob Gregory – an avid Nottingham Forest fan. I watched in awe as he whistled and hummed his way through reconstructing the most expensive ankle in football. He just popped his CD in the player and whistled as he twisted, cut, screwed and stitched. He looked at me when he'd finished. And spoke though his mask. 'All done. Very happy. Over to you.'

He became another part of our friendship group that day and someone I had enormous respect for.

'You happy you can do the rehab?'

Alan was sitting on the treatment table with a bundle of papers in front of him. He'd been recuperating at home for a while after his surgery but now it was time to get to work. He'd shown us the papers and I'd read them all and had become angrier by the second. I looked at Derek and spoke for both of us.

'Of course we can do it. That's our job. It's what I went to university for. It's what Derek's been doing for the past twelve years.'

I picked up the papers that had been delivered to his agent's offices and to his home. Every one of them was a letter written by some 'guru' or 'quack' promising to cure his ankle problem in double-quick time. All of them were claiming to know the secret to a full recovery and everlasting life. Each of them were warning of the doom and gloom that awaited him if he didn't allow their magic hands to cure him of all of his ills. Some names I didn't recognise, but others? Others were people we dealt with professionally and personally. 'Gurus' with one agenda and one agenda only – to use Alan Shearer's misfortune to further their own careers. The letters were making all sorts of claims way beyond the qualifications of the writers. We'd already had other people writing in the press about how they'd offered their services to the stricken England captain to make sure his glittering career wasn't over. These people made me sick to the pit of my stomach and were behaving in a way that I never would have.

'Listen, Alan. Do you trust me? Do you trust Derek?'

He was tapping the paper on the couch in front of me. 'Of course I trust you. But some of these look really good. They look like they could really help me. I think you should give them a call and we should get them in to have a chat? What d'you think?'

His eyes were fixed on me and his expression was stern. Was he not the man I thought he was, after all? Was he really that weak? I felt my stomach tighten and my palms moisten. All my training, all that struggle, all mine and Derek's quiet hard work and professionalism undermined by a bunch of egotistical wankers who'd written opportunistic letters to the England captain and he was so stupid he was falling for it! Seven years before I would have accepted it. Walked away meekly, not stood up for myself, but I'd been through too much, sacrificed too much to let these parasites undermine everything I'd worked for. I'd watched my ill mother stand up and fight for what she believed to be right, even when faced with the head of the local UDA in her own living room, whereas I'd allowed myself to be pushed out the back door of my career without even a whimper. It'd taken me so long and I'd worked so hard to fight my way back from that, I wasn't going to let these bluffers and a weak-willed footballer ruin all of that. I just blurted my anger out.

'Can't you see that these letters are just crap from a bunch of wankers who want a piece of you? They don't give a fuck about you or whether they can help you. They just want to be seen to help you in order to raise their own profiles. If you don't think we are capable of getting you fit then at least go and work with somebody credible instead of this lot. Fuck me, I thought you were better than that?'

When I turned to look at him he was smiling. Laughing.

'What's so funny?'

He grabbed the papers. 'You're a silly twat.'

I looked at Derek and he was laughing too.

'Why the fuck are you laughing? This is serious.'

Alan stopped laughing first. And handed me the papers. 'I'm winding you up, man. I showed these to Derek earlier. I would've thrown them in the bin already only I wanted to see you 'bite' first. You're too easy, man. Get rid of this shit.'

I tore up the letters and threw them where they belonged. He got off the bed and onto his crutches. He was out the door but popped his head back in.

'By the way . . . don't fuck up my rehab.'

He laughed all the way up the hallway.

I sat with Derek that afternoon and we meticulously planned our strategy to get him fit. There was no way we were fucking up his rehab.

We started out sharing the duties with him. One day Derek would take his rehab and the next day I would. That worked for a while until we decided that continuity was best for Alan and that one of us should concentrate on his rehab until we got him fit. At any other club in the country and with any other physio in the country, the longest serving one would never have even contemplated letting the other take over those duties. But I was working with Derek Wright. He wasn't interested in nonsense like that. He was interested in us getting our best player fit and back playing for the club.

'You take over the rehab work with Alan. You get on well together and he likes your sessions. I'll look after him in the treatment room.'

I was grateful for the gesture and from that day until he was fit, I devoted all of my time and energy into making sure Alan Shearer came back in as good a condition as he was before his ankle had been rearranged on the turf of Goodison Park. Every night I'd go home and make my plans, ready to give him something different the next day. I put a lot of time and thought into the sessions but would casually turn up the following day and put him through his paces as if I'd done this sort of thing a million times before. Good 'proprioception' was the key to his full recovery. His injury had robbed him of an innate ability we all take for granted. The ability to plant his foot with confidence. The ability to react and adjust to uneven surfaces or slight twists of his ankle. I had to be imaginative with my sessions. Our facilities were not up to the standard they should have been to rehabilitate the world's most expensive footballer. We were a long way from the Milan Lab. So I improvised with what we had. He'd be balancing at various heights on upturned old school benches with a high jump mattress either side of him and I'd challenge his body to stay there under relentless provocation. He was like a tightrope-walking *It's a Knockout!* contestant. I'd bombard him with stimuli from all angles and simultaneously rob him of his senses through blindfolds, making him stand on tiptoes or on one leg, with his arms whirling like helicopter blades.

The bemused look on the students' faces as he'd regularly go tumbling unceremoniously on to the mats before getting back up and challenging me to do it again was compounded by his habit of singing Chumbawumba's 'Tubthumping' at the top of his voice. But he was getting better and better every day. Our low-tech, but enjoyable, sessions were working. I wasn't fucking up his rehab. The boy who never quite made it was helping the superstar who was in danger of losing it. He became more than my star patient and I was more than his physio. He became my trusted friend and I became closer to him than any other player I'd worked with. There were dark days when he couldn't see the finish line, when the pain in his ankle burned all the way up his shin. When he couldn't run without a pronounced limp. He'd just look at me.

'Are you sure?'

I'd tell him the answer he needed to hear. 'Never been surer in my life.'

When he made his first appearance as a substitute I sat on the side-lines alongside Derek simmering with quiet pride that the superstar who was now my friend had made it back on to the stage where he belonged. I was also scared rigid that anything would go wrong and he'd be back to us with a problem. I just didn't tell him that. He was barely on the pitch when a cross was floated into the box. I didn't even watch the ball. I watched his familiar early push on the defender's back, putting him off his stride, long before the ball reached him. As the ball flew over the stricken centre half Alan leapt, made contact with it and it ended up where it always ended up. I jumped high in celebration, landed awkwardly and twisted my ankle. My proprioception was always pretty bad and I was always prone to injury. But I didn't feel any pain.

The work I did with Alan Shearer in the winter of 1997 was the best I'd ever done for the club. Better than anything I'd ever accomplished as a player. It fulfilled me as a physio and made me feel like I'd made a small contribution to the club I'd worked at for nearly ten years as a player and member of the backroom staff. Little did I know then that the work I did on those long winter months with our star striker and the bond that we developed would almost cost me my job.

Kenny Dalglish was sacked in the early part of the following season. Ruud Gullit was his replacement. It was August 1998.

He did not like Alan Shearer.

CHAPTER 33

WHEN A football club turns sour it's a hideous place to be. Paranoia reigns, cliques develop, and the air is thick with mistrust and discord. The truly terrifying aspect is that it can happen in a heartbeat. What was once the best place in the world to earn a living can suddenly become a living nightmare. The Newcastle United that Ruud Gullit presided over fleetingly in 1998/99 was just such a place. When this state of affairs develops, only one person is to blame. That person is the manager.

It all started well enough. The new boss was charm personified in the first weeks of his tenure. He was open, friendly, and was given the respect he was due for his achievements as one of the greatest players of his generation and, more recently, his successes at Chelsea where he'd won the FA Cup in his first managerial role. I warmed to him immediately and enjoyed hearing of his exploits when he ruled the football world with the great Milan and Dutch sides of the late 1980s. He was good company and I was excited to see where he could take the club. I was also delighted when he promoted John Carver, my long-time friend, to his senior staff alongside his former Chelsea team-mate Steve Clarke. Steve and his family moved into a house next to ours in Horsley and Geraldine and I had gone out of our way to make them feel welcome. With a charismatic young manager, England's best striker, a clutch of top-quality senior players and memories of Kevin Keegan's success still fresh in the mind of players and staff alike, we seemed well placed to challenge at the top end of the Premier League.

I heard the first rumblings of discontent only a matter of weeks into Ruud's tenure in the sanctuary of the treatment room. The treatment room is a place where players feel free to talk. Usually the talk is nothing more than typical football chatter, merciless ribbing of some unfortunate, a joke or two, or a story of someone's exploits that more often than not are exaggerated for dramatic effect. A physio who repeats any of it outside the confines of the room wouldn't last ten minutes in the job. We had some great individuals at the club at the time. Genuine people, intelligent men, exemplary professionals. John Barnes, Gary Speed, Stuart Pearce, David Batty, Rob Lee, Shay Given, Steve Harper, Alan Shearer and others. They were the lifeblood of the club. No fan would be disappointed if he'd spent time in their company as I did every day and got a feel for where their loyalties lay or what their desires were for Newcastle United. They were committed to the cause and understood the privilege they shared of representing the hopes and dreams of the city. It was therefore a shock to me that the early murmurings about our new manager emanated from this group. There was a theme developing to the daily rants:

He's too arrogant. He wants us all gone. His ego's too big. He hates Alan. He can't cope with anyone at the club with a bigger profile than him. He hates the city. He thinks it's a backward place. He misses the lifestyle in London.

No doubt some of it was probably justified, but a lot of it sounded a little petty to me as I'd seen no evidence of it myself. I challenged one senior player on some of his more outrageous suggestions.

'He won't have said that. I get it that you haven't warmed to him yet but give him a chance. He seems a decent bloke to me.'

He looked at me like I had two heads. 'What would you know? You're stuck in the treatment room every day while we have to deal with his crap on the training ground. You haven't seen him stop a training session in front of watching fans and tell Steve Howey very loudly to show Alan onto his left 'cos he has no left foot. There's only one purpose in doing that in my opinion, and that's to make a twat out of Alan. Oh ... and you can ask Alan and Steve themselves and half of the people watching if you don't believe me.'

As results deteriorated and the atmosphere at the training ground became ever more toxic I invited Alan to my local pub to spend an evening in the company of Ruud's assistant, Steve Clarke. I hoped a few pints in the quiet country pub would help ease the growing tensions that were all too evident and affecting everyday life at the club. We had a great night. They got on well, aired their differences and shared lots in common. When my drunken head hit the pillow I was satisfied that things would change after the meeting. I was happy that I'd made a small contribution towards restoring some sanity. I was confident things couldn't stay the same at the club after this meeting had taken place between the club's best player and Ruud's right-hand man. And change they did. Just not in the way I'd imagined.

If anything, in the weeks and months that followed the mood in and around the training ground plummeted. The fissures became cracks, and the cracks developed into one giant fracture. The club was broken. If I was in any doubt as to what side of the fracture I was perceived to be on, then Derek Wright clarified matters for me.

'I need to speak with you in private, Paul.'

Derek's expression suggested it wasn't good news he wanted to share with me. I followed him into the tiny cupboard adjacent to our treatment room.

'I've been asked to distance myself from you. The perception is that you are too close to Alan.'

I slumped down on to a box of strappings and tried to fathom what exactly I'd done wrong. My loyalty had always been to Newcastle United. I regarded myself as an employee who could always be relied on to give my very best to whatever task I was asked to perform. If I was close to Alan that was only because I'd put my heart and soul into getting him fit from a career threatening injury. It was a natural by-product of that effort and commitment that we would develop a friendship based on trust and respect. That friendship didn't automatically make me the enemy of the manager. I was capable of forming my own opinions about the mess the club was in. I certainly wasn't interested in taking sides in any arguments. If anything I'd tried to bring the two factions of a divided dressing room together in the hope of uniting them and making Newcastle United stronger for it. How could that be anything other than a good thing to do? How could my actions be interpreted in any other way? My attempts to help the situation had backfired spectacularly on me. I was now perceived as Alan's friend and that was not a good place to be in those cancerous times at the club. I wanted to go and speak with the manager. Tell him how disgusted I felt about the situation. Derek stopped me from making matters much worse for myself. Instead I sat in the cupboard until my pulse had settled and my anger had turned to disdain. I was grateful for Derek's decency and loyalty. I stored the information and got on with doing the job I was being paid to do. I had a mortgage and bills to pay; I couldn't afford to lose my job. Managers and players could come and go. They could love each other or hate each other. They did so with enormous salaries and bank balances to fall back on. The money that was pouring into football in the 1990s was hitting a dam before getting anywhere near the medical department. I hated that my

future could be decided on a whim. It felt unjust and unnecessary. I began to dread going to work.

'When Alan Shearer and Rob Lee speak in the treatment room, you
don't answer.'

Ruud was sitting opposite me in the cramped changing room at
our latest training base in Chester-le-Street. I looked up from tying
my laces. He was smiling. There was no malice in what he was
saying to me. There was also no sense in what he was saying to me.

'I don't know what you mean.'

He was on his feet now and walking out of the door, his short
dreadlocks bouncing in rhythm as he strode past me. 'That's all I'm
saying. When Alan Shearer and Robert Lee speak in the treatment
room, you don't answer. See you later, lovely boy.'

And with that he exited and left me a little puzzled. I spoke with
Derek and I managed to confuse him too. Late that afternoon as I
was leaving the training ground, the receptionist stopped me at the
front door.

*She was sorry to bother me. It was probably nothing. A bit silly really
but Ruud has been coming back in the evenings and disappearing into
the treatment room. It's all just a bit peculiar.*

I turned and made my way to the treatment room to find Derek.
He was cleaning. He was always cleaning. I passed on her message
to him. His thoughts mirrored mine. 'Fuck me, you don't think he's
bugging the treatment room, do you?'

It felt like we were being ridiculous but the manager's comments
to me in the changing room and him coming back into our room at
night when we'd all gone home were harmless enough in isolation,
but together? Together they were enough to have the club's long-
est-serving and most dedicated member of staff finish his day at

work with his head stuck through a hastily removed roof tile with his flashlight in hand while I felt my way around the skirting boards, under the treatment tables and behind the desks. We didn't find any bugs and through our laughter we agreed that we were now in danger of becoming ridiculously paranoid.

I got some respite from the madness when my father's health deteriorated and Denise said it would be a good idea if I came home. He'd suffered from heart failure for many years. I got home just in time. Denise brought me into his room in a downstairs bedroom in her house. The single bed he was in dwarfed him. Never a tall man, he now looked more like a baby who was spending its first night in the big bed after outgrowing its cot. I knelt by his bed and he opened his eyes. 'Paul. You're home, son.'

I told him I loved him but don't think he heard me. He didn't speak another coherent sentence in the morphine-induced stupor he spent his last week on earth floating in. My whole family were with him when he took his final breath. I cradled my niece Coleen as a hideous rattle signalled his end. As my family gathered around him to kiss him goodbye I slipped unnoticed around the back of them and left the room. For the three days he lay in his open casket I stayed out of the room. The image of one dead parent burned into my skull was enough for one lifetime. He'd finally gone to where he wanted to be since the day the light left his life twelve years before. I was happy for him. He was finally at peace.

Denise's house and garden were awash with flowers and wreaths. I read them all and then read them all again. They were from family, friends, distant relatives, my brothers' employers, which were mostly local taxi firms. There were wreaths from Ireland, England and New Zealand. It was like everybody wanted to pay their respects to him and to my family for our loss. The only one missing was the Newcastle United wreath. There was nothing. Not a flower, a card, a phone call. Nothing. I was embarrassed more than anything. An acknowledgement would have said so much. It would have meant so much. Instead its absence told me everything I already knew.

I was still raw from nursing my father in his final days when I arrived back for work in Newcastle. I was getting changed on my first morning back after my week long absence when Ruud strolled in.

'So. Also. How is Didier Domi's calf this morning?'

I stared at him. 'Sorry, I don't know.'

I knew it was probably nothing more than absent-mindedness on his part. He was a manager of a Premier League football club and had enormous demands to contend with every day. It was a perfectly legitimate question to ask of a physiotherapist sitting in front of him in the dressing room. But at that moment – that very moment – I knew I needed to get out of professional football. I was done with it. Having spent the past week nursing my father, and being surrounded by the love and support of my family, I could no longer stay in the world I'd worked so hard to be a part of. It suddenly felt pointless to me – a cold and harsh place that I needed to escape from – and all because the manager had asked me an entirely reasonable and innocent question. 'You don't know? What d'you mean you don't know?'

'Sorry, I don't know. My father died and I've just come back today. I'll ask Derek for you.'

Ruud offered his condolences and disappeared. I left the room and made my way to the treatment room. Thoughts of my father, my family, and just how exactly I was going to find my way to a better world accompanied me with every step I took.

The prospect of an FA Cup semi-final lightened the mood but I was still unsettled at times by some of my conversations with the manager. I made my way into the shower the day before we set off for our meeting with Tottenham Hotspur. Ruud was already there.

'So. Also. Tell your friend he's the best centre forward in England.'

I turned the handle and was hit by a jet of ice-cold water. 'What?'

He turned his off and grabbed a towel. 'Tell your friend he's the best centre forward in England. I think he's lacking a bit of confidence at the minute.'

I stepped back from the icy torrent. 'Are you serious?'

He grinned. 'Of course I'm serious. Tell him.'

I lost interest in the shower. 'You want me as a physio to tell the England captain he's the best centre forward in England? He'd tell me to fuck off and mind my own business and he'd be right. I don't think Alan Shearer has ever lacked confidence. I won't do that.'

He dried himself off while humming a tune I didn't recognise.

I left without showering and spent the rest of the day trying to understand the point he was making. Alan's spectacular goal to win the semi-final was achieved all on his own without the pep talk from a confused physiotherapist.

It wasn't the only time I was bemused by Ruud's actions. I arrived at Wembley Stadium for the FA Cup Final against Manchester United, the biggest game of our season. I sat on the bench to get changed and felt grains of sand beneath my thighs and on the floor at my feet. Ray Thompson, the kit manager, came in with a cup of coffee in his hand. I raised my palm with the grains stuck to it. He looked over his shoulder to make sure we were alone.

'You're not going to believe this, man.'

He sat down beside me.

'Why's there sand everywhere, Ray?'

He shook his head. 'It's not sand, man. It's salt.'

'Salt?'

'The manager's had me sprinkle salt everywhere to ward off evil spirits 'cos he thinks the club's cursed.'

'Fuck off.'

'Seriously, man. I've been chucking it everywhere.'

We were well beaten by Manchester United on the day. I don't think a 'curse' had anything to do with the result.

The summer came and those staff members who'd aligned themselves to Ruud's regime were quietly rewarded with pay rises, doubling their salaries in some instances. By the time we came back for pre-season I was very clear about one thing. I wanted the manager sacked. I hated myself for it but I wanted him gone. My relationship with John Carver was strained to breaking point. He was part of a regime that was making my life a misery and in my opinion ruining the club. I'd watch my long-time friend regularly disappear into Steve Clarke's house while I sat across the street and worried for my job and my family's future.

I had good reason to be worried. In the week leading up to playing Sunderland, our biggest rivals, I was at the training ground. I was chatting to my friend and colleague Kevin Bell. Ruud approached us and spoke through a beaming smile. He looked me in the eye.

'When I am in a stronger position, all of the shit will be gone from here.'

He held my gaze in uncomfortable silence before heading off and leaving us to stare at each other. Kevin fuelled my fears.

'Jesus Christ man. I think he means you.'

The day before we played Sunderland at home I walked into the staff canteen. Ruud, Steve and John were sitting on a table to the right as I made my way to the breakfast buffet. Ruud was leaning back on the chair, balancing it on two back legs. He had a wide smile on his face and spoke loudly so that I could hear. 'It's a new dawn for this club tomorrow. New day. Fresh start. The future is bright. The future begins tomorrow.'

It was unnecessary and childish. He was gloating over his decision to drop Alan Shearer for the big game. By all means do it if that's what you want to do but this sort of behaviour was crass and uncalled for. By the time I took my seat in the dugout I was desperate for our biggest rivals to beat us in our own stadium. I was ashamed of myself but I knew the heart and soul of the club was at stake. I felt my job was at stake. When I got home long after the monsoon had rained on Ruud's parade I watched the manager blame Alan Shearer for the result even though he'd left him out of the team in the first place. He gave the world a glimpse of the arrogance and wrong-headedness of his tenure at the club. I knew that once he'd done that there was no way back for him. The club would be better for it. I spoke with John after Ruud left. I fully understood the awkward position he'd found himself in and his duty to be loyal to the manager who'd given him his first senior position. I was glad our friendship survived the absurdity of his tenure. I was relieved it was over but apprehensive about who would replace him.

CHAPTER 34

IT WAS late in the afternoon when he came in and sat on the treatment table. He was immaculately dressed, tanned, and was handsome for his age. His white hair had been freshly cut for the occasion. His crisp, grey suit was being worn for the first time. His legs were swinging back and forth as he sipped the tea I'd made for him. He asked my wife's name, how long we'd been married, if I had any kids, if my parents were still alive, whereabouts I was from in Ireland, and how long I'd worked at the club. He told me about leaving home as a boy and playing for West Brom and Fulham before moving into management. He'd been sacked at Fulham, which hurt him. Moved to Ipswich, which was the making of him, and then onto England, PSV, Sporting, Porto, and Barcelona – they were too quick to discard him – then finally PSV again. But through it all, Newcastle United was always his club. It had been since he was a knock-kneed boy kicking a ball around Langley Park. He talked for an hour drinking his tea and swinging his legs.

That was the first time I met Bobby Robson. It was August 1999. The last time I did so was nine years later when he was close to losing his battle with the disease that would eventually claim him. He was attending an awards dinner and was already resigned to his fate. I stole a brief moment with him. He asked me how my wife was keeping, how old my children were now, how I was getting on, and he talked about Newcastle United.

My biggest regret is that he arrived at the club when I'd already decided that my future lay elsewhere. I worked for him for his entire time as manager and I found him to be an incredibly honest and very fair man. Someone who'd travelled the world yet never strayed too far from home. He turned a cancerous atmosphere on its head the minute he breezed through the door with a warm smile and a ready handshake. Newcastle was united again and the rollercoaster was on the ascent. But something had changed inside me.

The death of my father and the sickening, unnecessary stupidity of the previous year had left their mark. As I climbed out of bed in the mornings I was stepping over books by Kierkegaard, Kant and Nietzsche – some completed and others partially read, discarded, and only half-understood. In the corner of our bedroom were some unopened boxes containing the materials for a distance-learning conversion course in law. I'd enrolled after seeing Marty Crossey standing beside my father's grave. He looked every inch the success-ful intelligent man I wanted to be. My nerve had failed me again as soon as the boxes arrived. I still didn't believe I was capable of study-ing law – especially now that I was working full time as a physio and raising a young family. So instead I bought book after book. I was searching for something – I didn't really know what. But there was something gnawing inside of me that just wouldn't leave me alone. Events that I once took pleasure from – the match, a meal with Geraldine, a night out with Derek, Roddy and Ray – became some-thing less than they were before. I was still present and still enjoying them on some level but they'd lost their shine. I felt an emptiness right at my core that was robbing me of once-meaningful pleasures. The treatment room, which was once my sanctuary, became a living Hell for me. Where once players like John Barnes would sit and argue the hot topics of the day, and I'd love to lock horns with him, there was now a new breed – a different animal in the room.

There was nothing wrong with these new flashier models as such. They were just so young. And I wasn't. Tales of girls, cars, houses, girls in cars, and girls in houses, just left me completely cold. I couldn't wait to get home to Geraldine in the evenings, and talk about something – anything – other than the pointless ramblings of young boys with too much money, too much fame, and too little common sense. Previously I'd have been the first to join in with conversations on any topic, but now I found myself snapping and arguing with young footballers who were doing no harm but just living a life that I knew little of and didn't want to know anything about. The influx of players of every nationality added to my malaise. It was different to when Philippe Albert had injured his cruciate ligament and trusted us to bring him back to fitness. The new foreign players wanted to go home to their own physios for treatment. Even the most minor of injuries merited trips across the world, while I stood in the treatment room and learned the price of the latest imported Hummer or how many drunken girls fitted in one. I needed to find a way out. I wanted out of the world I'd fought so desperately to be in.

I overdosed on music and chocolate but they only gave me fleeting moments of happiness. I played with my children and could get lost briefly in that. I offered my services at the soup kitchen in Newcastle but wasn't needed. I finally found my escape in books. Not just any books. They had to have meaning. Not just 'puff'. There was no logic behind my choices. I'd spend my evenings browsing the shelves of the many bookshops in the city. I didn't really have a structure to my learning. I was more like a blind drunk stumbling along the street with no destination in mind but moving one foot in front of the other just to stop myself from falling down.

The club under Bobby's guidance was going from strength to strength but the knowledge that everything could change in an instant and a new manager could signal another period like the last one was all the motivation I needed to keep searching. I wanted out of football with all of its money, fame, egos, and hangers on. I wanted more. I was unhappy and bitter with where I was at in life and I knew that the only person who could change that was me. I just didn't know how. I spoke with Peter Hampson, a good friend who was a lecturer at the university. We discussed my choice of reading materials. He sent me a prospectus for a Master's degree. I enrolled immediately. I was a physiotherapist in professional football. I knew lots of other physios who'd undertaken Master's degrees. They'd studied sports medicine, manipulation or physiotherapy and enhanced their career prospects and earning capacity the moment they got their certificate.

When I graduated from mine I knew it was unlikely to enhance my career in football. An MA in History of Ideas – where 'Interpretations of the Cosmos' was one of my modules – was not likely to enhance my career as a physiotherapist. But three years of studying the Renaissance, the Enlightenment, Modernism and Post-modernism broadened my horizons and gave me something on which to focus my restless mind. I studied Irish history and wrote my thesis on James Fintan Lalor – an agrarian revolutionary whose writings inspired the leaders of the Easter Rising in 1916; an event that ultimately led to the partitioning of the troubled country of my birth. The day I graduated was a very proud one for our young family. Not because of me, but because on that same day Geraldine graduated as a teacher after four long years on her own journey. We'd put the kids to bed, open a bottle of wine and sit next to each other at the dining table studying towards changing our lives for the better. But not long after graduating I realised my Master's degree wasn't my way out after all.

Derek and I sat in front of Russell Cushing, the chief executive of the club. We presented our case for a pay rise. *We were loyal servants. We were the lowest paid physios in the Premier League. The club was in the Champions' League. We hadn't had a pay rise in the last five years. We only wanted a small increase and then yearly increments. It would cost double to get replacements of the same quality.*

All of it was met with a poker face and it seemed the only word in his vocabulary was no. We were getting up to leave, defeated and dejected, when I blurted it out. 'But I've got a Master's degree now.'

It stopped Russell in his tracks. He was interested. 'Oh . . . that's different. I didn't know that. What's it in?'

I wished he hadn't asked that bit, and stumbled over my words. 'It's in History of Ideas. The Study of Western European Thought over the last 500 Years.'

There was a pause while he digested my achievements in philosophy and the history of art. He rose to his feet and shook my hand. 'Well, that will get you 50 per cent of fuck all then, Paul, won't it?'

I didn't appreciate his manner. But it was a great retort. And in my heart I knew what I had to do. What I should have done fifteen years before but lacked the courage, what I'd tried to do five years before but my nerve had failed me yet again. I needed to study law. I wanted to study law. I needed to be a lawyer. Not just a lawyer. I needed to be a barrister. I needed to believe that I could do it; the shy boy who'd sat on the shed who'd failed his 11-plus and hadn't stayed at school to complete his O levels. I had to have the courage of my convictions or risk being a resentful and bitter old man telling my kids and grandkids how 'I coulda been a contender.' I'd sat at the back of too many meetings listening to managers and coaches believing I could speak better than them, could think quicker than them, was smarter than them. So many times in the past I'd made excuses and ducked out of speaking engagements – all because I was too afraid to stand up and back myself. Then I'd beat myself up about it because something inside me desperately wanted to do it. To speak, to argue, to think on my feet, to stand at the front of the room and hold everyone in it in the palm of my hand, enthralled by my every word. It was now or never for me. Put up or shut up.

The day after our meeting with Russell Cushing I enrolled on the Common Professional Examination distance learning course, for those with an existing degree to study for a postgraduate diploma in law. When I'd completed it I was going to leave Newcastle United and football for good and go to bar school. I hadn't worked out how I was going to afford giving up my job now that our third child, Ciaran, had come along and we'd recently moved into our dream home, courtesy of a sizeable mortgage. But I didn't really care. Geraldine said that if that was what I wanted then we'd work it out. The shy boy with no belief in himself, who could never quite find his voice, was about to take the gamble of his life: that if and when he did find it, he'd be good enough to make a living out of using it.

When I walked into my first lecture I was terrified and electrified. Terrified that the other ninety-four people in the room were all better than me – cleverer than me. But electrified that I'd finally had the courage to try. Throughout the two years I watched them fall away one by one. I could see why. It was a slog, an endless grind just to keep up. I studied every night after the kids had gone to bed. I spent every away trip with my head buried in my books. I spent a week in Dubai with the team and never left my room. But I got there in the end.

Only twenty-five of us completed the course and only five of us did so with a 'commendation'. I finally had my graduate diploma in law.

I wished I could have phoned Marty Crossey to tell him. Tell him that *I did it*. But he was gone. In the prime of his life he'd suffered a heart attack while on a treadmill at his local gym. I travelled home for his funeral and sat at the back of the church watching his wife and children's worlds fall apart. I didn't know them but I wanted to tell them what he meant to me. He was always an inspiration to me. He was my hero as a boy and my friend. I wish I'd told them.

My two years on the course coincided with yet another managerial change at the club. In August 2004 I turned up early for training one morning to find Bobby sitting alone in the half-light in the corner of the canteen. He was never normally there so early. He didn't see me as I approached him. His hair was a mess, his shirt button was undone, and his tie was pulled to one side and in a tight knot like he'd needed to loosen it from his neck in a hurry. He was holding a piece of limp toast in his right hand. He never moved. It was as if he'd forgotten what to do with the bread somewhere between lifting it from his plate and reaching his mouth.

'Everything OK, Gaffer?'

It took him a moment to respond. 'Morning, son. Sit down.'

I sat my tea on the table. He dropped his toast onto his place. He looked his age. 'I think I'm gone, son. I've had a call from Russell this morning. They want to meet me at the ground in twenty minutes.'

He caught me by surprise and I muttered something about not being silly. But he knew. After more than fifty years in football he knew. He was hurt and he was broken. I slid back out of the chair to let him move past me. He stopped, brushed his fingers through his hair, straightened his tie and marched off to meet his fate. He was broken but the world wouldn't get to see it.

By the time he came into the treatment room that afternoon the news had reached us that he'd been sacked. He came in with a golf club in one hand and his bag in the other. He shook Derek's hand and then mine. He thanked us for our loyalty and hard work and then asked us to help him with his things. When we were done he spoke to both of us.

'Where did I fail, boys?'

Derek looked at me and I looked at him. He spoke first. 'You didn't fail, Gaffer. You've been a great manager for this football club.'

He took no consolation from Derek's words. I shook his hand for the last time.

'Derek's right. This isn't failure. This is far from failure. The last five years have been some of the best times this club's ever had. When they write about this time it'll be about success, not failure.'

He looked at me, raised an eyebrow and gave me a rueful grin. 'Do you really think so, son?'

He bit his lip, shook his head and left Newcastle United as the most successful failure I'd met in all my time at the club. Three years after he'd left I phoned Judith, his PA. 'D'you know that Bobby's still sending flowers to Geraldine at Christmas? He must've forgotten to cancel the standing order.'

She laughed down the phone. 'I do know, yes. It's not a mistake. He wants her to have them. He wishes you and your family a Merry Christmas.'

A great man first and foremost – a great manager a close second.

My pathway into law would have been much smoother had Bobby stayed in the job for another two years. He was honest, fair, a great leader, and untangled the club from the mess created by his predecessor. He brought back the glory days of Keegan when we all thought they were gone for good. He left a very good team, good staff, and a well-run football club for the next incumbent. Graeme

Souness began dismantling it from the first day he entered the building.

I never quite trawled the depths I reached under Ruud Gullit, but that was solely because I could now see a way out of the club. If I'd had nothing else to focus on other than the football club, I'd have been driven to despair. Graeme arrived with three others. He held a meeting with all of the staff shortly afterwards. *He was bringing in someone to help us in the medical department.* We asked what his qualifications were. He gave us short shrift. 'Don't worry about that. He has all the qualifications, and more importantly, he's a good lad.'

Being a 'good lad' got Phil Boersma an untitled role in our department. Graeme was right. He was a good lad. He possessed qualifications also. He had an FA diploma in Physiotherapy which to my understanding, was a six week course offered to ex-professional footballers to ensure they could stay in the game after retirement. In recent years physio roles had been filled more and more by individuals with degrees attained after three years of university education. This was the route I'd followed and I felt strongly it was the route professional clubs should be going down. Phil was a very likeable man – the problem was he'd just been shoe-horned into our treatment room. We didn't really know what to do with him and he didn't really have a role. It led to some uncomfortable and comical moments. When I was conducting a fitness test with Shola Ameobi, Phil was setting up cones next to us. We'd just finished when he called Shola over. He had this 'special drill' he always did. If Shola completed it then he was fit to play. I told him Shola had already proved his fitness. He did 'the drill' anyway.

I found the manager in the gym. *Didn't he think it was a bit undermining for me and confusing for the players to be doing two fitness tests?* He shook his head and smiled.

'He's a good lad.'

Graeme wasn't interested in anything I had to say. *It wasn't about whether or not he was a good lad.* The problem was that the 'good lad' was repeating a fitness test I'd just completed. It was unnecessary, confusing and completely pointless. I thought it was going to be a long slog but thankfully that wasn't the case in the end. Phil left the club by mutual consent after our FA Cup semi-final defeat to Manchester United. His role was never filled again.

I liked Graeme. He was intelligent and personable. I could see that if things were going well he'd have been a great man to work for. But things weren't going well and I think in many ways we saw the worst of him. He undermined the staff who weren't part of his inner circle and did it publicly in front of the players, which was as disappointing as it was uncalled for. I overheard him ranting in the gym that he wasn't 'having us' (the medical department), or the fitness coach. He did it privately too. He once organised an appointment for a player to visit a physiotherapist in Nottingham while I was sitting in the training ground waiting to take him to his meeting with the leading neurosurgeon in Newcastle.

I coped with it only because I was getting out. I tolerated it because I knew that this would be the last time my livelihood would ever be affected by the irrational behaviour of an under pressure manager. He wanted the injured players treated morning noon and night –'to inconvenience the shirkers'. We agreed that we'd use Durham County Cricket's physio in the evenings because it meant a long drive to Chester-le-Street for the 'shirkers' but also to give us some time to be with our families. The idea was to inconvenience the players and not the medical staff.

I met with Graeme in the gym on a Friday before the team set off for an away game. It was Geraldine's birthday. He'd asked to see me. I walked over to where he was cycling on his static bike. He didn't look at me.

'Injured players getting treatment tonight?'

'Yes, all sorted.'

'Who's treating them?'

'Nigel is – at the cricket ground.'

'I'd rather you did it.'

'I thought the idea was to inconvenience the players and not me? I haven't had a day off for three weeks and it's my wife's birthday.'

'He costs money and you don't. I'd rather you did it.'

'He doesn't cost any more money than we've already agreed. We pay him his fee regardless.'

'OK – as long as it's all sorted.'

That was it. There was nothing to it. Just an explanation on my part that I was carrying out the agreed agenda. *Inconvenience the players but not the staff.* There was one thing that troubled me: he made no eye contact with me during the entire exchange.

I thought no more about it until the club doctor spoke with me on the Sunday after our exchange. *Graeme had never had a member of staff speak to him like that before. He'd known physios not have a day off for six weeks. That was 'the price on the ticket'.*

The doctor was surprised by my shoulder shrug.

I found it all a little pathetic. If that was the price on my ticket, I was glad I would soon no longer be part of the circus.

CHAPTER 35

I STARED OUT of the window and watched the river flow gently by. My shirt collar was biting into my neck, and my waistcoat felt tighter than when I'd bought it last year. My head itched and my shoulders were heavy from the layers of clothing bearing down on them. I watched a group of Japanese tourists who were crammed into a small boat and were pointing their expensive cameras at anything that caught their eye. My mother's image flashed across my brain, momentarily obscuring the bobbing Japanese cameras. Not the dead one. The living one. It was always the same image now. She was behind the kitchen window and I was looking down at her from my perch on the shed. I hadn't invited her. I hadn't conjured her up. She'd just decided to join me there gazing out of a window at some tourists gazing back at me. She'd been gone now for over twenty years. But she was here with me at what was my proudest moment. I got to share it with her after all. Standing there, itchy and uncomfortable, I was proud. Prouder than I'd ever been and I was happy she'd come along to share it.

The last two years had been the most challenging of my life. We'd converted our home and sold half of it so that we'd enough money to survive. I'd left Newcastle United, where I'd worked for eighteen years as a player and physio. I'd gone to bar school and finally overcome my fears of standing up and speaking in public. The first time I did it I thought I was going to faint with fear. But when I'd sat down I wanted to get up and do it all over again. I hated the fear but loved the excitement of it. I'd always hoped I'd be good at it. I'd secretly believed I would be. When I eventually did it *I knew* I was good at it. I was in the right room at last. I was forty-one years old when I finally stood up for myself for the very first time. I was able to think quickly and articulate clearly. I could anticipate my opponent's argument and counter it instantly. The thing I'd feared most in my life, speaking in public, was the thing that I was actually best at. I never had a doubt I'd get through bar school after I stood on my feet for the first time.

The really hard work began after I had qualified as a barrister. The competition to secure a pupillage was more intense than any football match I'd ever played in. Trying to earn a place in a prac-tising chambers was a hideous and nerve-wrecking experience. There were too many barristers and not enough pupillages. Only 5 per cent of us were able to get one. I made twelve applications and got nine rejections within a day of doing so. I got first interviews in three others; two in London and one in Park Court Chambers in Leeds. There was nothing available in Newcastle.

After my first interview in Leeds I drove to York on the way home and bought a three-piece pinstriped suit. Geraldine thought I was being premature but *I knew*. I knew after the first interview that I'd get the pupillage. There were more than 300 applicants but I just knew. I didn't care that they'd all had better educations – public school and Oxbridge – and, in lots of instances, were no doubt following in Daddy's footsteps. They didn't have my history. They didn't have my background. Most importantly, they didn't have my ability to present an argument. I was offered another pupillage in one of the London sets too. This time there were 600 applicants. I knew I'd get that one too. *I just knew*. The frightened little boy who was too shy to speak had come a very long way. The young man who'd lacked the courage of his convictions and postponed studying law for fear of failing was now firmly consigned to my past. Putting my wig and gown on for the first time and being called to the bar in Middle Temple was all the confirmation I needed that I was finally good enough. Even *I* couldn't talk myself out of that reality. Every day I got out of bed in the middle of the night to get the early train to Leeds. Every night, regardless of the time, I made the reverse trip and would climb into my own bed with Geraldine. Sometimes by the time I'd finished my notes for the following day I'd get two or maybe three hours sleep. The five hour round trip from my door to my Chambers was just part of the journey I was on.

Park Court was one of the premier criminal law sets in the north of England with some brilliant barristers and outstanding QCs. My pupil master, Paul Greaney, was the shining star of the set. He worked alongside Robert Smith QC, and I spent my time learning how to be the best from the very best. They were two like minds and two brilliant minds. They were generous with their precious time and were nurturing me along and without doubt had my best interests at heart and high hopes for my future.

Today they'd brought me to the House of Lords. *The House of Lords.* I was gazing out over the Thames, sweltering in my wig and gown and ill-fitting suit, while the five Law Lords I'd just been mesmerised by were having a short break to let their giant brains rest before the afternoon session. Robert Smith QC and his equally eloquent opponent had spent the morning arguing a case that would change the very law of the land we live in. I stood behind them in silent awe waiting for someone to tap me on the shoulder and tell me I'd stumbled into the wrong room – the wrong life. The boy on the shed, who had wet the bed fearing his council house would be burned to the ground, who had played football until his body had let him down and who had spent his working life nursing footballers back to health shouldn't really be standing in the highest court in the land wigged and gowned. Yes, I was proud all right.

That's what I was thinking when my mother made her way into my head uninvited to join me at my finest hour. I was finally on my way. Deep down, I knew I would get there in the end. I wouldn't have even tried otherwise. I was only sorry that she wasn't able to stay around long enough in this world to see me find the courage to follow my dreams. That she'd gone when everything was such a mess for me. But that was all in my past. I was finally where I wanted to be. My future would be determined by me. I'd live or die by my abilities as a barrister. I was content with that thought.

I was still reliving my experience in Westminster when my phone buzzed in my pocket. I was running through Leeds station. I was always running through Leeds station. I'd walk from Chambers every day and tell myself to take my time – that there was a train every thirty minutes. Then I'd get to the station and look at the Departures board. There was always one leaving in the next five minutes. I'd quicken my step, and then break into a jog, weaving my suitcase in and out of the throng that always seemed to be coming the other way. Once through the barrier I'd take the stairs two at a time and usually arrive in a sweaty mess to find there were no seats on the overcrowded cattle truck home. I'd just jumped the stairs when my phone vibrated. I fumbled in my pocket and checked the number in case it was someone from Chambers requiring anything from me. It wasn't my Chambers calling. It was Alan Shearer.

I hadn't heard from him for a while so I took the call, and missed my train.

'What's up? Thought you were in Vienna for the Euros?'

'I am.'

I sat down on a bench to catch my breath and loosen my tie. A button flew off my waistcoat and landed at the feet of a sprinting woman. Without breaking stride she kicked it over the railings and on to the track below.

'Everything OK?'

'Everything's better than OK. I've got a proposition for you.'

He sounded upbeat. 'I've been offered the Southampton manager's job. I think I'm going to take it. I'd like you to come with me. I'll look after the football side and you manage the sports medicine side and make sure we are as good as we can be.'

I was pleased I was sitting down. I didn't answer.

'You still there?'

'Yes, I'm still here.'

'What do you think?'

I wasn't sure. I wasn't sure what to think or whether I wanted to do it or not. But I had to say something.

'It's a bit of a surprise.'

He laughed. 'I was always gonna ask you, man – you must've known that? It's not just this one. I want you to do this with me wherever it takes us.'

I didn't know that. 'I'm a barrister now. Couldn't you have asked me before I sold half my house and studied law for the last three years?'

He laughed again. 'So are you up for it or not, man?'

The knot in my stomach and the nausea rising in my throat told me I probably wasn't. I'd worked too hard and come too far to go back. Back to a world that hadn't really been that kind to me. I'd been robbed of one career as a player and been forced into desperate measures to extricate myself from my second as a physio. But I didn't want to say no. Not to him. I needed to buy some time.

'It's come as a bit of a shock. Can I have some time to think about it?'

'Absolutely. It's a big decision. Take your time. They're coming to my house at ten on Saturday.'

It was Thursday evening and I'd just missed two trains. I got on the next one and tried to work out how I would say no to him. I'd tell him I'd moved on. That football wasn't for me anymore. Law was my future.

I'd just come back from the House of Lords. I'd spoken with Robert Smith, the head of Chambers, about writing a sports law book. With my background as a player and physio and now a barrister, I was uniquely placed to carve out a career for myself as a sports lawyer. Alan would understand. My mind raced faster than the train that took me home. In the time it took to travel from Leeds to Newcastle, I knew in my heart what I wanted to do. There was no doubt what I was going to do. I'd regret it for the rest of my life if I didn't do it. *I was going to sit on the right shoulder of Alan Shearer while he made his way in the game as a bright young manager.* He'd be Southampton manager, Newcastle manager and England manager. If I'd been a boy educated at public school and had gone to Oxford, Cambridge, or even a good red-brick university there would have been no debate. No turmoil. Law would've won every time. But I wasn't that boy. Football had been my life for so long; since I was old enough to remember. Yes, I'd been tarnished by my experiences, but this was my chance to rectify that. I was getting the chance to shape the culture and practices of whatever club I worked for. I'd be answerable only to Alan. I could live with that. I trusted him implicitly. If it was anybody else in the world asking me the question then I'd have said no. But it wasn't. It was him. So I said yes.

We met three businessmen from Southampton in Alan's living room. They were buying the club from the current shareholders. It was imminent; a matter of days – a week or two at most. Alan would have £26 million to spend to get the team out of the Championship. I could have the salary I'd asked for plus a bonus and a pay rise if we were promoted. It would change my life over-night. We'd sign for three years with an option of a fourth. By the time I'd sat down for dinner with Geraldine, Alan and his wife Lainya in my favourite bistro in Wylam village that night, I was bursting with excitement at the thought of what the future would bring for me, Geraldine and our three boys.

Monday morning came around and the alarm seemed to go off an hour earlier than I expected. The station was colder, the journey longer. The day in court was never-ending and the train home slower and more crowded than ever. As the days passed and I waited for the takeover to happen I began to feel uneasy about what I was contemplating. I wasn't having doubts about the decision I'd made, but I was feeling dishonest with the people at Chambers who were putting their time and energy into making me the barrister I no longer intended to be. The guilt burrowed and gnawed away at me until I finally walked into Chambers and told Paul Greaney I was leaving. I was giving up the pupillage I had been awarded over all those people who had never gotten the opportunity I'd been given. He was shocked and disappointed in me. He never said that but I could tell. I couldn't even give him a valid reason for leaving. What could I say? *I'm just passing time here until the news breaks that Alan Shearer is the new manager of Southampton and Paul Ferris is going with him.*

I felt more honest for telling him and leaving Chambers with nothing than waiting for confirmation of the takeover and walking out and then straight into the job with Alan.

I'd only just left when the worrying calls from the Southampton businessmen began. *The recession was delaying the funding but it was still on its way. They were borrowing from the Far East so there was no problem. The recession had reached the Far East but we shouldn't worry. We should keep watching for breaking news.* So I did. Every day I watched the TV waiting for the story to break that Southampton had been sold to new owners. I watched and waited; getting more and more anxious, until one day it finally happened. It was the top story on the sports channel. The announcer with the annoying habit of shouting at everyone like we were all deaf screamed the news that Southampton had been sold. I turned him up even louder. Southampton had been sold all right – just not to the consortium we were talking to!

I turned the TV off and collapsed onto the settee. I sat there motionless until I felt Geraldine's hand on my shoulder when she came in from work. What had I done? I was a physiotherapist who wasn't practising physiotherapy, I had a Master's degree in History of Ideas that would get me '50 per cent of fuck all' and I was a barrister who'd given up my only route to having a career at the bar. On top of that I'd butchered our dream home, and spent almost all of the money we'd made from the sale on chasing my dream of being a barrister, only to discard it all on one ninety-minute train journey. Only I could hatch a plan like that. I'd taken Geraldine and my children on a one-way ticket to nowhere. And for what? For nothing more than a *promise of a potential job?* I'd signed nothing. I'd been guaranteed nothing. Any sane person would have said no in the first place, or at least, after saying yes, would have stayed where they were until the contract was signed. Any person in his right mind wouldn't have allowed a few pangs of Catholic guilt to ruin everything he'd been striving to achieve for the past three years. He'd have stayed in Chambers until the 'deal' was formally concluded.

In the weeks and months that followed, my settee became my prison and my own mind my warped jailor. Some days I'd say goodbye to Geraldine and the kids and then sit down and not move again until I'd hear a key turn in the door to signal their return. I'd get up and make dinner and listen to the stories of their day and have nothing to add. Geraldine would drag me to The Lion and Lamb pub next to our house. I'd talk to my friends and lie to them all when they'd ask how my legal career was going. I went to the doctor and came home with some pills to help with my 'low mood'. The next morning I opened the packet and put the first one in my mouth. I tried to swallow it – I knew if I did it would help. I tried to swallow it. I knew if I did it would change things. I tried to swallow it but I couldn't do it. I didn't want my mind altered by pills. I didn't want artificial help to change how I felt. I spat it down the sink and threw the packet into the bin. I went to the cupboard below the stairs. I found an old pair of trainers. I walked out into the fresh air and jogged until my lungs hurt. I walked home and refused to sit on the settee. Every day, after Geraldine went off to work, I jogged a little further. By the time I got the call I'd been dreaming of I was two stones lighter and running 7 miles a day.

It was Alan again. He was going into Newcastle United for the last eight games of the season. Iain Dowie was going to be his assistant. He'd rather have waited until the end of the season when most probably the team would have been relegated. But the opportunity was here and now. And in football they don't come along every day. My role wouldn't really bear fruit until the summer when we'd rebuild all aspects of the club. But I'd go in with him now and start plotting our way forwards.

When Alan Shearer walked back into his beloved Newcastle United alongside Iain Dowie on 1 April 2009, I was there too. The third man. Invisible to all but those who mattered.

CHAPTER 36

MICHAEL OWEN'S private physiotherapist was in the treatment room when I'd gone in to find Derek. I wanted to see my old friend, to speak with him privately about my new role. I didn't want him to be uncomfortable that the young player he had treated, and the young physio he had once mentored, was now back at the club as his boss. He was my friend first and foremost; the circumstances of our employment were different, but that was an irrelevance. Instead of Derek I found the physio, paid for privately by Michael but treating him publicly in the club's medical department. I didn't like it. I thought it was disrespectful to the hardworking staff – Derek included. I wouldn't have accepted it if I'd still been a physio at the club. So I didn't accept it now either. I had a meeting with him where I asked him to leave. Not to return to the club. Not to undermine fellow professionals. If he wanted to take Michael's money then he could do it elsewhere. I eventually found Derek. He agreed with my actions and was grateful for them. He accepted the situation we now found ourselves in with the good grace I knew he would – no matter how hard that was for him.

Before we arrived, just getting people to turn up for work on time was a problem, it seemed. Players were late for training; injured players were late for treatment sessions and often didn't turn up in the afternoon. Only a few stayed behind and ate together after training. This was something Bobby Robson had insisted upon and we very quickly put in place again. We insisted that any player who was injured and wanted to miss an afternoon session had to ask the manager's permission to do so. That one simple act reduced the numbers on the injury list almost overnight. Five of our six top earners were regulars on the physio's table instead of the pitch – Mark Viduka, Joey Barton, Alan Smith, Geremi, and Michael Owen commanded phenomenal salaries and two would play no part for us in the short time we had. Michael's salary was almost double the others. Alan felt that keeping him fit was crucial to our chances of survival. They had history and Alan was banking on Michael in many ways.

I embarked on a project that we hoped would help us be as professional as we could be, not just until the end of the season but beyond. We were there for the long term and not just eight weeks. I made it a priority to speak with all the senior players and staff. I canvassed their opinion of what was fundamentally wrong and shared with them our vision for the club moving forward. I'd spoken to everyone I needed to and only had Joey Barton left – he'd been away for some 'one on one' rehab in the warmth of Dubai in a bid to speed up his return to fitness.

Watch out for Joey. Be careful with Joey. Don't get on the wrong side of Joey. He's a nice lad Joey but when he loses it he's a lunatic. The warnings came from players, support staff, coaches, security staff and canteen staff. He'd not long come out of prison for beating a young boy senseless in an act of thuggery outside a fast food bar in the early hours of the morning after a drunken binge in Liverpool. I wasn't particularly looking forward to meeting him. Certainly not after watching the brutish savagery on the blurry CCTV footage that I'd watched when someone shoved it in my face while I was eating my lunch. I was pleasantly surprised when I did meet him, however. I spoke with him at the same table where

I'd once watched Bobby Robson forget how to eat toast. I told him of our plans for the short-, medium- and long-term future of the club. He told me how happy he was that we were there. He spoke of 'the shambles' the club was before our arrival and of how refreshing it was to be part of a professional club again. He talked of how prison had changed him and made him a better man. He spoke with sincerity and passion. I left the meeting buoyed. There was no problem with Joey after all. What had all the fuss been about?

'You're the same as all the rest. No different from Keegan. One rule for one and one for the other. The lads aren't happy. They're fuming. It's not on. Alan needs to know. I'm the only one who'll speak up. It's fuckin' shit.'

I was in a cupboard next to the main gym. Shola Ameobi had brought me there. *Joey wanted to speak with me and he wasn't happy.* It was a week after our initial conversation and two days after we'd picked up a valuable point at Stoke. I let him speak. And speak and speak. Building his case for the prosecution based on completely flawed logic. We'd given two of the older players – Michael Owen and Nicky Butt – an extra day off after the Stoke game to rest their ageing, and, particularly in Michael's case, fragile bodies for the battles that lay ahead. Joey said he and everyone else were fuming that we'd given them special treatment. I let him finish his speech and made two observations. The first was that Alan was free to manage the team in the best way he saw fit. The second was that he himself was currently injured and had only recently come back from a warm weather break in Dubai while all of the other injured players had remained in Newcastle. He and no one else had complained of special treatment then. He didn't accept my logic and presented his case on behalf of the other disgruntled players to the manager as well. He got the same answer from Alan.

I was concerned that we'd upset the harmony of the dressing room by our well-intentioned actions to save Michael and Nicky's legs for the challenges ahead. I spoke to the senior players. Not one of them had a problem. None of them knew what I was talking about. Everyone didn't have a problem after all. Only Joey had a problem. So my conversation in the cupboard was entirely point-less. Everyone wasn't furious after all, with the exception of the unelected shop steward. Joey was the only one, but he believed he spoke for everyone else too.

We faced an uphill task to turn the club's fortunes around and in the end we weren't able to do it. We were the fourth management team of a disastrous season. Some players had already 'downed tools' when we got there, others hadn't, but some were low on confidence and others were lacking in ability and desire. We tried to instil some discipline, and bring order to the chaotic mess we'd walked into. I've never worked so hard in my life, or seen so little of my family during those eight weeks. They felt more like eight months. I'd pop my head into Alan's office to say goodnight after a long day and be met with the same sarcastic remark from him every time.

'Early finish, is it?'

I'd remind him it was after nine o'clock and I had a family to go home to and I'd suggest he did the same. I don't know if he paid attention to me or how long he and Iain stayed watching videos of games and players after I'd gone. I do know this, though. He threw his heart and soul into the job of trying to keep the club in the league. He looked like he was born to sit in the manager's chair and we spoke often of what could be possible once this season of misery and failure was out of the way. He tried everything and anything to formulate a winning mentality from a losing one. To build some momentum where inertia had prevailed all season.

'I'm going to play Joey at Liverpool.'

We were sitting in his office late in the afternoon. Alan was leaning back on his chair with his foot on the desk. A portrait of Bobby hung behind his head. Iain responded.

'Not sure he's fit enough. Been out a while and won't last the ninety minutes.'

I offered my opinion after Iain. 'The last time he was in Liverpool he beat up some young kid. Is putting him in the team away at Liverpool of all places such a good idea?'

But Alan's mind was made up. The following day we got Joey into the office. Alan told him he was playing and raised our concerns about his temperament. He responded as we'd hoped he would. He'd learned his lesson. He wouldn't let anybody down. He wanted to be part of the fight.

The day before the game he arrived late for training and sneaked out just as the warm-up began. Ten minutes into the game at Liverpool he aimed a kick at Xavi Alonso and missed again. I looked at Chris Hughton sitting next to me on the Anfield bench. 'What the fuck was that?'

He just shook his head. 'That's Joey.'

We were losing 2–0 with ten minutes remaining. The game was beyond us but we lived to fight another day, or three days, as that's how many games we had left to save our club from oblivion. Alonso had the ball in the far corner of the pitch. It was caught between his legs. He was half turned toward the crowd. Joey timed his tackle to cause maximum damage to him. He flew off the ground and lunged at him when Alonso was facing the other way. It was a tackle designed to deliberately hurt a very talented fellow professional. The inevitable red card followed and the player who'd sworn he wouldn't let anyone down had just let himself down, his manager down, his club down, and the thousands of people who'd travelled to watch down as well. The game was already dead. But we had three more left. He'd just guaranteed he'd play no part in any of them. It was an idiotic and selfish act. After the game Alan addressed the team.

'Not good enough, boys. We didn't compete. But let's not dwell on it. This game was not the one to keep us up. Middlesbrough mid-week is the one that really matters. Let's prepare properly from now and go and win that game in front of a full house at our place.'

He turned to Joey. 'It was a stupid tackle, Joey. He was going nowhere and now we've lost you for the last three games.'

I waited for the remorse. Surely he'd apologise to his manager and his team-mates for letting them down? For making his mates run around like demented dogs chasing a ball they could never quite reach? The remorse would be as predictable as it'd be pointless but it would still be the right thing to do. Only it didn't come. There was none. Instead he looked at the floor. 'It was a fair tackle. Never a sending off.'

He'd barely finished justifying himself when Alan, hands on hips, shouted across the room. 'Aw, fuck off with that shit, Joey. It's a red card. Come and see for yourself.'

He turned to the laptop behind him. Joey walked across to it. Alan slowed the footage down to show the moment of impact. *The red-card tackle.* Joey looked at the evidence stacked up against him. He turned to walk away. 'It was a fair tackle. Never a sending off.'

In all my eighteen years in football and my very short time as a barrister, I'd never before seen anyone argue black was white when it was clearly black. Completely ignore the evidence against him. The proof was right in front of his nose but he refused to acknowledge it. Alan shouted after him. 'You've let your team and the club down. It's a coward's tackle. A 'shithouse' tackle and you know it.'

It was as if a switch flicked in Joey's head. His mouth started spewing insults at Alan and then at Iain. So much shit. I'd never heard so much shit come out of the wrong hole before. It was like his fragile grip on reality had been shattered by Alan's words. As if Alan had flipped his fingers off the ledge he was desperately clinging to. Everything just came spilling out of him on to the dressing room floor. He was a jabbering mass of incoherent vitriol and bile. Like the possessed girl in *The Exorcist*, head swivelling and spitting venom and needing to be put out of her misery. Iain moved towards him to quieten him in the old-fashioned way, but Alan's hand stopped him in his tracks.

By the time Joey was finished I felt sorrier for him than angry with him for what I'd just witnessed. He was a deeply unhappy man and a worryingly deluded one. His only response to any kind of challenge to his warped world view was to pour scorn on anything or anyone around him that dared to prick his alternative reality bubble. I left the changing room convinced he needed some help from professionals outside of football. Without it he was lost. He was unstable. A ticking time bomb. Anyone who crossed his path was in danger of being beaten to a pulp as his hands tried to mask the insecurities and demons that ran riot in his head. The warnings about him were right. Our biggest mistake was in not heeding them.

The win against Middlesbrough felt like the momentum-changer we'd been searching for. A text from the owner Mike Ashley telling Alan how much he loved him suggested he thought so too. The salvage job was now a real possibility. A win at home against a Fulham side with nothing to play for would almost certainly be enough, taking into account the form of Hull City who were in freefall and the most likely side to go down at our expense. The mood around the club and the city was buoyant. Then we hit a buffer. A huge one.

The doctor and the three physios were sitting to my right in the medical office. Opposite me sat Michael Owen. I liked Michael and regarded him as a good professional. He'd complained of a 'feeling' in his groin after training, 'like it was going to go'. He'd had a career ravaged by muscle injuries so I fully understood his caution. We'd had a scan on the area and it had picked up nothing. That was good news. Whatever it was, it wasn't a muscle tear, which would've ended our best striker's season and our best hopes of scoring goals in the last two games of it. The doctor relayed the positive news to all in the room.

I spoke to Michael first. 'In light of the clear scan results do you think you'll be fit to play against Fulham? It's the most important game of the season. A win might be enough for us.'

Michael placed his hand over his groin. 'Not sure, to be honest. It doesn't feel too bad. But I'm out of contract at the end of the season. What if I rip my groin on Saturday? I'll not get a contract at another club if I'm injured.'

I was a little taken aback by his reply. I didn't share his reasoning. 'But you already have a contract, Michael. You have a contract here now with us.'

He didn't like mine either. 'I want to speak to Alan about this.'

I leaned forward and pointed at my chest. 'You're speaking to Alan – he's here.'

He looked behind me and pointed. 'Is he in the cabinet?'

It was getting silly now.

'No, Michael. He doesn't want to deal with this bit as he wants me to do it and that's why I'm here. But if you want to speak with him let's go.'

It hadn't been my intention to offend him. I certainly didn't doubt that he was genuinely feeling something. He was an honest lad and I respected his professionalism. I was simply desperate to have our best goalscorer on the pitch for a game that could save our season. I didn't care about next season or even next week. We needed to score goals and win the game against Fulham. Michael was by far our best goalscorer.

He spoke with Alan. *He was desperate to play.* He'd have a fitness test on the morning of the game. When the day arrived we travelled to the training ground in Longbenton from our hotel base in Jesmond. It was five hours before kick-off of the biggest game of our season. Michael, Iain Dowie, me and the physio Davy Henderson shared a car. When we reached the training ground Michael and Davy started off on a gentle jog, running to the opposite end of the pitch from where we stood. Iain turned to me, hand outstretched.

'A fiver says he passes.'

I took his hand and looked at Michael's face as he jogged back to us. 'A tenner he doesn't.'

Michael stopped beside us and put his hand over his groin again. He shook his head. I felt a knot in my stomach. 'No point in going on. I can't really feel anything but I just have this sensation it's going to go. I don't want to risk it.'

I looked into his eyes and I could see genuine disappointment. I understood his caution. His fragile body had let him down on too many occasions. He was understandably frightened to take the risk. For me to try to push him to play would have been futile and wrong. He knew his body better than anyone. I understood that. That acceptance didn't stop me from feeling physically sick that we would face the biggest game of our short tenure without the one world class goalscorer we had at the club.

Iain slipped me a tenner on the way back to the hotel. I would much rather have given him his fiver. We lost the game and lost again on the final day against Aston Villa. A single point would have been enough in either game. Michael played for twenty minutes in the final game. He made little impact but came through with his groin intact. If we'd had him for both games then I believe we'd have gained the points we needed. Michael's agency produced a glossy brochure to send to prospective clubs. His physio contributed a lengthy piece on his fitness record. He signed for Manchester United.

We were relegated.

CHAPTER 37

'WHAT ABOUT head of performance?'

We'd been discussing my job title for the last fifteen minutes. 'Head of performance' was my latest effort and my favourite. We knew the role, just not the appropriate title for it. Alan nodded in agreement. Iain liked it too. We could hear the helicopter approaching. He was two hours late but we didn't mind. It gave us extra time to revisit and solidify our position before the negotiations. All of Mike Ashley's statements, both privately and publicly, after our relegation indicated that he wanted Alan to be the next permanent manager of Newcastle United. He'd told the press only the day before that he'd made too many mistakes, especially in the season just ended, but appointing Alan Shearer wasn't one of them. In fact, his only regret was that he hadn't done it sooner. Derek Llambias, the managing director, was quoted in the morning papers confirming that they wanted Alan to be the manager and thanking his staff for all of the hard work put into trying to prevent the club from slipping out of the top division. Senior players were lining up to testify to the professionalism and discipline of the last few weeks in contrast to what had gone before. We'd fallen just short, but after the initial disappointment, we were meeting the owner in confident mood that we could take the club back up at the first attempt. More than that, we believed we were capable of creating something really special.

Having worked with Alan over the past two months I was more convinced than ever that my decision to sacrifice a career at the bar and embark on this journey with him was the right one. He was a natural leader who commanded respect from players and staff alike. He wasn't afraid of hard work and he loved the club with a passion. As we watched the helicopter land and the three men duck their heads and emerge from beneath its blades, we recognised the owner and the managing director, but not the smartly dressed man who walked two paces behind them as they approached. We shook hands warmly and were introduced to our unexpected guest. He was Keith Harris, a name that meant little to us but we were curious as to why he was here today. We made our way to the deserted canteen to begin our conversations, which we expected would end with Alan being appointed as the next manager of Newcastle United and me earning a salary for the first time in three years, under the newly created title of head of performance. Alan's agent was the seventh man in the room. He was with us to negotiate the finer details of the contracts for all three of us. I was glad he was there. I was never comfortable negotiating on my own behalf. Not since Neil McDonald had gained his ten grand signing-on fee and I'd got nothing all those years ago.

Mike Ashley sat slumped in the chair in front of us. He took a packet of sandwiches out of a plastic supermarket bag. He peeled the wrapper off and ate half the contents in two bites. He devoured it like he hadn't eaten all week. His hair was unkempt and his shirt was tucked into his jeans on one side but flapped loosely on his thigh at the other. He spoke as he swallowed. 'I'm selling the club. I've had enough. I'm a businessman. I've had great success in business, but not this business. This business is unique. I don't understand it and I never will. It's oil and water for me and I want out. Keith is here because he is going to help me sell it.'

I watched him with a mixture of emotions. I felt genuinely sorry for him. He looked exhausted, like he hadn't slept since we'd been relegated three days previously. He was a shy man who I'd only spoken to on one or two occasions during the past two months, but when I had done, and here again now, he seemed like he desperately wanted to do well for the club. He just didn't know how.

I was astonished when he dropped his bombshell about selling the club. This wasn't on the agenda. This meeting was where we were supposed to be negotiating the agreement for Alan to become manager of his hometown club for the foreseeable future. We were there to discuss our plans to drive the club forward in the short and long term. What did the owner's words mean for us now? Was the job no longer on offer? If not, how long could I realistically remain in my home without a regular salary to pay my mortgage? That thought nearly had me excusing myself from the room, but before my insides left me Alan responded.

'I don't really care who owns this club. I want to be the manager.'

He fixed his stare straight at the owner, who placed the other sandwich on the table. Mike glanced at Keith Harris. 'Will that work, Keith?'

Keith ran his fingers through his perfectly coiffured hair. 'If anything, Mike, that makes my job a lot easier. I can sell the club with Alan as its manager as a far more attractive entity than I can with no manager.'

Mike was satisfied with that. 'Great. Let's get on with making this happen then.'

Alan asked to speak with the owner in private. Mike followed him into his office. I sat with Iain drinking coffee until my head hurt while Alan's agent negotiated with Derek Llambias. We hung around for what seemed an eternity. It was probably less than an hour but it felt like time stood still for me. So much depended on the conversations taking place in Alan's office that I could barely swallow the biscuit Iain offered me. I was excited more than apprehensive about Alan speaking with the owner. I knew Alan well and I was convinced that nothing but good could come out of an honest conversation between him and Mike. The owner would see his passion, vision, and love for the club. More importantly, he'd see his honesty. When they finally emerged, and the day was drawing to a close, I sat with Alan in his office. He was confident we'd reached an agreement in principle. We'd have total control of all aspects of the footballing side of the club and a budget of £10 million to spend on new players. This was in addition to any money we made from transfer sales. We'd sign contracts in the coming days that would keep us at the club for the next three years.

I couldn't wait to tell Geraldine. Tell her that the gamble to go back into football was the right one. That I'd known all along this would be the outcome. A three-year contract to be part of the management team at the only club I'd ever worked for, or ever really wanted to work for, was within touching distance. I couldn't have been happier. I was coming to the end of a long journey. One that had started while I was still employed as a physio and had subsequently turned into a living nightmare where I was rapidly running out of money and worrying daily about losing the roof over our heads. I was relieved it was nearly over.

I was daydreaming about a brighter future when Alan began relaying the details of his private meeting with Mike. 'I told him to get rid of Llambias. Replace him with someone who understands football. Like Rick Parry from Liverpool. The club needs someone at the top who is steeped in football. Without it we'll always struggle.'

I sat up in my chair. 'Really?'

He leaned forward. 'Yes, really.'

'You do know he's his mate, don't you? You're asking him to sack his mate?'

Alan put both hands on the table. 'I know what he is, but he's not the right man to run the club. That's how I feel. So I gave my honest opinion.'

I admired him for his honesty but selfishly I was worried that suggesting sacking Llambias might be a step too far for the owner. The door opened before I could share my concerns. Keith Harris poked his head through it. He fixed his eyes on Alan.

'Just popped in to say we're off. Thank you for your time and I'm sure we'll speak soon.'

'When do you think you will have the club sold?'

Alan was straight to the point as always.

Keith was caught off-guard by the bluntness of the question. He stuttered a little in his response before regaining his composure. 'I'll have it sold by the end of June or the middle of July. You have my word on that. If I don't keep my promise, you can go the press and tell them.'

It was a peculiar response; full of unnecessary self-importance. It got the response it deserved and the one I expected from Alan. 'In all honesty, who cares about you in the press?'

There was silence. Then the perfect hair and cufflinks disappeared and the door closed behind him. I got up to watch them walk towards the helicopter.

'Don't apply for a job in the Diplomatic Service any time soon, Alan.'

He was walking around the table to join me and Iain. 'It's the truth, man. I'm only being honest.'

'Yes but there's a . . . never mind. You're gonna be manager of Newcastle United. We're in for a hell of a ride.'

As the helicopter disappeared from view the three of us shook hands. We were nearly there. It was almost a year since I'd left the bar. Another year without earning that I hadn't factored into my grand plans. I needed this to happen, and quickly. I was convinced it would now. Not only because Alan and the owner had spoken at length with each other but also because of the demeanour of Mike Ashley. He looked like a man in need of redemption. He'd already sacrificed one idol at his altar when he'd made Kevin Keegan's position untenable and had felt the wrath of the fans in the fallout. He wouldn't do it twice, surely? He wouldn't do the same to Alan? Alan was going to be the next manager of Newcastle United. I was sure of that.

I've never seen anyone fidget so much. It was like his chair was alive with biting ants. He shifted one way, then the next. He crossed one leg over the other and uncrossed them again. He tapped his papers on his lap and then pushed them down the side of the chair. He pulled them back out, folded them and slipped them into his jacket pocket. His eyes were a whole different show of their own. They were darting around the room as if he was chasing the fastest invisible fly known to mankind. I tried to catch it – not the invisible fly, his eye. I tried to make eye contact with him but my sockets hurt. He'd slipped into Alan's office and into a chair directly behind me. I turned mine around, as did Iain, so that all three of us were facing him to hear his update. It'd been two days since he'd flown off with Mike Ashley and Keith Harris. Now Derek Llambias, the managing director, was back. But he was different. Two days ago he'd been full of bonhomie. Not today. It was like he'd been sent to do his duty against his will. He proceeded to deliver the short straw he'd been given.

'There's been a bit of a problem with Barclays. They won't approve the overdraft now that we've been relegated. It's gonna hold us up a little. Nothing to worry about. We just don't know what we're gonna do if we don't get it. Anyway, I'll keep you posted.'

With that he jumped up to escape his ant-ridden chair, and the sauna that Alan's office had suddenly become for him. He closed the door behind him and scurried away.

'Fuck me, what was that all about?'

Alan was laughing behind his desk. Iain answered. 'There's a rabbit off, I think.'

In the short time we'd been at the club I'd never really had the chance to get to know the managing director. When I had spent time in his company it was usually when he visited Alan's office for a weekly briefing. He'd always been calm and measured in those dealings and was keen to ensure we had everything we needed to try to get the club out of the mess we'd inherited. His demeanour on this occasion was unlike anything I'd witnessed before. I felt very uneasy when he was in the room and even more so when he eventually departed.

'I feel very uncomfortable. I agree with Iain. Something is clearly not right.'

As I left the training ground that evening, I had a sinking feeling it might be for the last time. I established that fact for certain when I picked up a newspaper two days later. I called Alan.

'You're not getting the job.'

'Go on. Why's that then?

'Cos I'm sitting looking at a newspaper headline and it's calling you a greedy bastard.'

He laughed. 'Not the first time I've been called that.'

'No, you don't understand. It's the article below it that's the issue. My name's in it. The salary I asked for is in it and they list my job title as head of performance.'

There was a silence.

'You still there?'

'Fuck me. I didn't expect that. Fuck's sake man. This is not good.'

I agreed with him. It could only have come from one source.

I was right about the job. Alan was never contacted again about the manager's role at Newcastle United, in spite of the handshakes and promises. There was a charade played out in the press that they still hoped to have him as the manager, but that's all it was. The sensible thing to do would have been to contact him and say there'd been a change of heart in the two days between shaking hands and Derek Llambias coming to see us again to talk about Barclays and loan delays. The right thing to do would have been to tell the press that they were looking elsewhere for their manager. The objectionable thing to do was to shake hands on an agreement, leak details of that agreement to the press, and not contact Alan Shearer or any of us again. Alan, and all of us, deserved to be treated with more respect than that. The owner had changed his mind. He was entitled to do that. No one can dispute that. The actions of the club after the change of heart were unfathomable, unwarranted, and uncalled for.

In the weeks and months that followed, many opportunities presented themselves. Alan would ring and I'd feel a surge of excitement but ultimately nothing materialised. We were going here, there and everywhere, but in the end we went nowhere. I would have bet my house Alan would end up as a great manager. I eventually did. After holding on for as long as I could, I had no choice but to put what was left of our home up for sale. The alternative didn't bear thinking about. Geraldine accepted it in the way she always did, with grace and understanding, but that just made the pain of failure harder to bear. And it was a catastrophic failure. Only I could leave my job, embark on the hard slog to become a barrister, gamble it all on Alan becoming a manager, and end up with nothing to show for it. I was a physiotherapist not practising physiotherapy, a barrister not practising law, had a Master's degree worth 50 per cent of nothing and I was a novelist with a book that no one had read. Yes, that's right.

A novelist.

After it dawned on me that I'd made such a mess of my career, one that would cost me and my young family our home, I spiralled deep into a place far darker than anywhere my mind had ever taken me before. Even the running stopped working. I was like an addict whose drug of choice no longer brings the anticipated high. I was running every day but my despair at the mess I'd got us into wasn't lifting. I could hear voices in my head. A single voice, to be more precise. I could see his face, I knew his name, and I knew his story. I sat numbed at my keyboard for a week. Every night his story got more and more interesting and every day I tried to write it. I wrote an outline on a pad of paper; a start, middle, and an ending. I ripped it up and did it again, and again, until I had a small mountain at my feet. I wanted to write, but I was scared to write, scared I couldn't do it, that everyone would laugh at my work. Until one day I realised I could just write it. I didn't actually have to show it to anybody else. In fact I wouldn't show it to anybody else.

So I started.

And something amazing happened.

I couldn't stop.

Every day I wrote and every night I thought about what I'd write tomorrow. The character in my head came alive in front of my eyes. I could see him, feel him, and wanted to know more about what would happen to him. After a few weeks I plucked up the courage to let Geraldine read what I'd written. She liked it, really liked it, and not just because she was my wife and had to say she liked it. I'd write with tears in my eyes at certain points and then just to check I wasn't just clinically depressed I'd sneak a peek at Geraldine as she read what I'd written that day. I'd see a tear appear and feel exhilarated that 'I'd gotten her.' In no time I had a manuscript for my first novel. *An Irish Heartbeat* was a romantic thriller set in Ireland, that focused on the trials and tribulations of a central character called Cormac. His love interest was Bernadette. I gave her my mother's name because I just wanted to write the name on a page – to breathe life into it again. I'd written a novel. I just didn't know what to do with it.

CHAPTER 38

I DID NOTHING with the book in the end. Published it online and forgot it even existed. I was too busy flailing in open water – a drowning man, going under for longer each time. Getting desperately tired but still fighting with everything I had to get back to the surface and gasp in the air before sinking to the depths once more. Our home was going. I'd accepted that. It was a relief in the end. I needed to sell it before the bank did it for me. I tried to resurrect my legal career and could visualise a way to get there, but I no longer had the money to pay for the ride. The house sale would help, but I felt that using the proceeds to follow that route was just too much to ask of Geraldine. Not after everything I'd asked of her already. I thought about contacting football clubs. An ex-player, physio, and qualified barrister – surely I had something unique to offer on the administration side of a progressive club? I didn't know where to start though. I contacted Lee Charnley, the secretary at Newcastle. He thought my inexperience would work against me and couldn't help. I considered lecturing. I knew now for certain that I could talk and that I was good at it. I wasn't frightened anymore. I made some enquiries but that route would cost me too much money as well.

No matter how hard I tried I just couldn't envisage a way forward. So one day I just stopped trying to find one. I'd had enough of striving. I was fed up with trying. I'd lost the stomach for the fight. I'd stopped running, stopped writing, stopped caring and stopped fighting. I simply let go. I was sinking and I didn't care anymore. I did feel something. Definitely something. Anger. Rage even. How the fuck did it get to this? All of that useless striving, all of those stupid decisions. How did I end up here? With nothing to show for any of it. *I was done.* I was angry. I was bitter. I was beaten.

And then it happened.

At a birthday party. At Alan Shearer's fortieth birthday party. A hand reached into the darkness and pulled me up from the murky depths and brought me to the surface once more. I wasn't even going to go to the party. An hour after it had started I was in my bed, fully clothed, and telling a distraught Geraldine to leave me alone and that if she wanted to go so badly she could go on her own. I went there in the end only because I didn't want to let Alan down. I could let myself down but not him. Not anyone for that matter. I dragged myself from bed, to taxi, to party, and there I met a man who gave me my life back.

His name was Graham Wylie, a well-known businessman in the North East. He'd been a co-founder of SAGE Software and was the most unlikely person in the world to require the services of a confused ex footballer, physiotherapist, History of Ideas graduate, non-practising barrister, unemployed head of performance, and unpublished novelist. Come to think of it, who'd be the likeliest person to make any kind of sense out of that confused mess?

A quiet and unassuming man, he didn't introduce himself as I stood in his company. Instead he listened as I talked gibberish about my time with Alan, my unpublished book, and all of the rest of it. Three days later I was sitting with him in a hotel he owned 10 miles outside the city, as he told me about his plans to invest in a medical tool being developed in the USA. I travelled to South Carolina to give him my opinion on it. He paid me a fee. I needed the money. I wrote him a report on my findings and thought I'd never see him again. But I did. He liked my passion for the product and asked me to give him one year of my life to see where we might take it together. I agreed. And threw everything I had into helping him turn a piece of medical equipment called Speedflex into a mainstream fitness concept. He sat by my side, encouraging, nurturing, and, most of all, believing in me, as I tried to navigate my way through a world that was completely alien to me. He watched me make mistakes and even learn from some of them and he pushed me forwards until I no longer needed his firm hand on my back. He became so much more than a business partner. He was my mentor, confidant, and friend.

All those skills that I thought would be redundant forever suddenly became relevant again; key to the success of our business. My physiotherapy background was vital for my understanding of just what Speedflex was capable of becoming and allowed us to develop it into something more than we originally inherited. My legal training helped me navigate my way around documents that would have bamboozled me ten years previously. Most important of all was my ability to talk about the concept we'd created. I was happy to talk to anyone in any setting: in the boardroom, in a hospital, in a gym, or in a presentation to anyone who'd listen. I talked and I talked and I talked again. I'd finally found my voice and I was using it to full effect. He did so much more than lift me out of the deep waters I was in, he gave me the opportunity to stand or fall by my own actions and abilities. We created a network of Speedflex Studios, generated jobs for lots of people, and we were growing a business together. Alan Shearer came on board as a director and ambassador. We still worked together, after all, just not in the way I had imagined.

Something else happened along the way. Something seismic. The fog that had hung over me thick and heavy, since I'd walked out of my Chambers for the promise of working with Alan in football again, had finally cleared. I could see clear sky again. I found a respect for myself that I thought was gone forever. I could, at last, see a future that I really wanted to be part of. It was a future that I could create. It was something that might change the lives of my children and their children. A legacy to be proud of. We bought a new home in the countryside – a new dream home to replace the one I'd butchered and eventually lost. I'd ended up where I wanted to be after all. I just didn't know this was the destination I was searching for until the day I arrived at it. I knew now for certain. I could once again look Geraldine and the kids in the eye and know that I was doing everything I could for them. I was finally happy with my position and my place.

Then I woke up one morning with an unusual feeling in my chest. It was the pain my cardiologist had told me not to worry about. The one that three weeks later caused my heart attack, and nearly ended my life just when I was really starting to enjoy it again. It had me lying in a hospital bed in the middle of the night with a stent in my main coronary artery, and a thousand memories and a million regrets fighting for space in my head.

I was fragile when I got home the day after it happened. I wasn't thinking clearly. I lied to Ciaran. I lied to my youngest son. He was twelve and I lied to him because I didn't want him to ever be me. *The boy on the shed*. I didn't tell him I'd had a heart attack. Geraldine thought he should know, but I didn't let her tell him either. He was such a shining light in our family. He was a loving, kind, and confident child and I didn't want to burden him with it in case it changed him somehow. I should have told him. If for no other reason than it would have stopped him jumping out of the darkness of our kitchen and scaring me half to death as I made my way to bed on my first night home. I nearly had another heart attack! He was only copying what I'd done to him two days before. I suppose none of us ever really grow up. Even on the day before we nearly die. So I sat him down and told him. As soon as I did, I recognised the look in his eye. I could see fear becoming a part of him. He was frightened. His perfect world was coming to an end. It felt like I'd stolen a little piece of his childhood that day.

It's been three years now since I walked out of hospital with a broken heart and the disease that stole my mother from me now working its way silently through me too. Her battle is now my battle. Her enemy is now my enemy. And it is a deadly one. All that time I was trying to make a life for myself and my family, my silent assassin was weaving its way through my body and into the very core of me. Secretly starving me of my life's blood.

I've spent those three years trying to give Ciaran back what I stole, not just from him, but from his brothers too. In spite of my best efforts I can feel him watching me sometimes. Making sure I'm still there and that all is well in his world. He checks what I eat, cooks with me and makes sure I'm exercising. I can still see a flicker of fear behind his eyes but I'm working hard on it. He's not the boy on the shed. But he's no longer as carefree as he once was. However, I'm confident he is not *me*. I am the boy on the shed and I always will be that boy – watching, worrying, and praying. But I am *her* now too. The one being watched. I know now what she felt. The fear wasn't all up on the shed after all. She was as helpless as I was as she watched her youngest boy fret his way through his child-hood. I feel her pain and her hopelessness and I love her more for it. I am her. Her killer is in me, but I have more resources to fight it than she did. It won't take me without a fight. Winter came far too soon for her. I've felt its icy chill myself now. But there is fight left in me yet. Ciaran is in his springtime. Everything is fresh and new

for him; life and all its wondrous mystery is revealing itself bit by bit
in front of him still. It's only just the beginning for him. Owen and
Conor are my boys of summer. Owen is at university now. Quiet,
but with the steel behind my mother's eyes that he looks through
every day. I hope he finds his voice earlier than I found mine. Conor
is about to have a daughter of his own now. He'll take her home
and lay her on his chest. He'll feel her heart beating next to his and
she will melt right through his ribcage. *Then he will know.*

I know now I'll never go home to Ireland. To the place where I
once belonged and will always belong. I used to dream that some
day I would. Go back to where it all started for me. But I know now
that I won't. Some nights I dream that I'm back there. Back home.
They're vivid dreams. Like I'm awake and not dreaming at all. Like
I never left in the first place. Sometimes I wonder what my life
would've been like had I stayed. Stayed with the people who loved
me most. The pain of leaving all those years ago has never left me.
I carry it with me. I miss the life I never got to have with the people
I left behind. And all because I could play football better than my
friends at school. Who would think that entire lifetimes can be
shaped on such small things? I know for certain now that I will
never go back to the world from which I came. Not while I'm living
anyway. I ache at the thought even now. I'd like to think I'll find my
way home in the next life. That my spirit will rest there alongside
my ashes. But I believe my spirit will die with my body. Despite all
my childhood brainwashing, I don't believe in the next life. I believe
in this one and this one only. I'd love to believe that somewhere in
the ether I'll be reunited with my beautiful mother again, in some
paradise where she's no longer ill and I'm no longer a lost boy terrified that she'll leave the moment she's out of my sight, but in my
broken heart I know she's gone forever. I've lived a lifetime without
her love. And when my time comes, then so will I disappear into the

nothingness from where I came. She did live on after her death, but only in the thoughts and actions of those she left behind. She is part of me and I am part of her. I will live on in my children and in a little girl who is yet to even be born. She might yet have my mother's eyes.

The house is quiet today. There's no one around. Well, there is one person. Geraldine is in the kitchen. I can hear her. I recognise how she moves across the floor, how she breathes. She is in her autumn now. The raw beauty that stole my heart when we were both in our springtime has faded but it's been replaced by something else. Something more. Much more. She's rich in colour and has a depth to her now that her youthful beauty could never hope to match. I believe I will live only one lifetime. No hereafter. No second chances. I've been gifted one small window in time to spend on this tiny planet. And when my story is told and if anyone should ever want to know it, it will be a simple one. It begins and ends with Geraldine. She was my love. She is my love. She will always be my love. That's all that really matters in the end.

I've felt the first chill of winter. I fear that it's just around the corner for me. But as I look outside I can still see sunshine, and bright blue skies are all around me. The leaves are falling onto the garden and finding their resting place on the shed.

It is only autumn still.

END